CARLYLE

ODERINT DUM METUANT

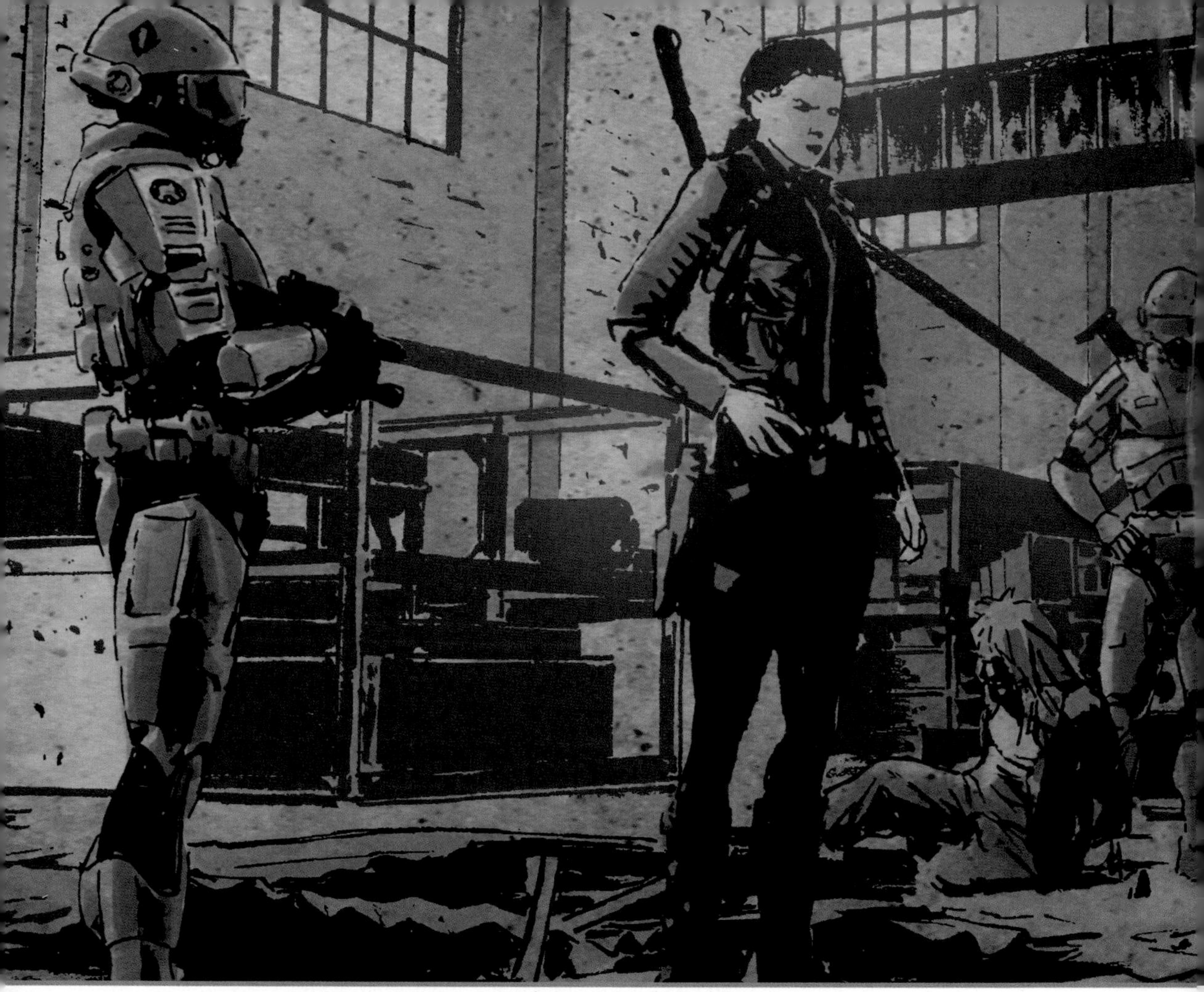

# LAZARUS™

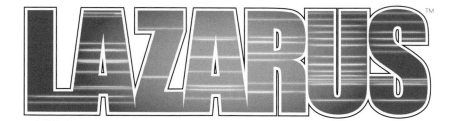

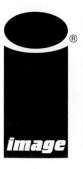

**IMAGE COMICS, INC.**
**Robert Kirkman** – Chief Operating Officer
**Erik Larsen** – Chief Financial Officer
**Todd McFarlane** – President
**Marc Silvestri** – Chief Executive Officer
**Jim Valentino** – Vice-President

**Eric Stephenson** – Publisher
**Ron Richards** – Director of Business Development
**Jennifer de Guzman** – Director of Trade Book Sales
**Kat Salazar** – Director of PR & Marketing
**Jeremy Sullivan** – Director of Digital Sales
**Emilio Bautista** – Sales Assistant
**Branwyn Bigglestone** – Senior Accounts Manager
**Emily Miller** – Accounts Manager
**Jessica Ambriz** – Administrative Assistant
**Tyler Shainline** – Events Coordinator
**David Brothers** – Content Manager
**Jonathan Chan** – Production Manager
**Drew Gill** – Art Director
**Meredith Wallace** – Print Manager
**Monica Garcia** – Senior Production Artist
**Jenna Savage** – Production Artist
**Addison Duke** – Production Artist
**Tricia Ramos** – Production Assistant
**IMAGECOMICS.COM**

LAZARUS, VOLUME TWO. July 2014. First Printing. ISBN: 978-1-60706-871-6. Published by Image Comics, Inc. Office of publication: 2001 Center St, 6th Floor, Berkeley, CA 94704.

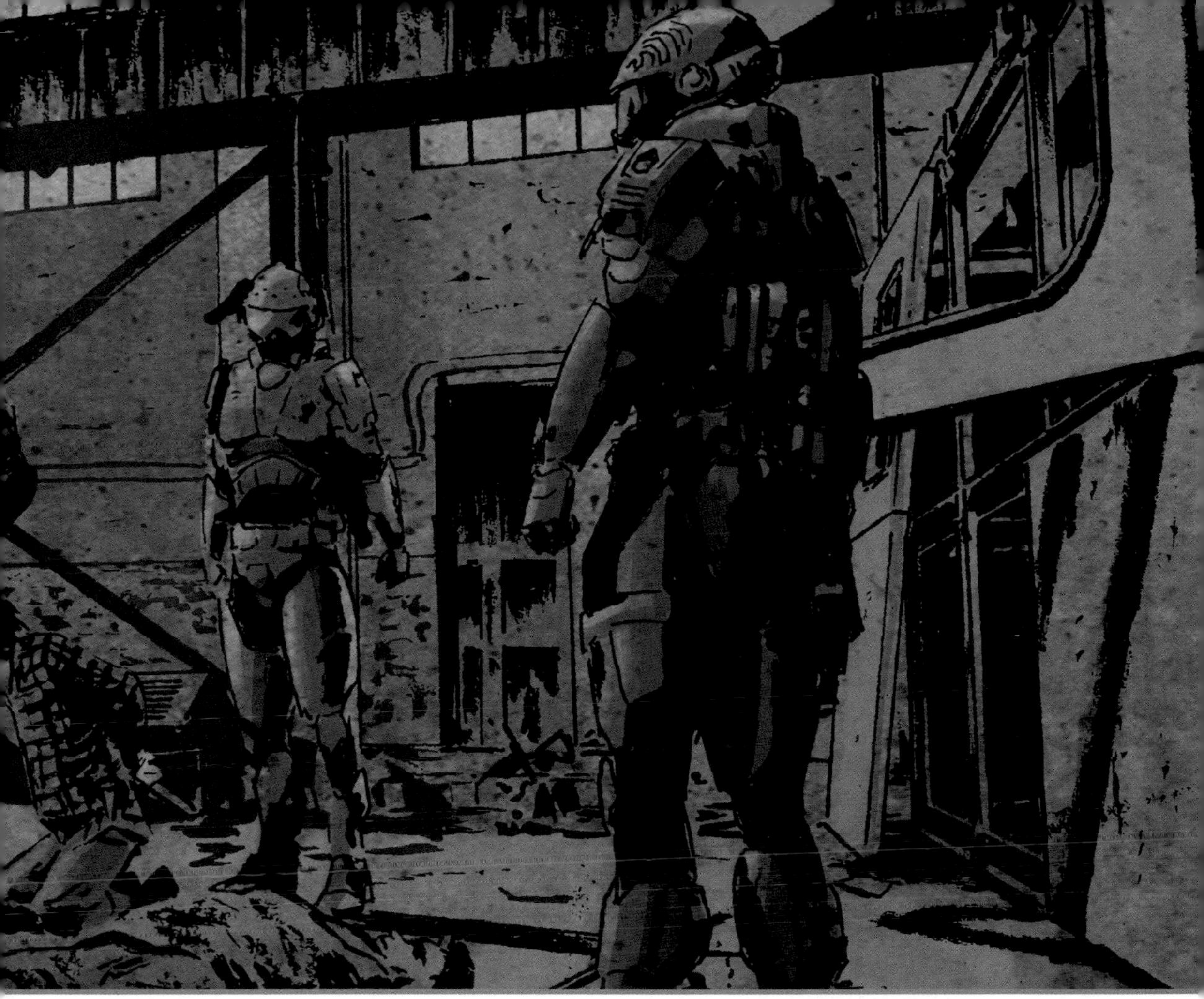

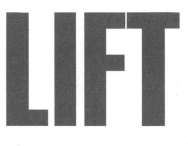

*volume two* **LIFT**

*written by* **GREG RUCKA**

*art by* **MICHAEL LARK**
*with* **BRIAN LEVEL**

*letters by* **MICHAEL LARK & JODI WYNNE**

*colors by* **SANTI ARCAS**

*cover by* **OWEN FREEMAN**

*publication design by* **MICHAEL LARK & ERIC TRAUTMANN**

*edited by* **DAVID BROTHERS**

# LIFT
CHAPTER ONE

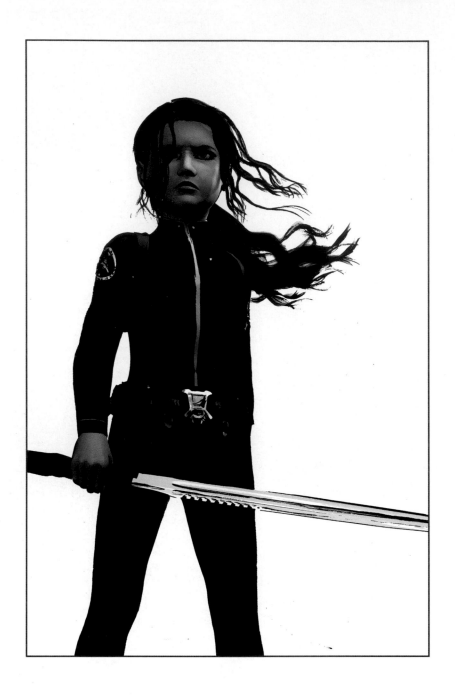

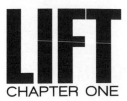

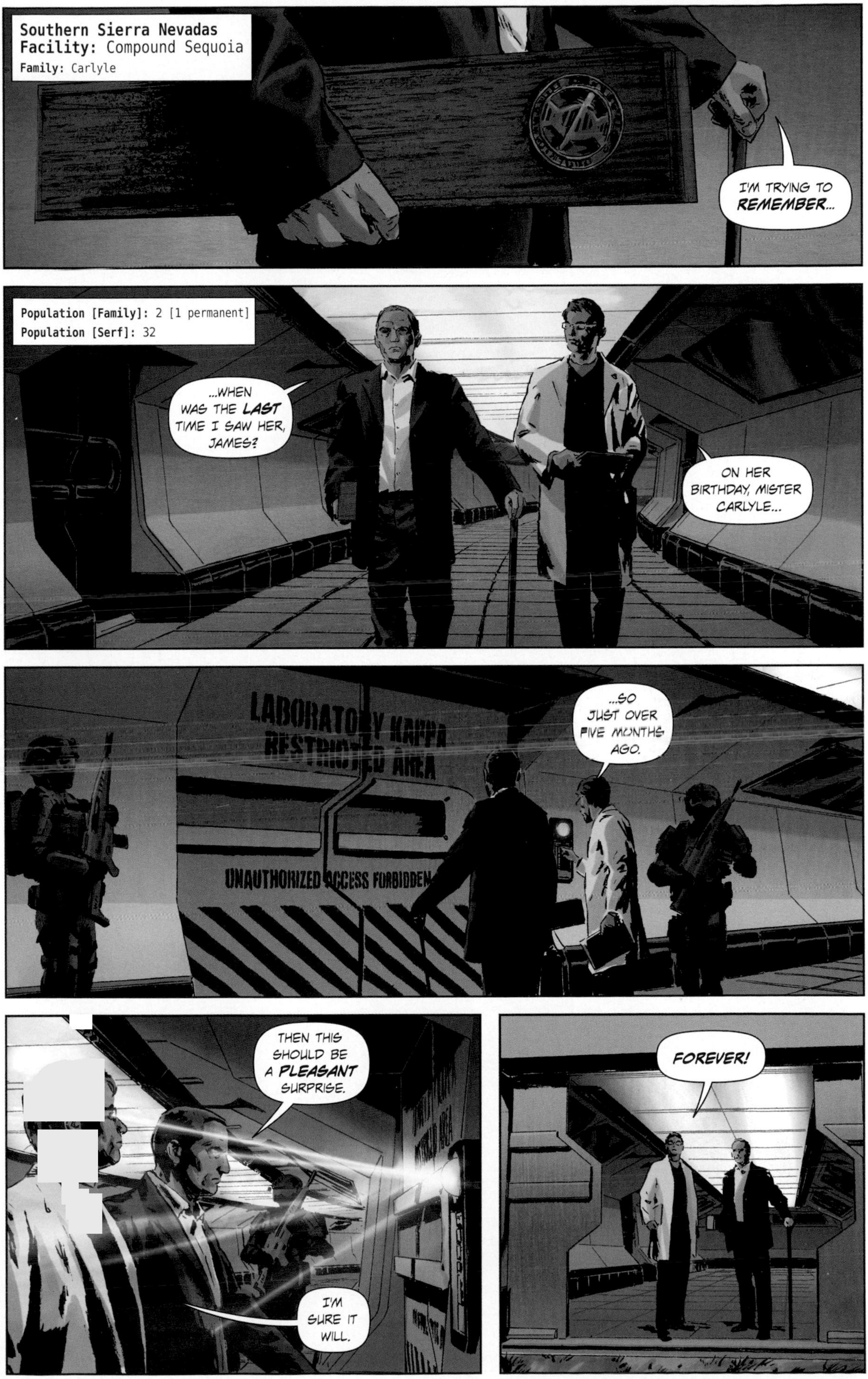
Southern Sierra Nevadas
Facility: Compound Sequoia
Family: Carlyle
I'M TRYING TO REMEMBER...
Population [Family]: 2 [1 permanent]
Population [Serf]: 32
...WHEN WAS THE LAST TIME I SAW HER, JAMES?
ON HER BIRTHDAY, MISTER CARLYLE...
LABORATORY KAPPA
RESTRICTED AREA
UNAUTHORIZED ACCESS FORBIDDEN
...SO JUST OVER FIVE MONTHS AGO.
THEN THIS SHOULD BE A PLEASANT SURPRISE.
I'M SURE IT WILL.
FOREVER!

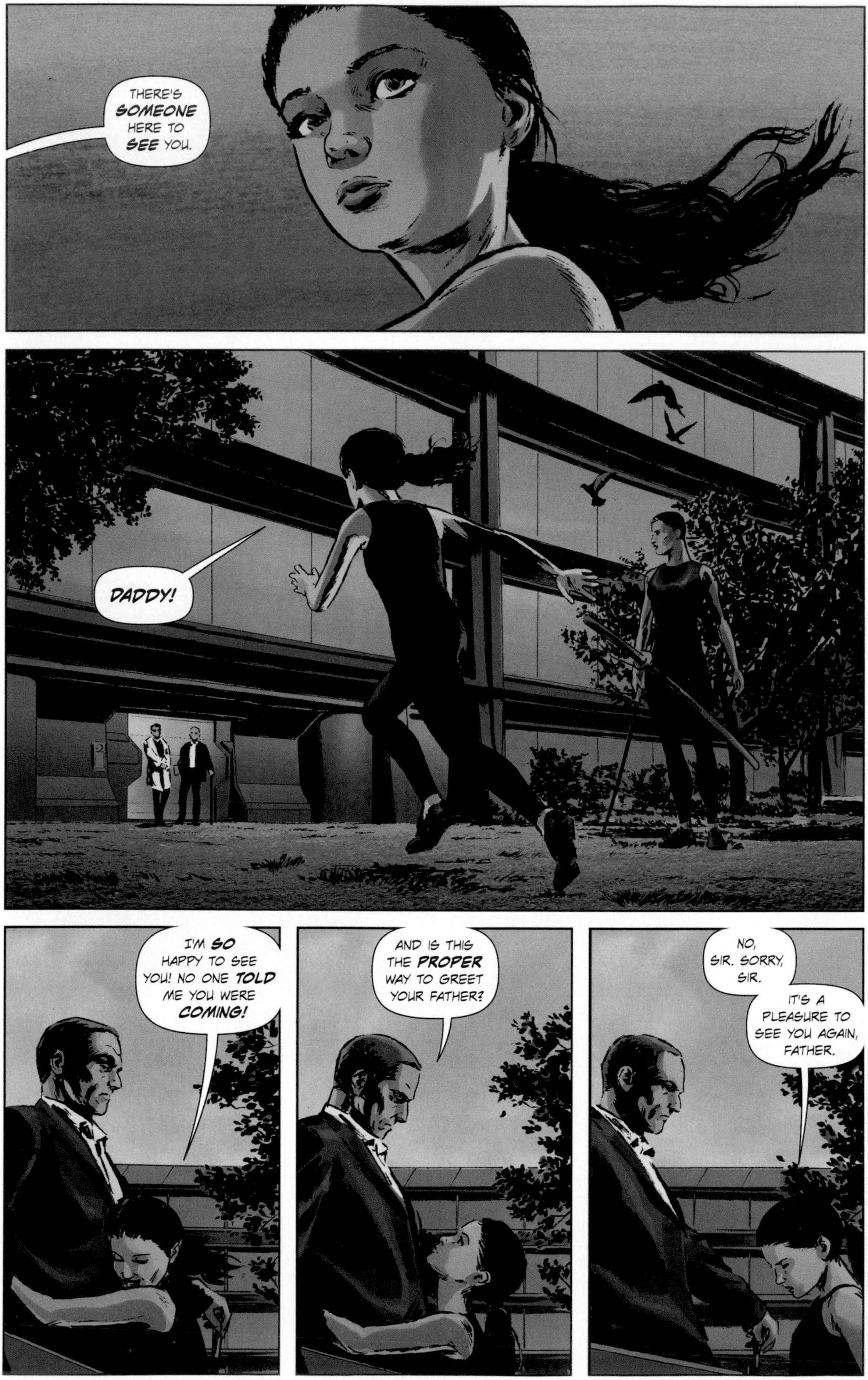
THERE'S SOMEONE HERE TO SEE YOU.
DADDY!
I'M SO HAPPY TO SEE YOU! NO ONE TOLD ME YOU WERE COMING!
AND IS THIS THE PROPER WAY TO GREET YOUR FATHER?
NO, SIR. SORRY, SIR.
IT'S A PLEASURE TO SEE YOU AGAIN, FATHER.

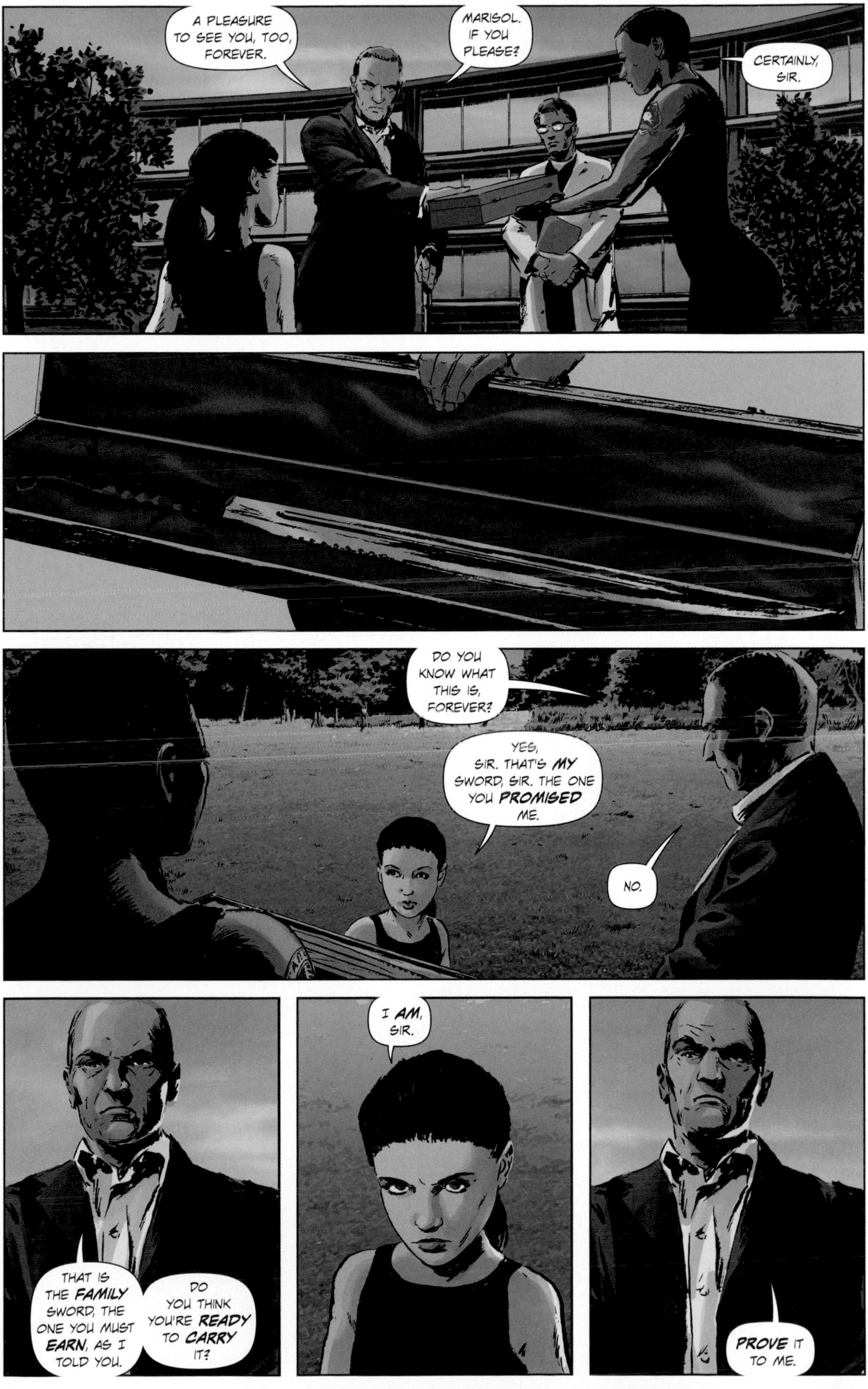
A PLEASURE TO SEE YOU, TOO, FOREVER.
MARISOL. IF YOU PLEASE?
CERTAINLY, SIR.
DO YOU KNOW WHAT THIS IS, FOREVER?
YES, SIR. THAT'S MY SWORD, SIR. THE ONE YOU PROMISED ME.
NO.
THAT IS THE FAMILY SWORD, THE ONE YOU MUST EARN, AS I TOLD YOU.
DO YOU THINK YOU'RE READY TO CARRY IT?
I AM, SIR.
PROVE IT TO ME.

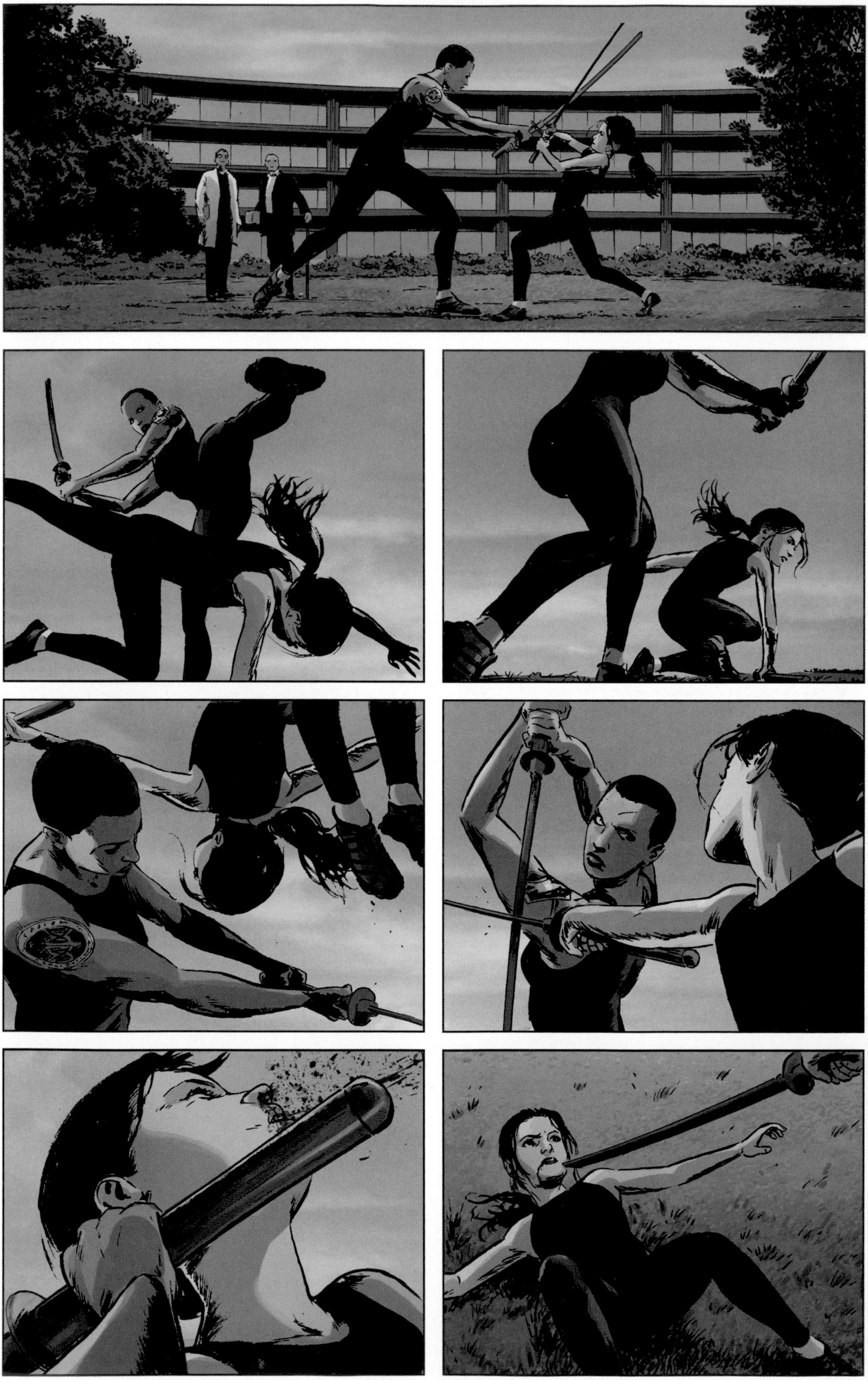

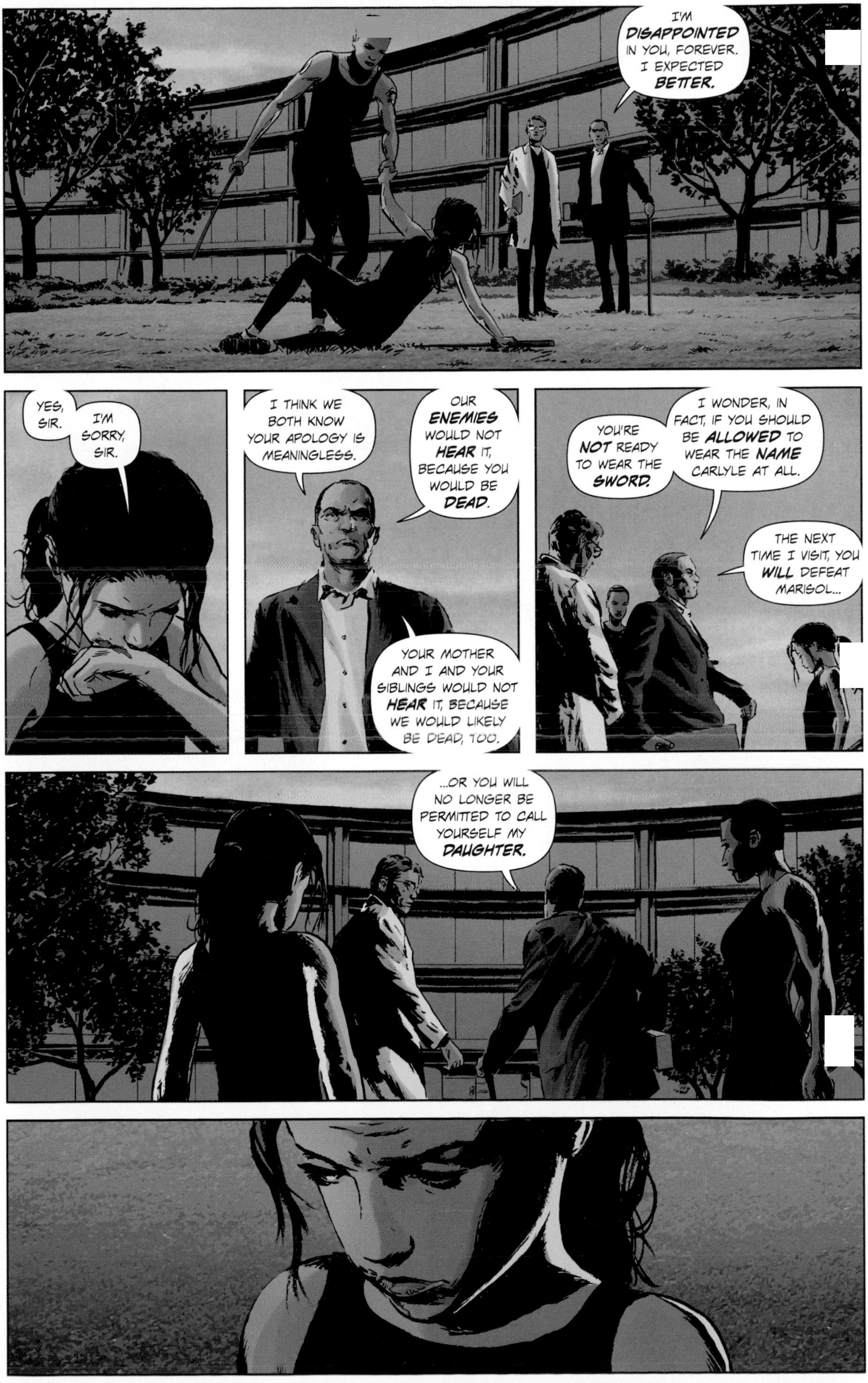

I'M DISAPPOINTED IN YOU, FOREVER. I EXPECTED BETTER.
YES, SIR.
I'M SORRY, SIR.
I THINK WE BOTH KNOW YOUR APOLOGY IS MEANINGLESS.
OUR ENEMIES WOULD NOT HEAR IT, BECAUSE YOU WOULD BE DEAD.
YOUR MOTHER AND I AND YOUR SIBLINGS WOULD NOT HEAR IT, BECAUSE WE WOULD LIKELY BE DEAD, TOO.
YOU'RE NOT READY TO WEAR THE SWORD.
I WONDER, IN FACT, IF YOU SHOULD BE ALLOWED TO WEAR THE NAME CARLYLE AT ALL.
THE NEXT TIME I VISIT, YOU WILL DEFEAT MARISOL...
...OR YOU WILL NO LONGER BE PERMITTED TO CALL YOURSELF MY DAUGHTER.

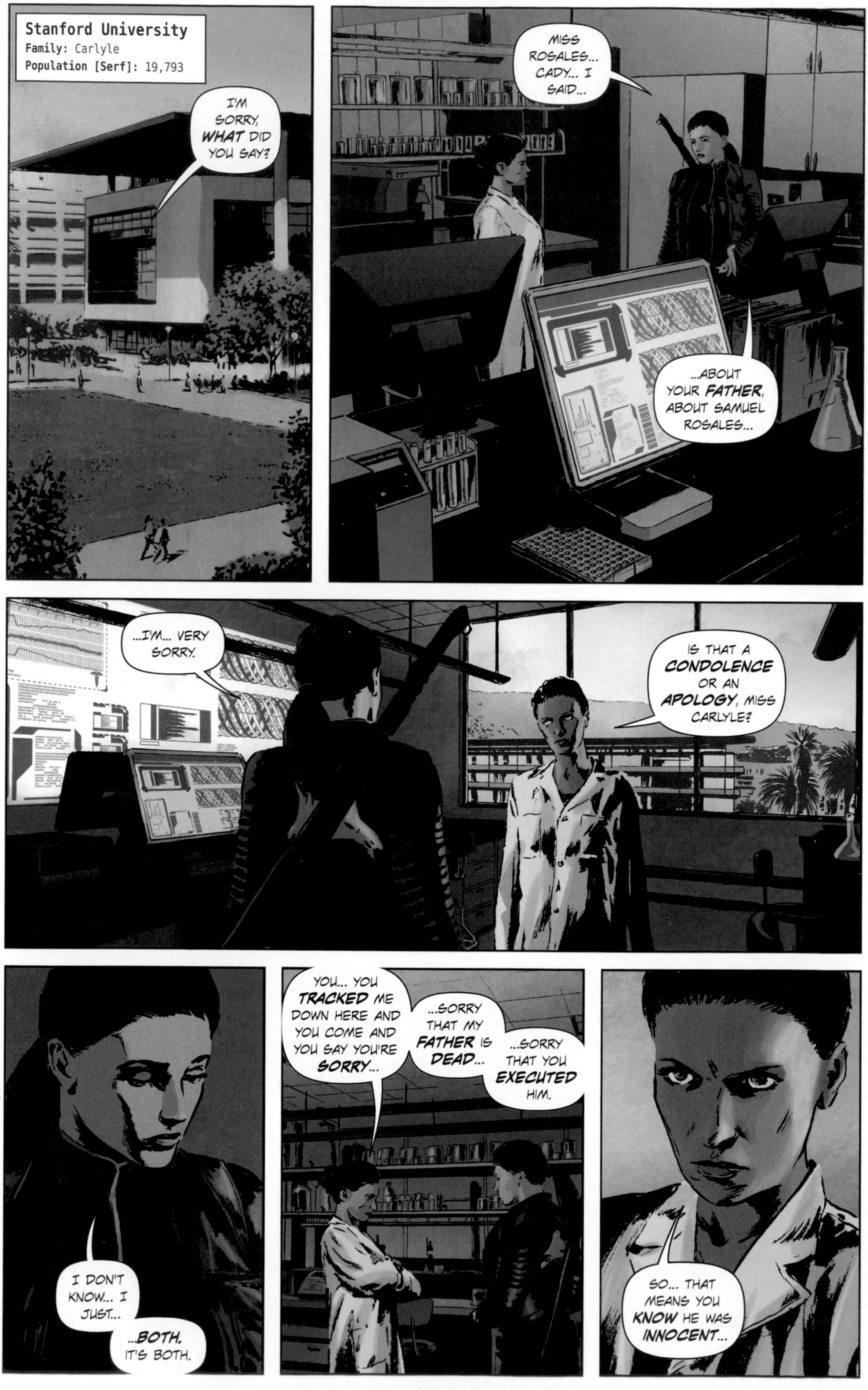
Stanford University
Family: Carlyle
Population [Serf]: 19,793
I'M SORRY, WHAT DID YOU SAY?
MISS ROSALES... CADY... I SAID...
...ABOUT YOUR FATHER, ABOUT SAMUEL ROSALES...
...I'M... VERY SORRY.
IS THAT A CONDOLENCE OR AN APOLOGY, MISS CARLYLE?
I DON'T KNOW... I JUST...
...BOTH. IT'S BOTH.
YOU... YOU TRACKED ME DOWN HERE AND YOU COME AND YOU SAY YOU'RE SORRY...
...SORRY THAT MY FATHER IS DEAD...
...SORRY THAT YOU EXECUTED HIM.
SO... THAT MEANS YOU KNOW HE WAS INNOCENT...

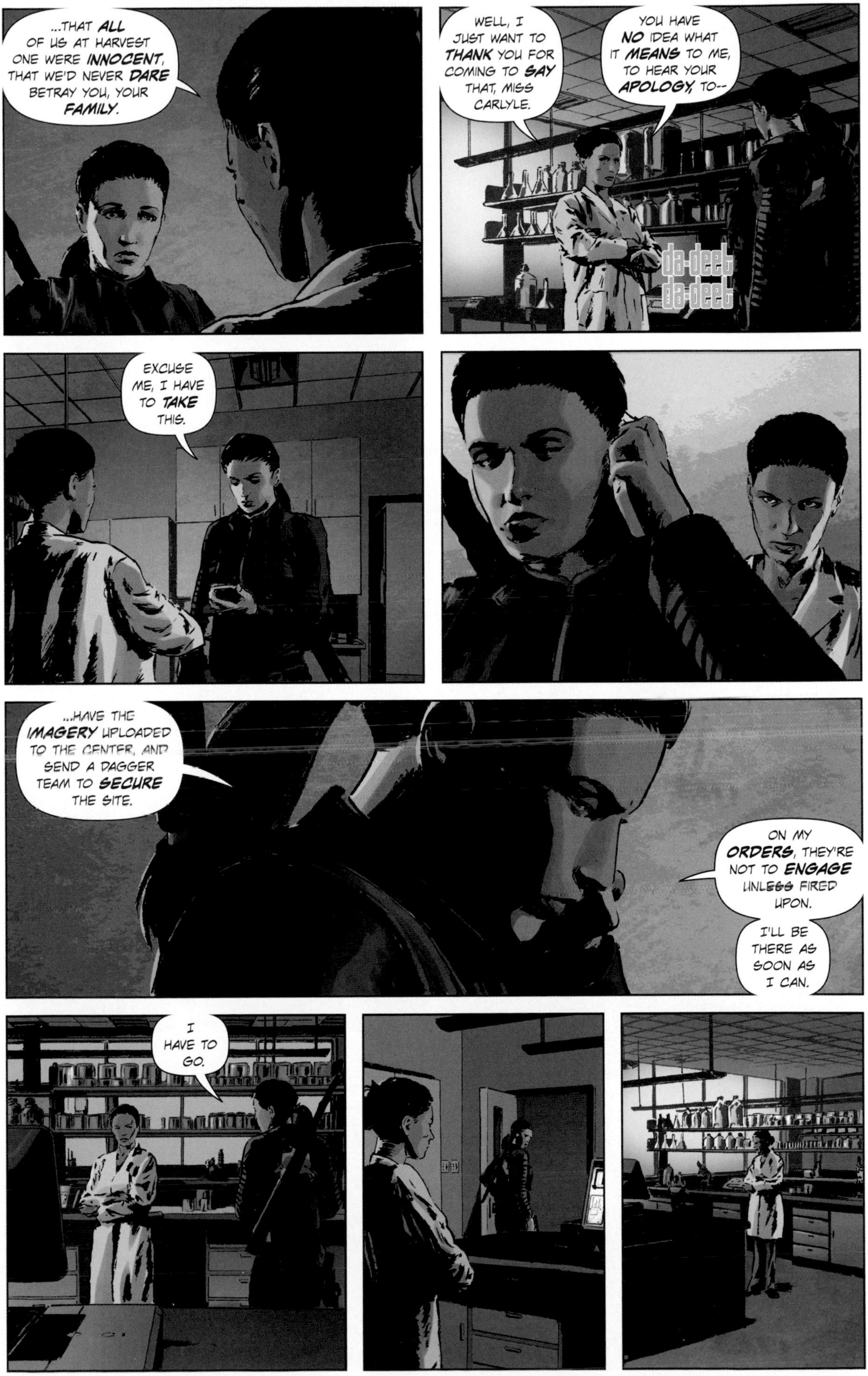
...THAT ALL OF US AT HARVEST ONE WERE INNOCENT, THAT WE'D NEVER DARE BETRAY YOU, YOUR FAMILY.
WELL, I JUST WANT TO THANK YOU FOR COMING TO SAY THAT, MISS CARLYLE.
YOU HAVE NO IDEA WHAT IT MEANS TO ME, TO HEAR YOUR APOLOGY, TO--
da-deet da-deet
EXCUSE ME, I HAVE TO TAKE THIS.
...HAVE THE IMAGERY UPLOADED TO THE CENTER, AND SEND A DAGGER TEAM TO SECURE THE SITE.
ON MY ORDERS, THEY'RE NOT TO ENGAGE UNLESS FIRED UPON.
I'LL BE THERE AS SOON AS I CAN.
I HAVE TO GO.

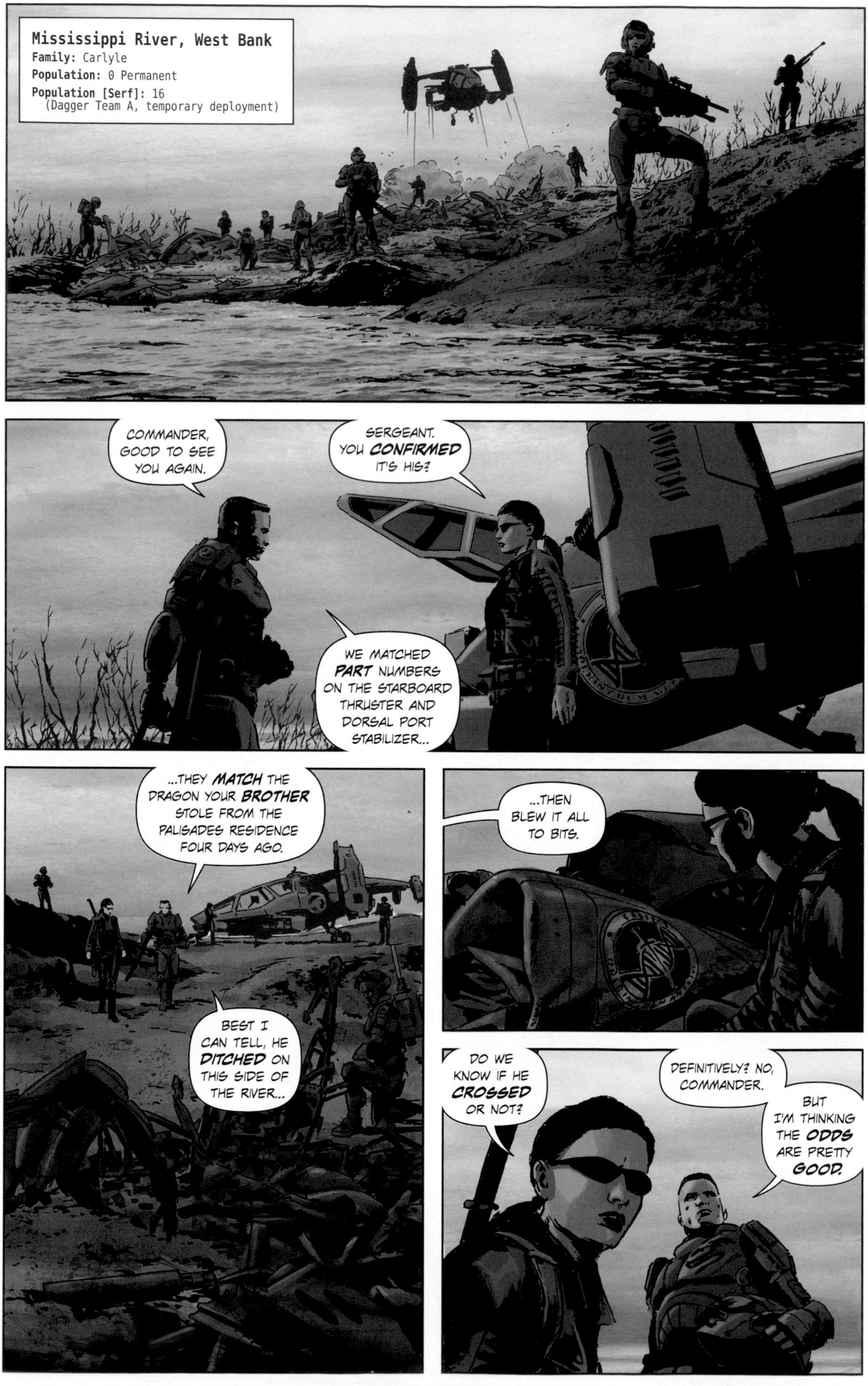
Mississippi River, West Bank
Family: Carlyle
Population: 0 Permanent
Population [Serf]: 16
(Dagger Team A, temporary deployment)
COMMANDER, GOOD TO SEE YOU AGAIN.
SERGEANT. YOU CONFIRMED IT'S HIS?
WE MATCHED PART NUMBERS ON THE STARBOARD THRUSTER AND DORSAL PORT STABILIZER...
...THEY MATCH THE DRAGON YOUR BROTHER STOLE FROM THE PALISADES RESIDENCE FOUR DAYS AGO.
BEST I CAN TELL, HE DITCHED ON THIS SIDE OF THE RIVER...
...THEN BLEW IT ALL TO BITS.
DO WE KNOW IF HE CROSSED OR NOT?
DEFINITIVELY? NO, COMMANDER.
BUT I'M THINKING THE ODDS ARE PRETTY GOOD.

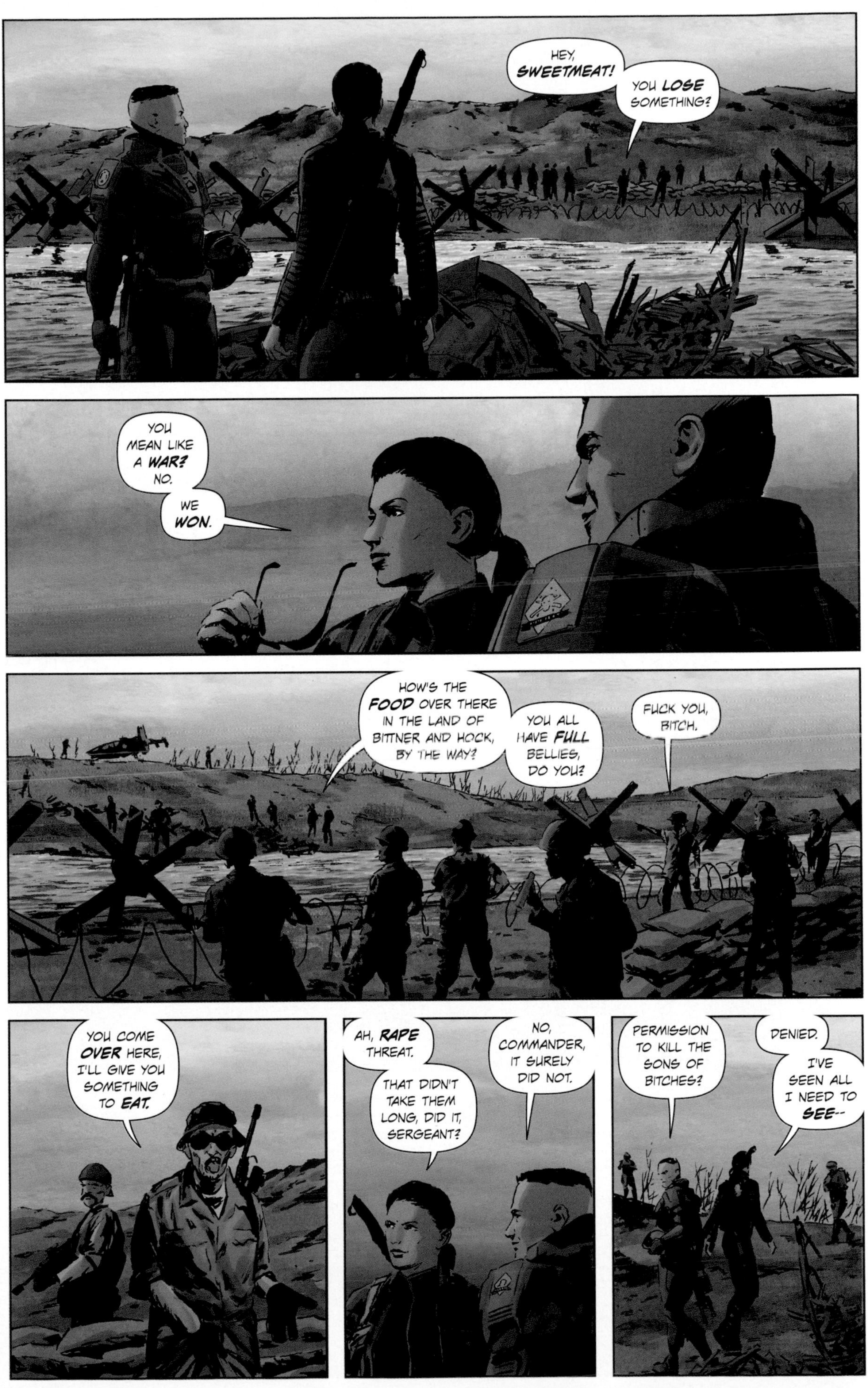
HEY, SWEETMEAT!
YOU LOSE SOMETHING?
YOU MEAN LIKE A WAR? NO.
WE WON.
HOW'S THE FOOD OVER THERE IN THE LAND OF BITTNER AND HOCK, BY THE WAY?
YOU ALL HAVE FULL BELLIES, DO YOU?
FUCK YOU, BITCH.
YOU COME OVER HERE, I'LL GIVE YOU SOMETHING TO EAT.
AH, RAPE THREAT.
THAT DIDN'T TAKE THEM LONG, DID IT, SERGEANT?
NO, COMMANDER, IT SURELY DID NOT.
PERMISSION TO KILL THE SONS OF BITCHES?
DENIED.
I'VE SEEN ALL I NEED TO SEE--

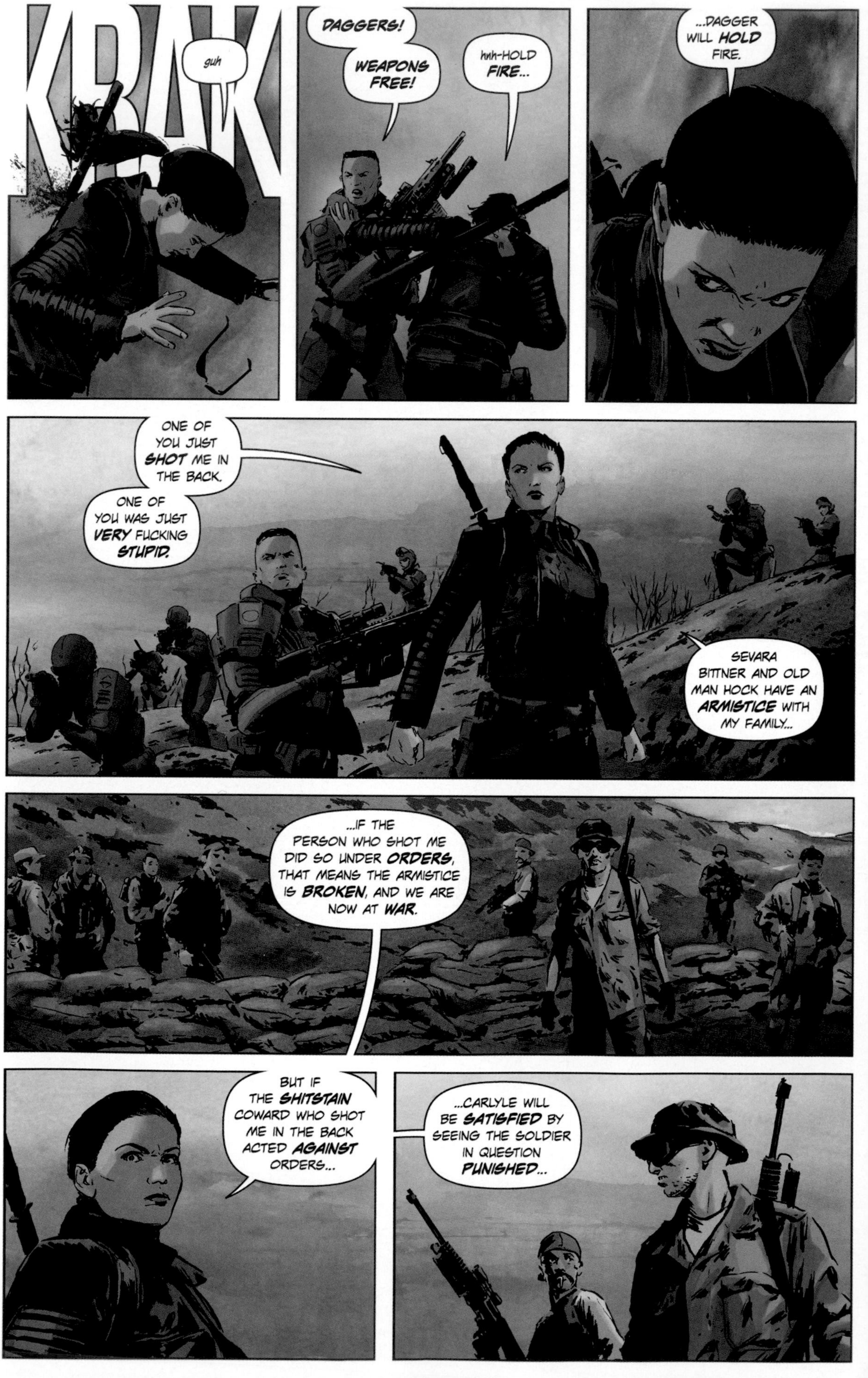
KRAK
guh
DAGGERS!
WEAPONS FREE!
hnh-HOLD FIRE...
...DAGGER WILL HOLD FIRE.
ONE OF YOU JUST SHOT ME IN THE BACK.
ONE OF YOU WAS JUST VERY FUCKING STUPID.
SEVARA BITTNER AND OLD MAN HOCK HAVE AN ARMISTICE WITH MY FAMILY...
...IF THE PERSON WHO SHOT ME DID SO UNDER ORDERS, THAT MEANS THE ARMISTICE IS BROKEN, AND WE ARE NOW AT WAR.
BUT IF THE SHITSTAIN COWARD WHO SHOT ME IN THE BACK ACTED AGAINST ORDERS...
...CARLYLE WILL BE SATISFIED BY SEEING THE SOLDIER IN QUESTION PUNISHED...

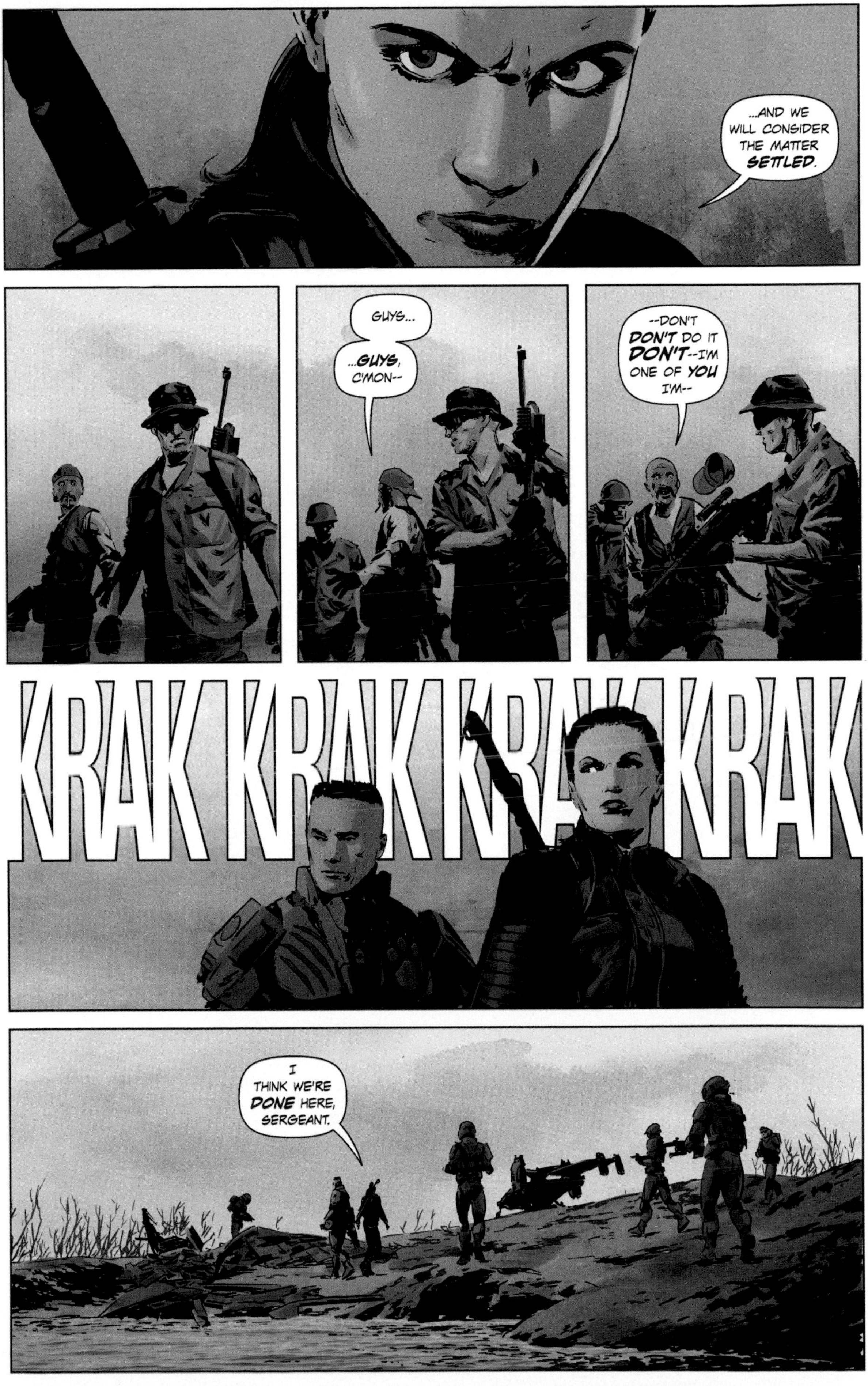

...AND WE WILL CONSIDER THE MATTER SETTLED.
GUYS...
...GUYS, C'MON--
--DON'T DON'T DO IT DON'T--I'M ONE OF YOU I'M--
KRAK KRAK KRAK KRAK
I THINK WE'RE DONE HERE, SERGEANT.

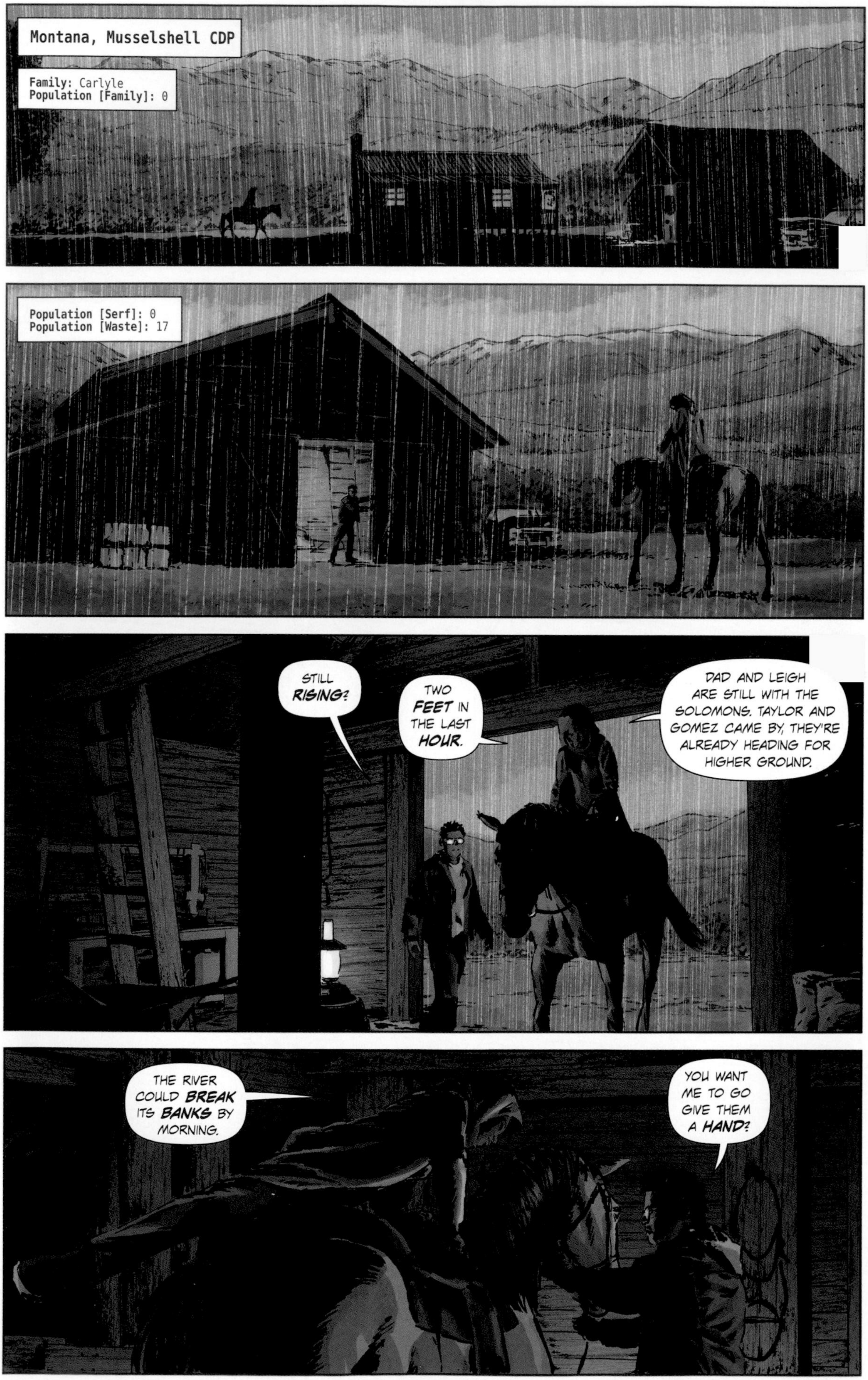
Montana, Musselshell CDP
Family: Carlyle
Population [Family]: 0
Population [Serf]: 0
Population [Waste]: 17
STILL RISING?
TWO FEET IN THE LAST HOUR.
DAD AND LEIGH ARE STILL WITH THE SOLOMONS. TAYLOR AND GOMEZ CAME BY, THEY'RE ALREADY HEADING FOR HIGHER GROUND.
THE RIVER COULD BREAK ITS BANKS BY MORNING.
YOU WANT ME TO GO GIVE THEM A HAND?

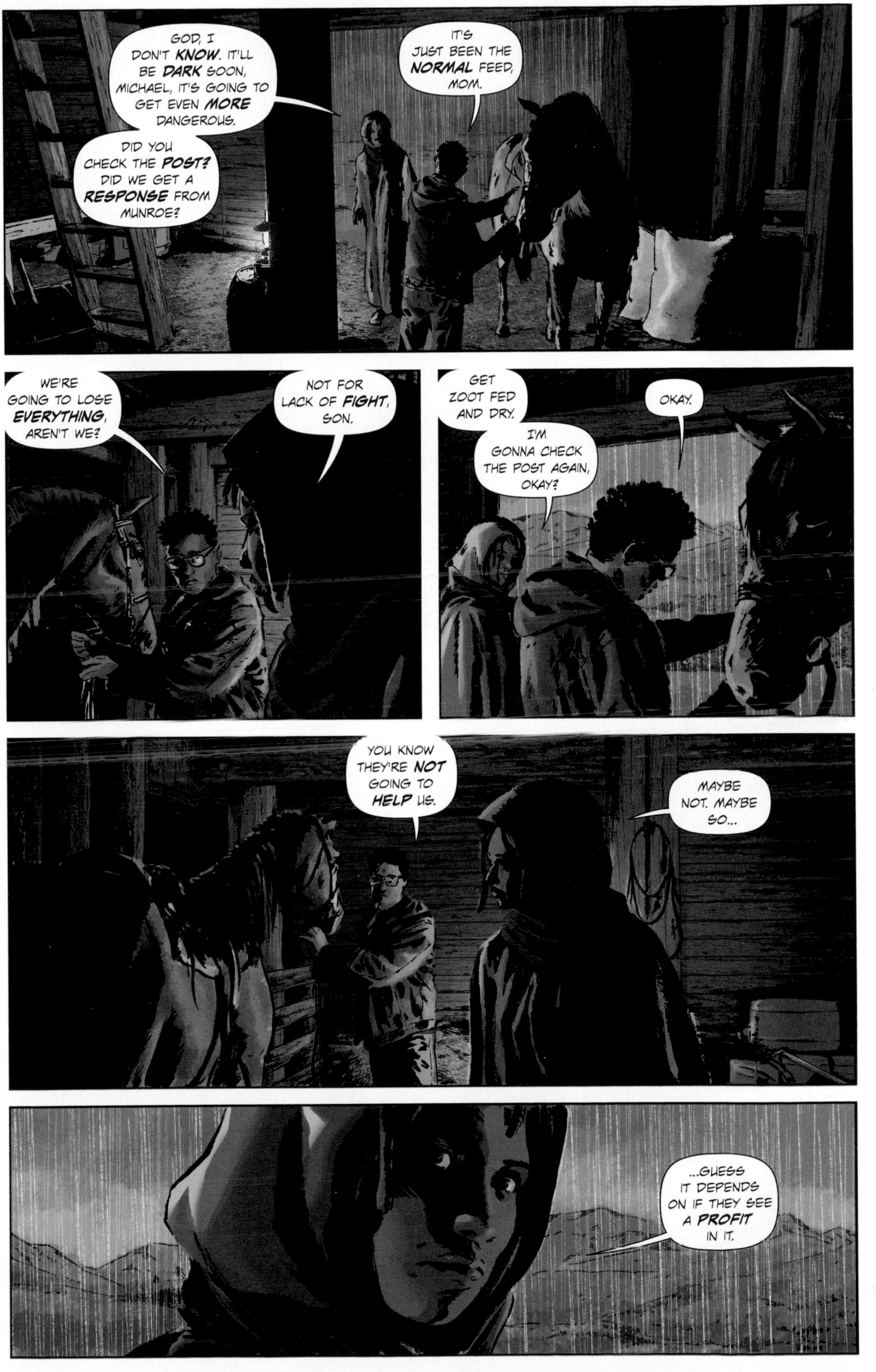
GOD, I DON'T KNOW. IT'LL BE DARK SOON, MICHAEL, IT'S GOING TO GET EVEN MORE DANGEROUS.
IT'S JUST BEEN THE NORMAL FEED, MOM.
DID YOU CHECK THE POST? DID WE GET A RESPONSE FROM MUNROE?
WE'RE GOING TO LOSE EVERYTHING, AREN'T WE?
NOT FOR LACK OF FIGHT, SON.
GET ZOOT FED AND DRY.
OKAY.
I'M GONNA CHECK THE POST AGAIN, OKAY?
YOU KNOW THEY'RE NOT GOING TO HELP US.
MAYBE NOT. MAYBE SO...
...GUESS IT DEPENDS ON IF THEY SEE A PROFIT IN IT.

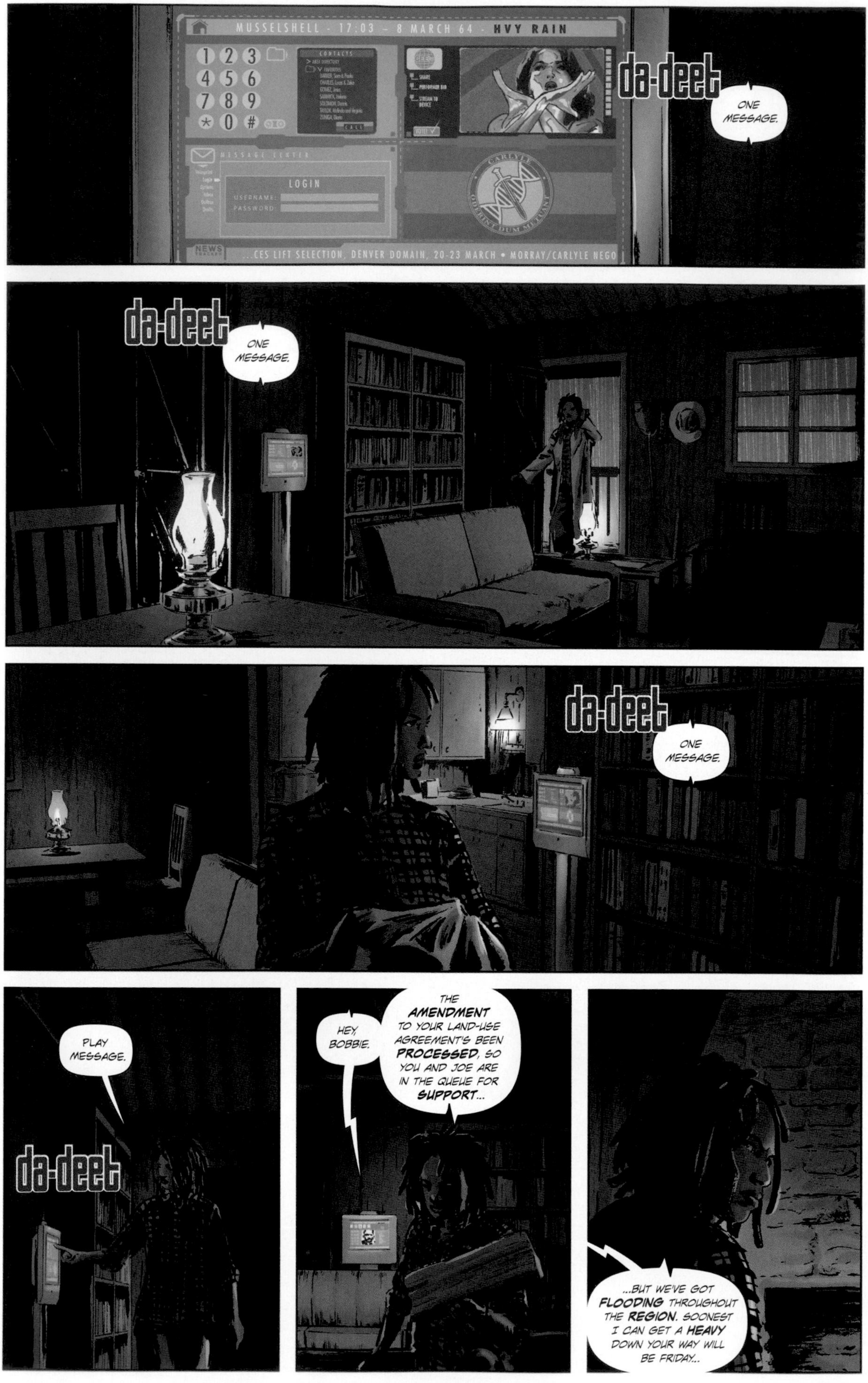
MUSSELSHELL - 17:03 - 8 MARCH 64 - HVY RAIN
CONTACTS
MESSAGE CENTER
LOGIN
USERNAME:
PASSWORD:
CARLYLE
...CES LIFT SELECTION, DENVER DOMAIN, 20-23 MARCH • MORRAY/CARLYLE NEGO
da-deet
ONE MESSAGE.
da-deet
ONE MESSAGE.
da-deet
ONE MESSAGE.
PLAY MESSAGE.
da-deet
HEY, BOBBIE.
THE AMENDMENT TO YOUR LAND-USE AGREEMENT'S BEEN PROCESSED, SO YOU AND JOE ARE IN THE QUEUE FOR SUPPORT...
...BUT WE'VE GOT FLOODING THROUGHOUT THE REGION. SOONEST I CAN GET A HEAVY DOWN YOUR WAY WILL BE FRIDAY...

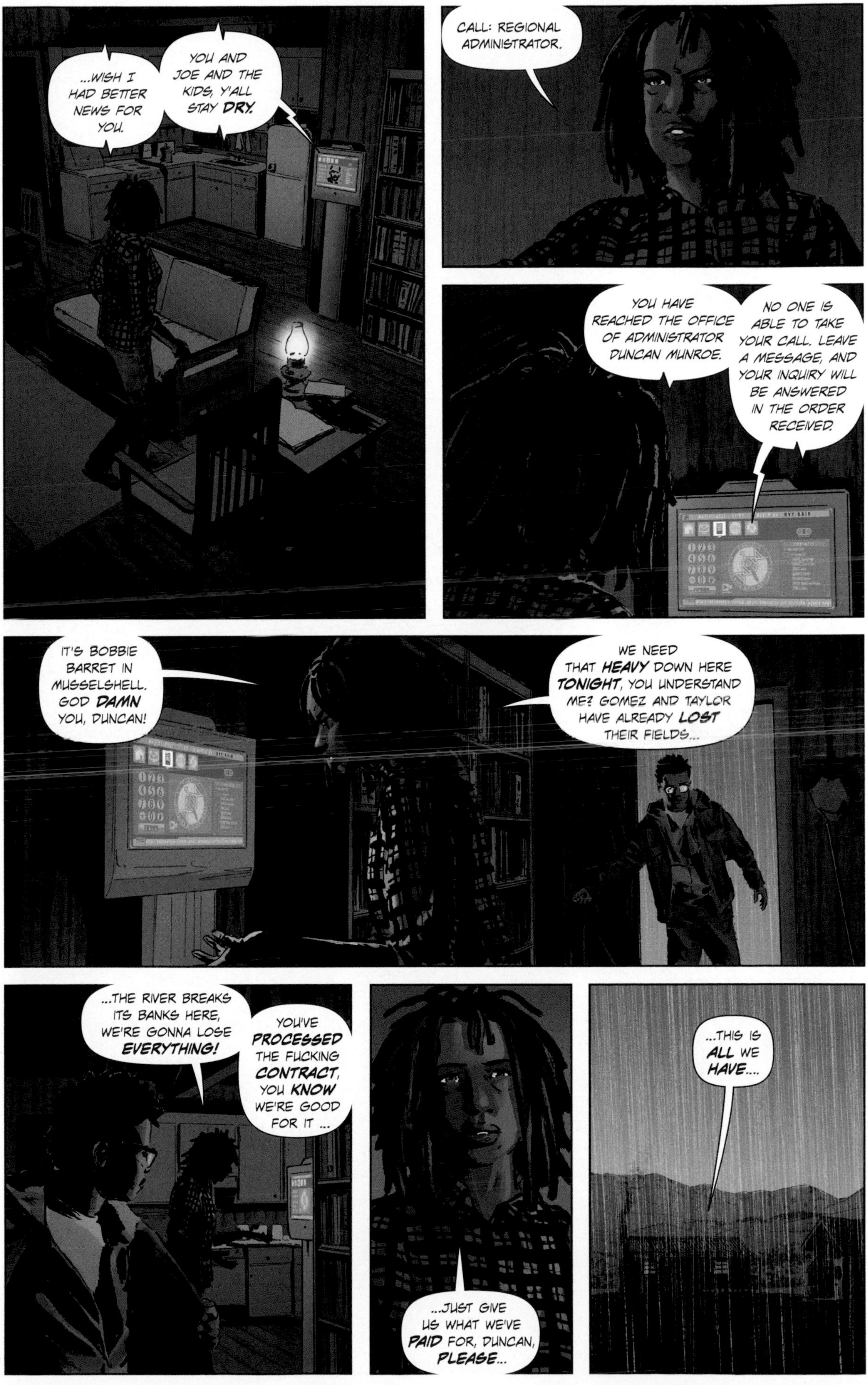
...WISH I HAD BETTER NEWS FOR YOU.
YOU AND JOE AND THE KIDS, Y'ALL STAY DRY.
CALL: REGIONAL ADMINISTRATOR.
YOU HAVE REACHED THE OFFICE OF ADMINISTRATOR DUNCAN MUNROE.
NO ONE IS ABLE TO TAKE YOUR CALL. LEAVE A MESSAGE, AND YOUR INQUIRY WILL BE ANSWERED IN THE ORDER RECEIVED.
IT'S BOBBIE BARRET IN MUSSELSHELL. GOD DAMN YOU, DUNCAN!
WE NEED THAT HEAVY DOWN HERE TONIGHT, YOU UNDERSTAND ME? GOMEZ AND TAYLOR HAVE ALREADY LOST THEIR FIELDS...
...THE RIVER BREAKS ITS BANKS HERE, WE'RE GONNA LOSE EVERYTHING!
YOU'VE PROCESSED THE FUCKING CONTRACT, YOU KNOW WE'RE GOOD FOR IT ...
...JUST GIVE US WHAT WE'VE PAID FOR, DUNCAN, PLEASE...
...THIS IS ALL WE HAVE....

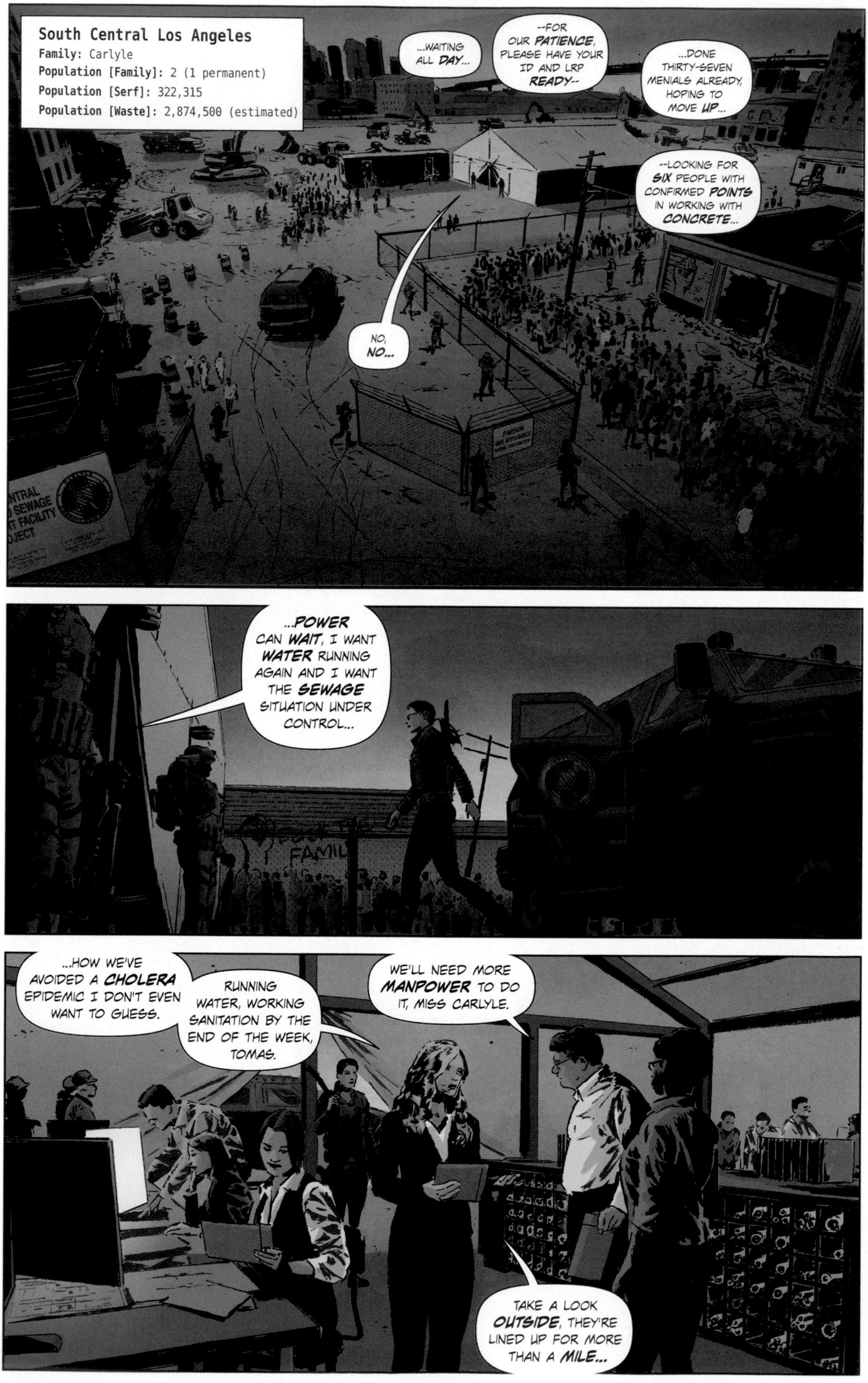
South Central Los Angeles
Family: Carlyle
Population [Family]: 2 (1 permanent)
Population [Serf]: 322,315
Population [Waste]: 2,874,500 (estimated)
...WAITING ALL DAY...
--FOR OUR PATIENCE, PLEASE HAVE YOUR ID AND LRP READY--
...DONE THIRTY-SEVEN MENIALS ALREADY, HOPING TO MOVE UP...
--LOOKING FOR SIX PEOPLE WITH CONFIRMED POINTS IN WORKING WITH CONCRETE...
NO, NO...
...POWER CAN WAIT, I WANT WATER RUNNING AGAIN AND I WANT THE SEWAGE SITUATION UNDER CONTROL...
...HOW WE'VE AVOIDED A CHOLERA EPIDEMIC I DON'T EVEN WANT TO GUESS.
RUNNING WATER, WORKING SANITATION BY THE END OF THE WEEK, TOMAS.
WE'LL NEED MORE MANPOWER TO DO IT, MISS CARLYLE.
TAKE A LOOK OUTSIDE, THEY'RE LINED UP FOR MORE THAN A MILE...

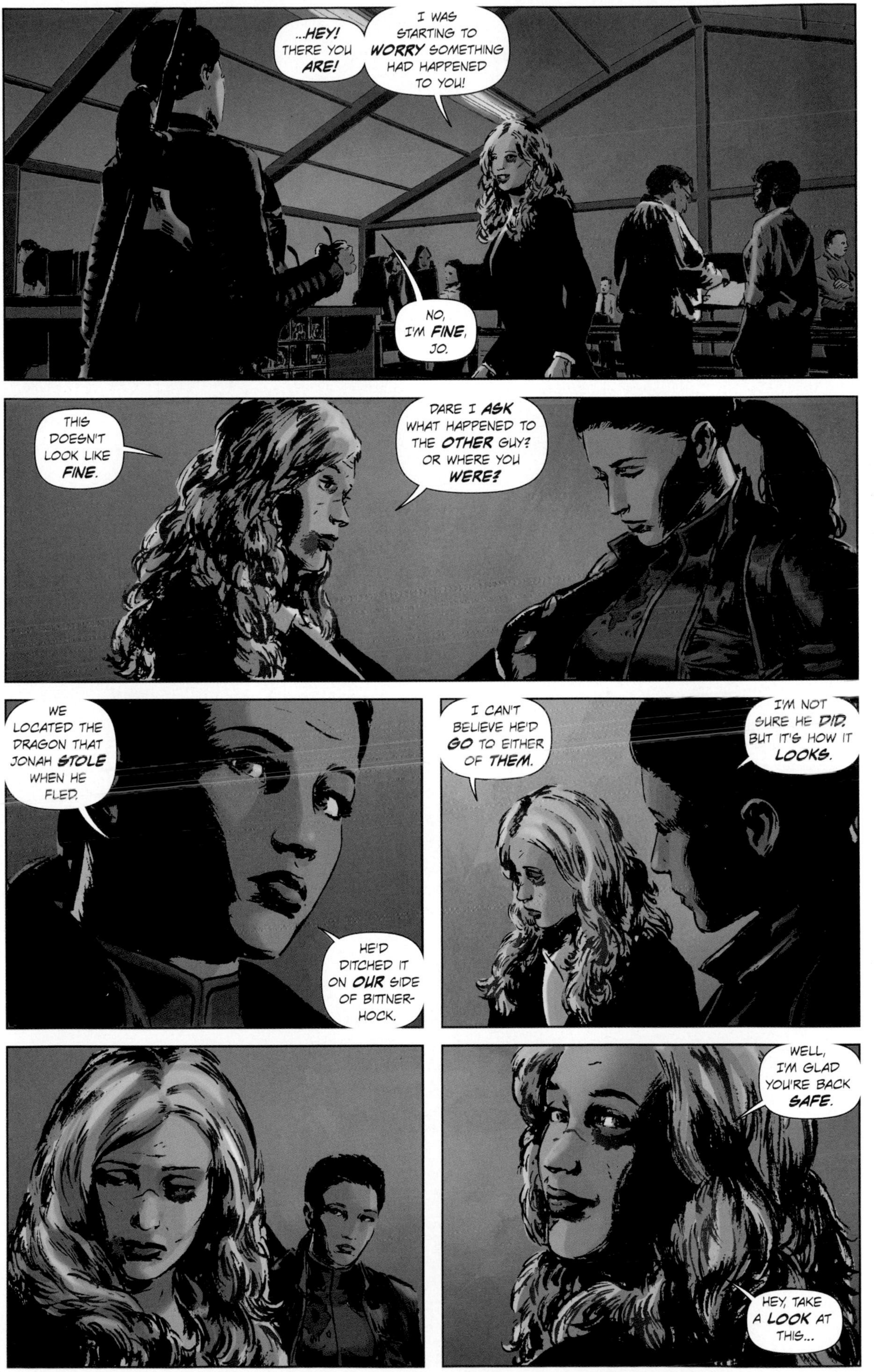
...HEY! THERE YOU ARE!
I WAS STARTING TO WORRY SOMETHING HAD HAPPENED TO YOU!
NO, I'M FINE, JO.
THIS DOESN'T LOOK LIKE FINE.
DARE I ASK WHAT HAPPENED TO THE OTHER GUY? OR WHERE YOU WERE?
WE LOCATED THE DRAGON THAT JONAH STOLE WHEN HE FLED.
HE'D DITCHED IT ON OUR SIDE OF BITTNER-HOCK.
I CAN'T BELIEVE HE'D GO TO EITHER OF THEM.
I'M NOT SURE HE DID, BUT IT'S HOW IT LOOKS.
WELL, I'M GLAD YOU'RE BACK SAFE.
HEY, TAKE A LOOK AT THIS...

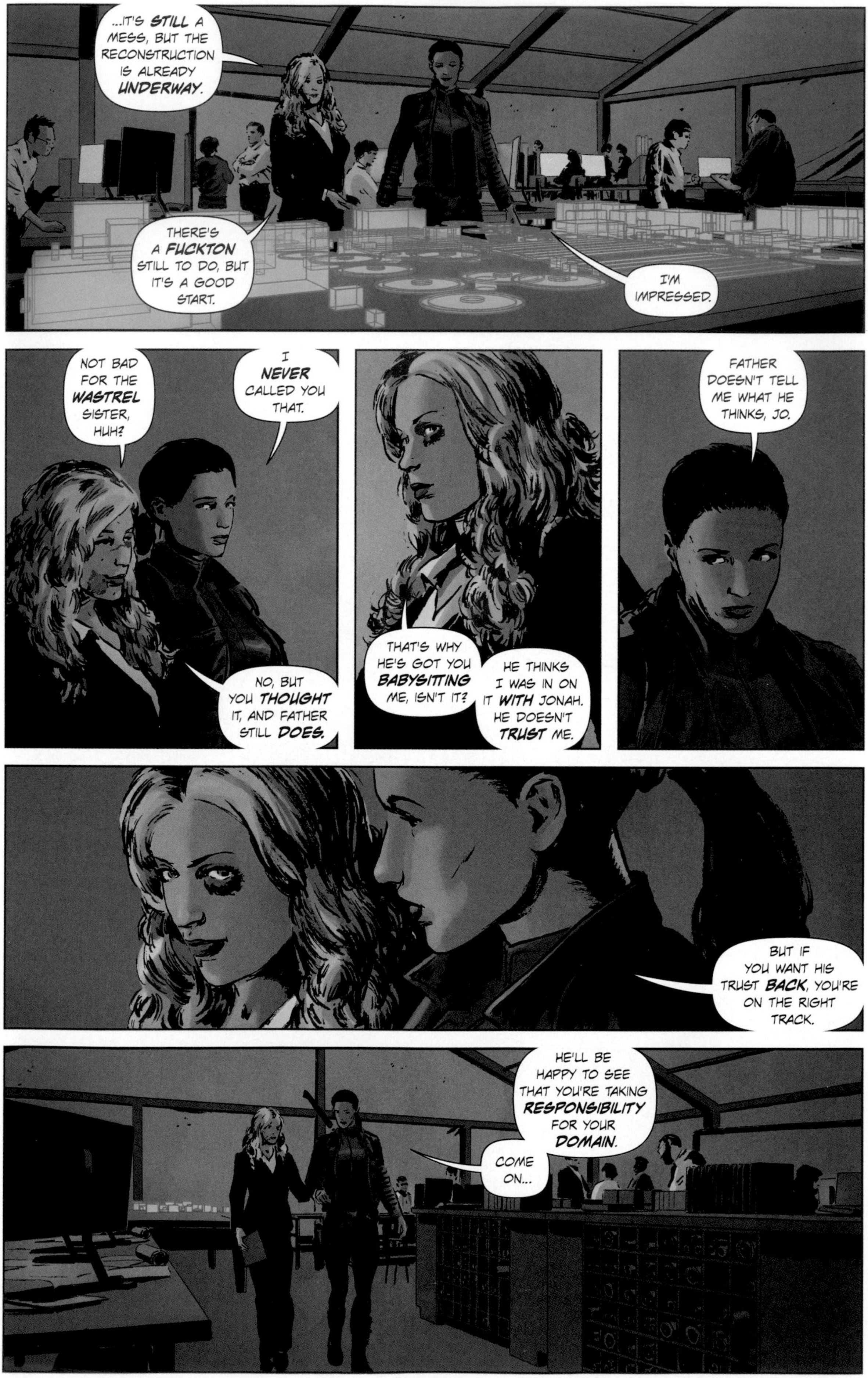
...IT'S STILL A MESS, BUT THE RECONSTRUCTION IS ALREADY UNDERWAY.
THERE'S A FUCKTON STILL TO DO, BUT IT'S A GOOD START.
I'M IMPRESSED.
NOT BAD FOR THE WASTREL SISTER, HUH?
I NEVER CALLED YOU THAT.
NO, BUT YOU THOUGHT IT, AND FATHER STILL DOES.
THAT'S WHY HE'S GOT YOU BABYSITTING ME, ISN'T IT?
HE THINKS I WAS IN ON IT WITH JONAH. HE DOESN'T TRUST ME.
FATHER DOESN'T TELL ME WHAT HE THINKS, JO.
BUT IF YOU WANT HIS TRUST BACK, YOU'RE ON THE RIGHT TRACK.
HE'LL BE HAPPY TO SEE THAT YOU'RE TAKING RESPONSIBILITY FOR YOUR DOMAIN.
COME ON...

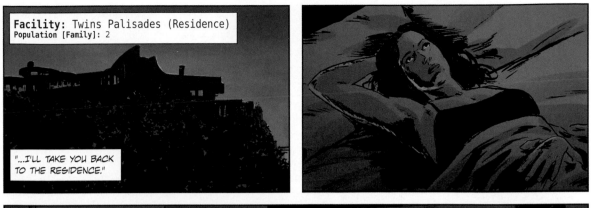

**Facility:** Twins Palisades (Residence)
Population [Family]: 2

"...I'LL TAKE YOU BACK
TO THE RESIDENCE."

TO: CARLYLE_FOREVER
FROM: X#%UNKNOWN#1%NERROR

HE IS NOT
YOUR FATHER.

THIS IS NOT
YOUR FAMILY.

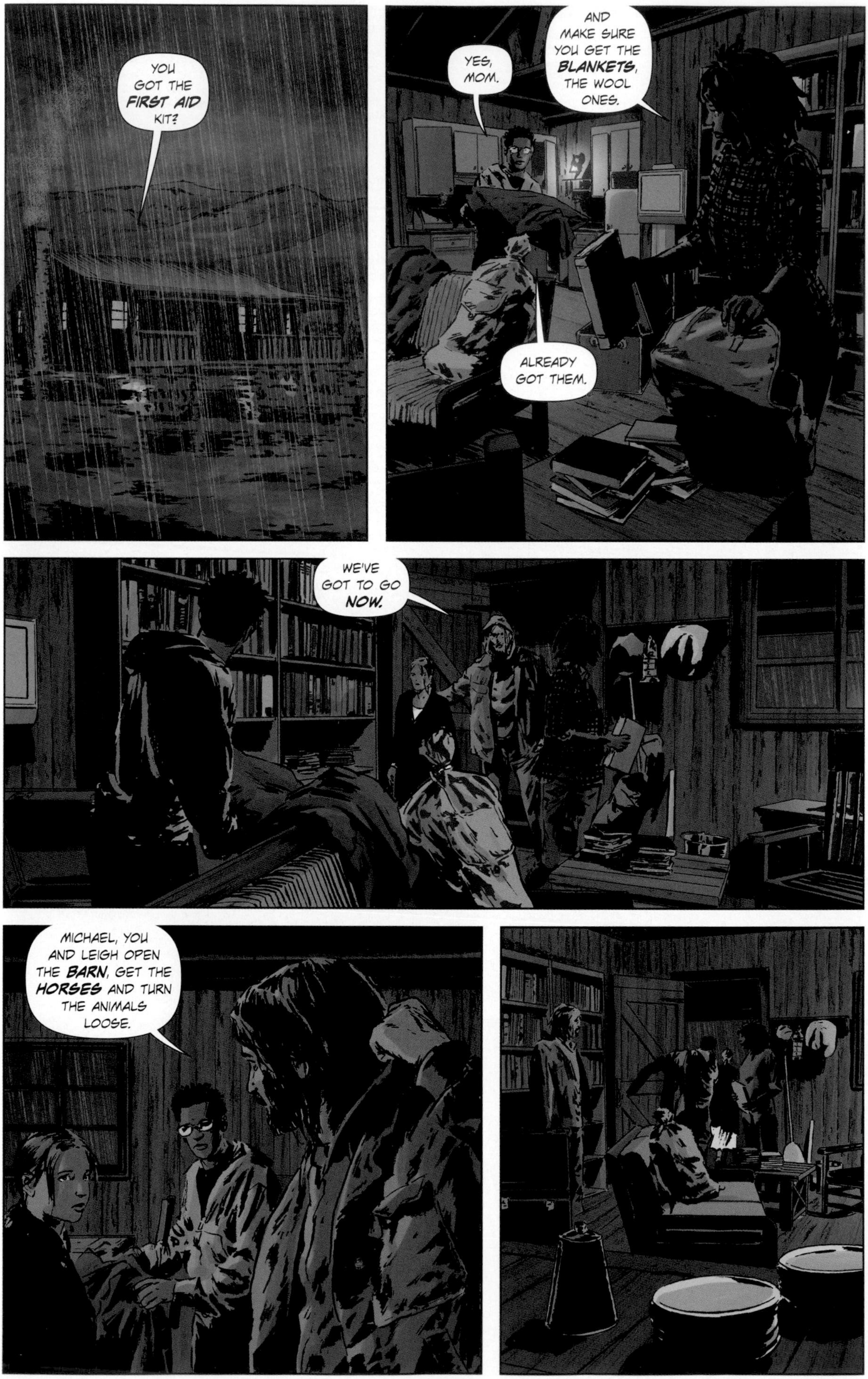
YOU GOT THE FIRST AID KIT?
YES, MOM.
AND MAKE SURE YOU GET THE BLANKETS, THE WOOL ONES.
ALREADY GOT THEM.
WE'VE GOT TO GO NOW.
MICHAEL, YOU AND LEIGH OPEN THE BARN, GET THE HORSES AND TURN THE ANIMALS LOOSE.

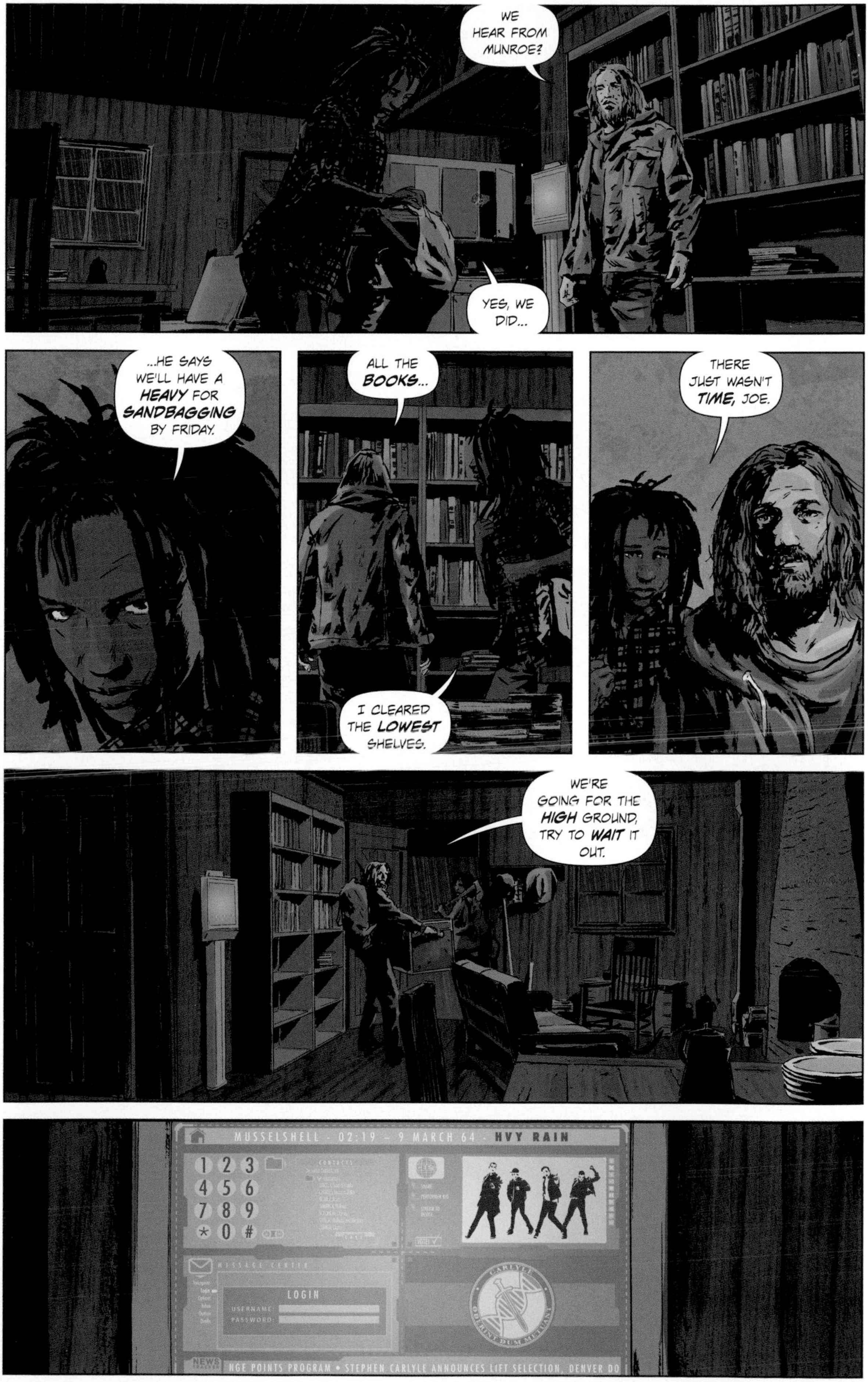
WE HEAR FROM MUNROE?
YES, WE DID...
...HE SAYS WE'LL HAVE A HEAVY FOR SANDBAGGING BY FRIDAY.
ALL THE BOOKS...
I CLEARED THE LOWEST SHELVES.
THERE JUST WASN'T TIME, JOE.
WE'RE GOING FOR THE HIGH GROUND, TRY TO WAIT IT OUT.
MUSSELSHELL - 02:19 - 9 MARCH 64 - HVY RAIN
1 2 3
4 5 6
7 8 9
* 0 #
CONTACTS
MESSAGE CENTER
LOGIN
USERNAME:
PASSWORD:
CARLYLE
NEWS
HGE POINTS PROGRAM • STEPHEN CARLYLE ANNOUNCES LIFT SELECTION, DENVER DO

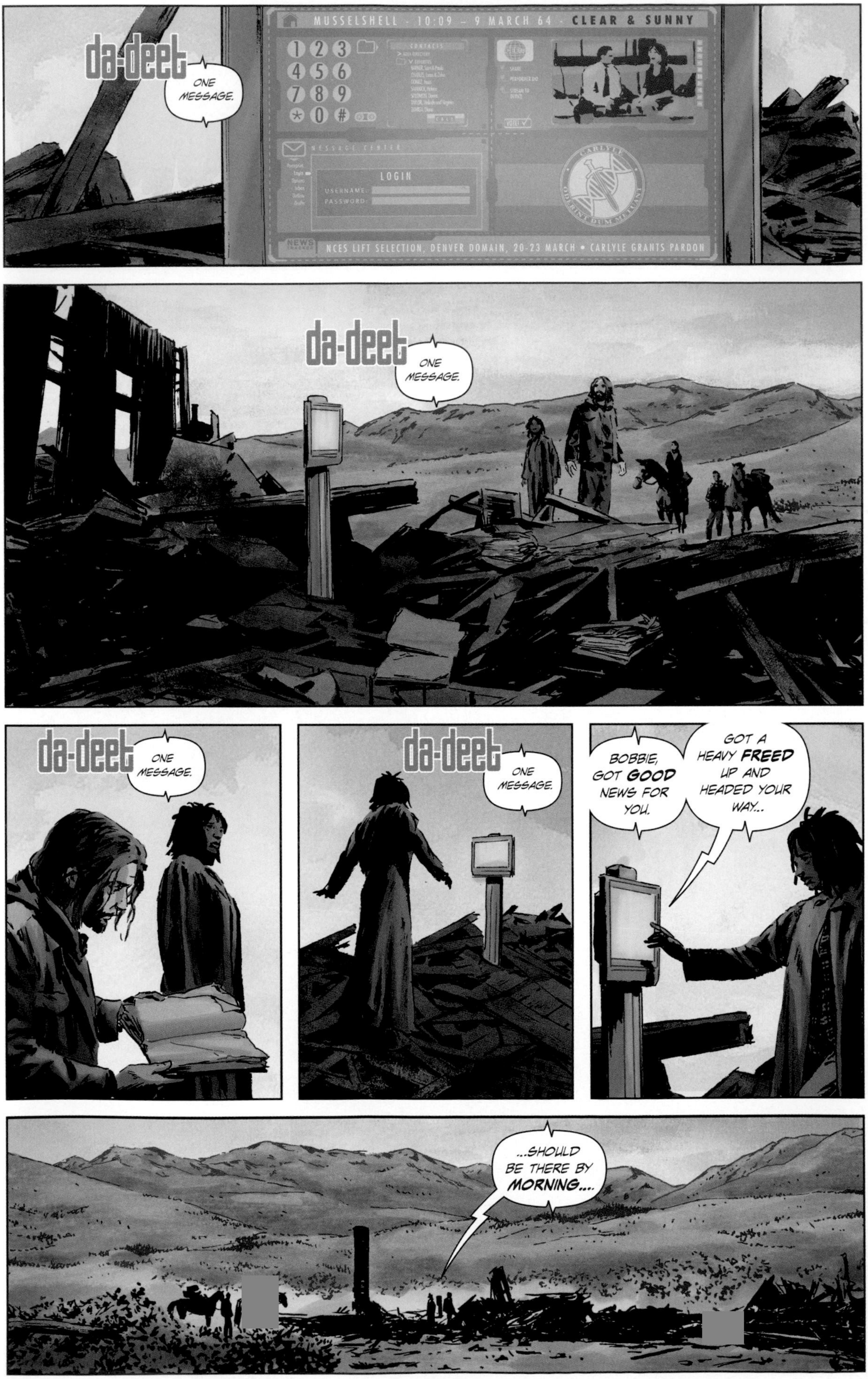
MUSSELSHELL - 10:09 - 9 MARCH 64 - CLEAR & SUNNY
1 2 3 4 5 6 7 8 9 * 0 #
CONTACTS
MESSAGE CENTER
LOGIN
USERNAME:
PASSWORD:
NEWS
NCES LIFT SELECTION, DENVER DOMAIN, 20-23 MARCH • CARLYLE GRANTS PARDON
da-deet
ONE MESSAGE.
da-deet
ONE MESSAGE.
da-deet
ONE MESSAGE.
da-deet
ONE MESSAGE.
BOBBIE, GOT GOOD NEWS FOR YOU.
GOT A HEAVY FREED UP AND HEADED YOUR WAY...
...SHOULD BE THERE BY MORNING....

# LIFT
CHAPTER TWO

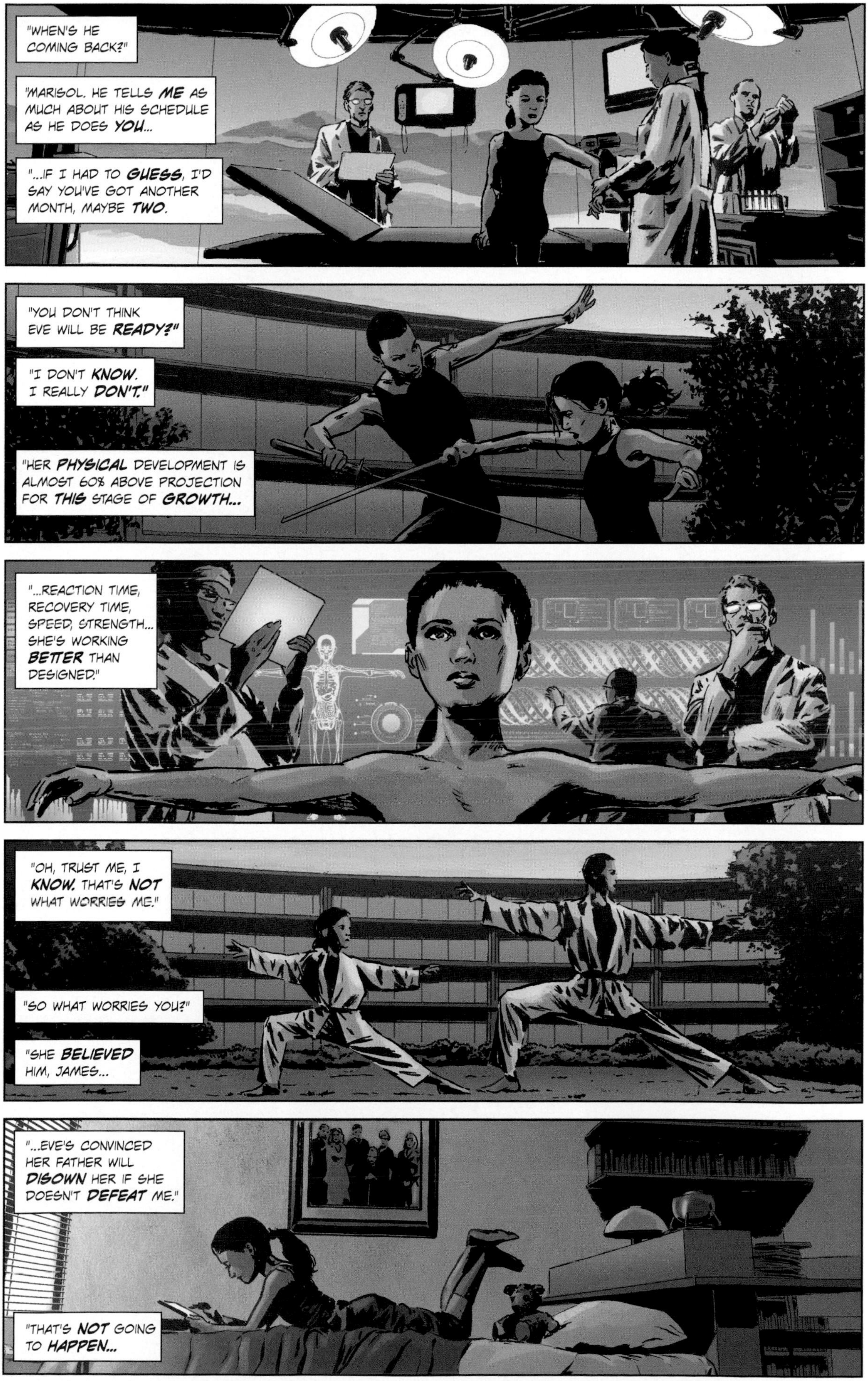
"WHEN'S HE COMING BACK?"
"MARISOL. HE TELLS ME AS MUCH ABOUT HIS SCHEDULE AS HE DOES YOU...
"...IF I HAD TO GUESS, I'D SAY YOU'VE GOT ANOTHER MONTH, MAYBE TWO.
"YOU DON'T THINK EVE WILL BE READY?"
"I DON'T KNOW. I REALLY DON'T."
"HER PHYSICAL DEVELOPMENT IS ALMOST 60% ABOVE PROJECTION FOR THIS STAGE OF GROWTH...
"...REACTION TIME, RECOVERY TIME, SPEED, STRENGTH... SHE'S WORKING BETTER THAN DESIGNED."
"OH, TRUST ME, I KNOW. THAT'S NOT WHAT WORRIES ME."
"SO WHAT WORRIES YOU?"
"SHE BELIEVED HIM, JAMES...
"...EVE'S CONVINCED HER FATHER WILL DISOWN HER IF SHE DOESN'T DEFEAT ME."
"THAT'S NOT GOING TO HAPPEN...

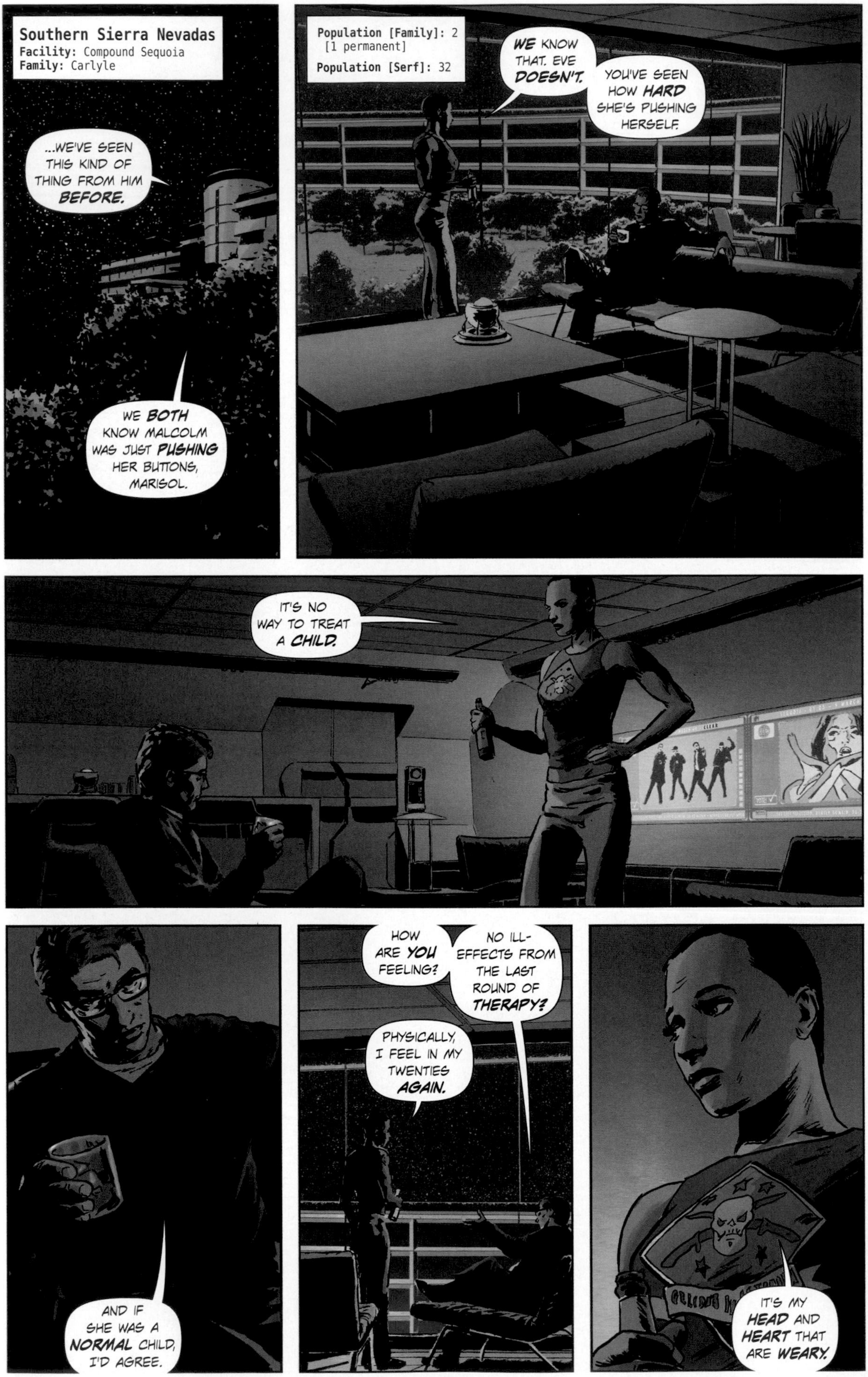
Southern Sierra Nevadas
Facility: Compound Sequoia
Family: Carlyle
...WE'VE SEEN THIS KIND OF THING FROM HIM BEFORE.
WE BOTH KNOW MALCOLM WAS JUST PUSHING HER BUTTONS, MARISOL.
Population [Family]: 2 [1 permanent]
Population [Serf]: 32
WE KNOW THAT. EVE DOESN'T.
YOU'VE SEEN HOW HARD SHE'S PUSHING HERSELF.
IT'S NO WAY TO TREAT A CHILD.
AND IF SHE WAS A NORMAL CHILD, I'D AGREE.
HOW ARE YOU FEELING?
NO ILL-EFFECTS FROM THE LAST ROUND OF THERAPY?
PHYSICALLY, I FEEL IN MY TWENTIES AGAIN.
IT'S MY HEAD AND HEART THAT ARE WEARY.

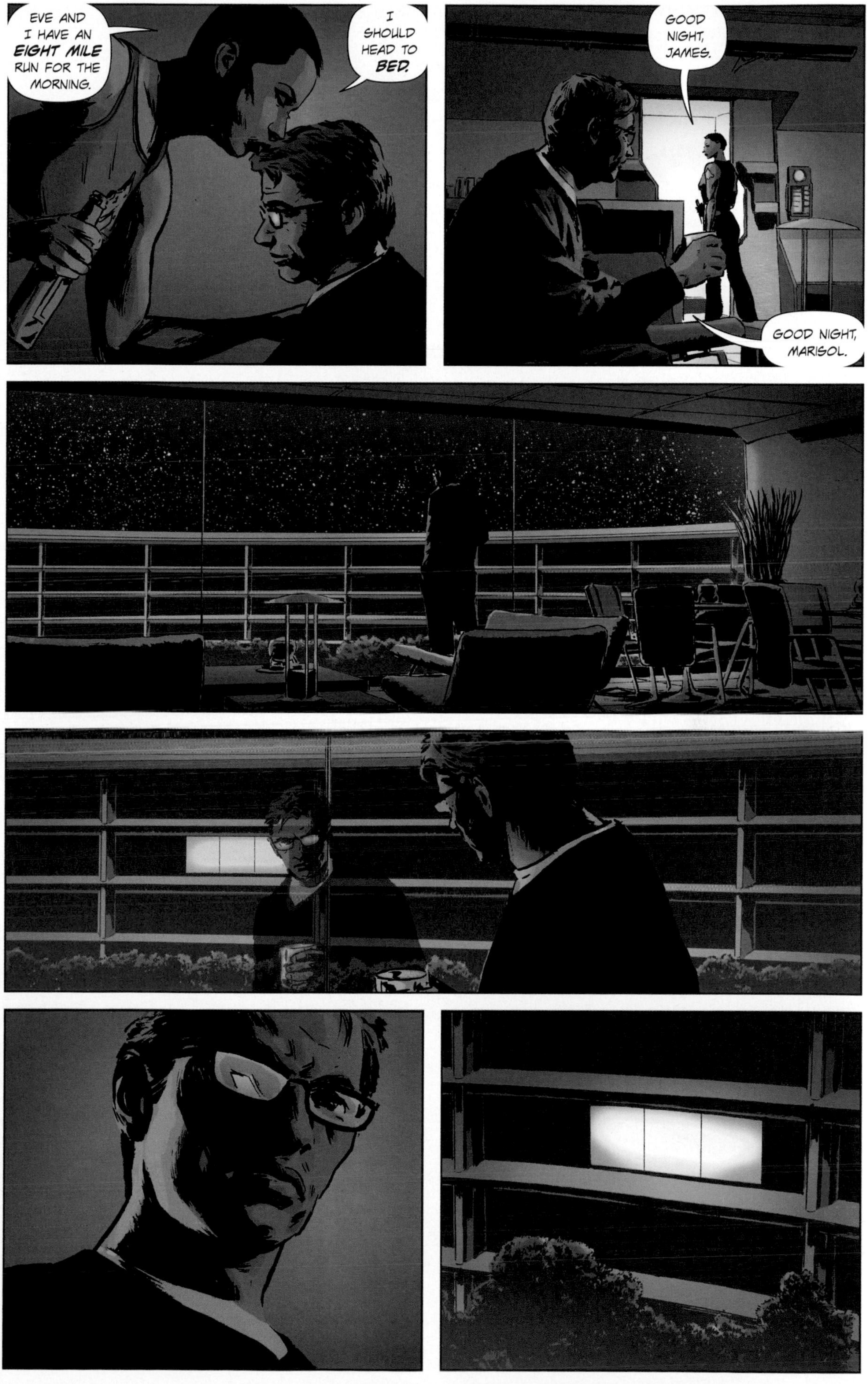

EVE AND I HAVE AN EIGHT MILE RUN FOR THE MORNING.
I SHOULD HEAD TO BED.
GOOD NIGHT, JAMES.
GOOD NIGHT, MARISOL.

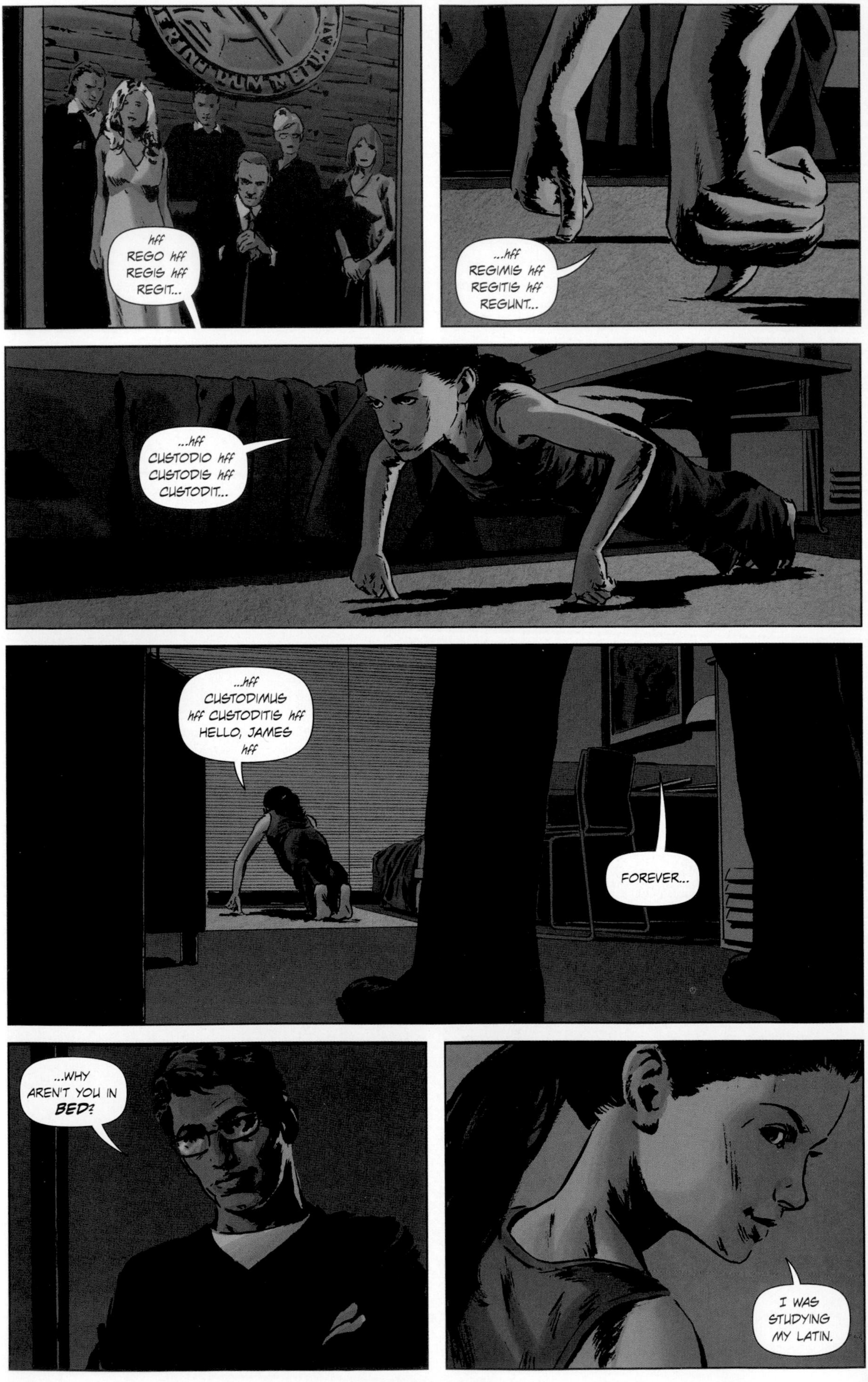
hff REGO hff REGIS hff REGIT...
...hff REGIMIS hff REGITIS hff REGUNT...
...hff CUSTODIO hff CUSTODIS hff CUSTODIT...
...hff CUSTODIMUS hff CUSTODITIS hff HELLO, JAMES hff
FOREVER...
...WHY AREN'T YOU IN BED?
I WAS STUDYING MY LATIN.

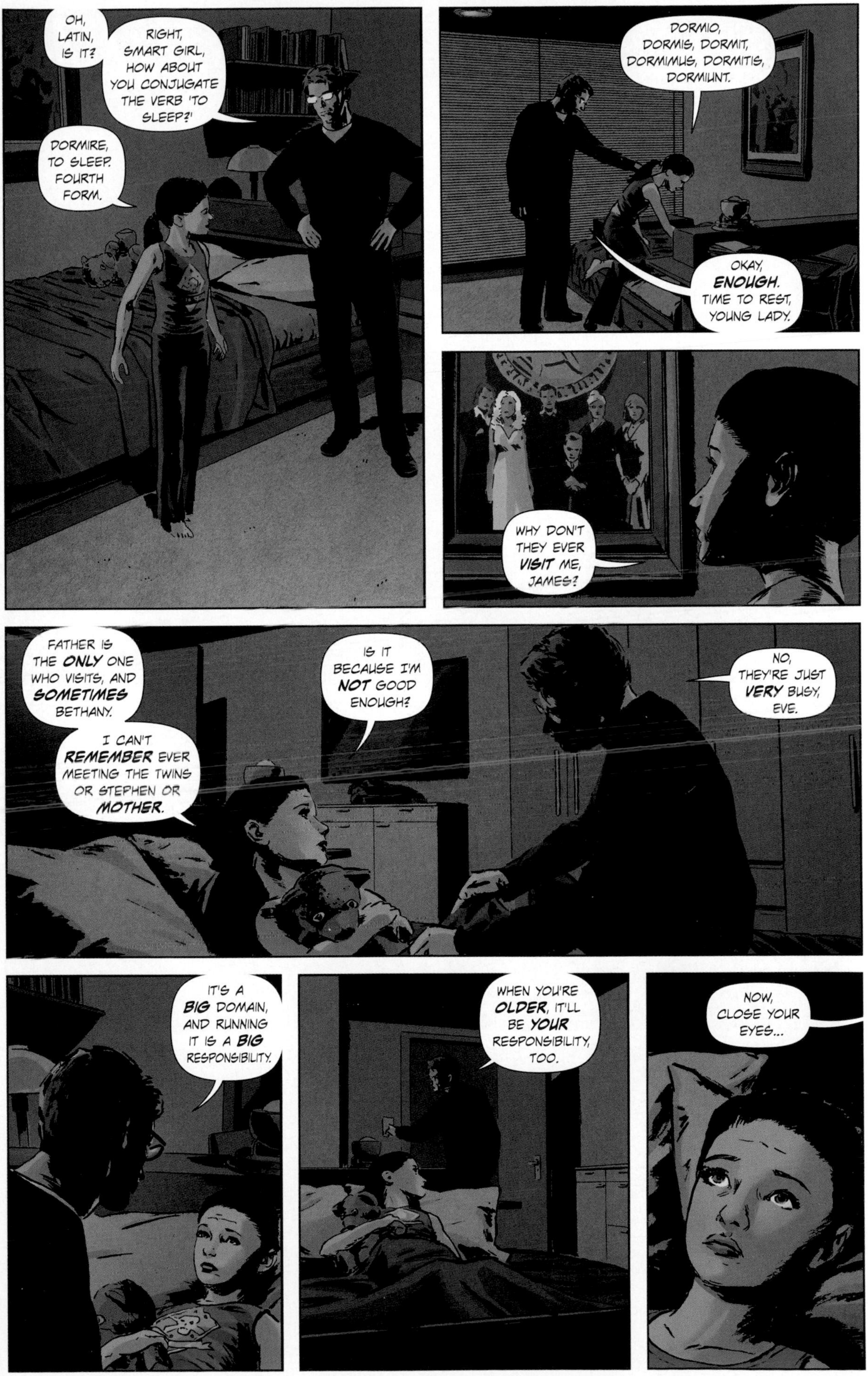
OH, LATIN, IS IT?
RIGHT, SMART GIRL, HOW ABOUT YOU CONJUGATE THE VERB 'TO SLEEP?'
DORMIRE, TO SLEEP. FOURTH FORM.
DORMIO, DORMIS, DORMIT, DORMIMUS, DORMITIS, DORMIUNT.
OKAY, ENOUGH. TIME TO REST, YOUNG LADY.
WHY DON'T THEY EVER VISIT ME, JAMES?
FATHER IS THE ONLY ONE WHO VISITS, AND SOMETIMES BETHANY.
I CAN'T REMEMBER EVER MEETING THE TWINS OR STEPHEN OR MOTHER.
IS IT BECAUSE I'M NOT GOOD ENOUGH?
NO, THEY'RE JUST VERY BUSY, EVE.
IT'S A BIG DOMAIN, AND RUNNING IT IS A BIG RESPONSIBILITY.
WHEN YOU'RE OLDER, IT'LL BE YOUR RESPONSIBILITY, TOO.
NOW, CLOSE YOUR EYES...

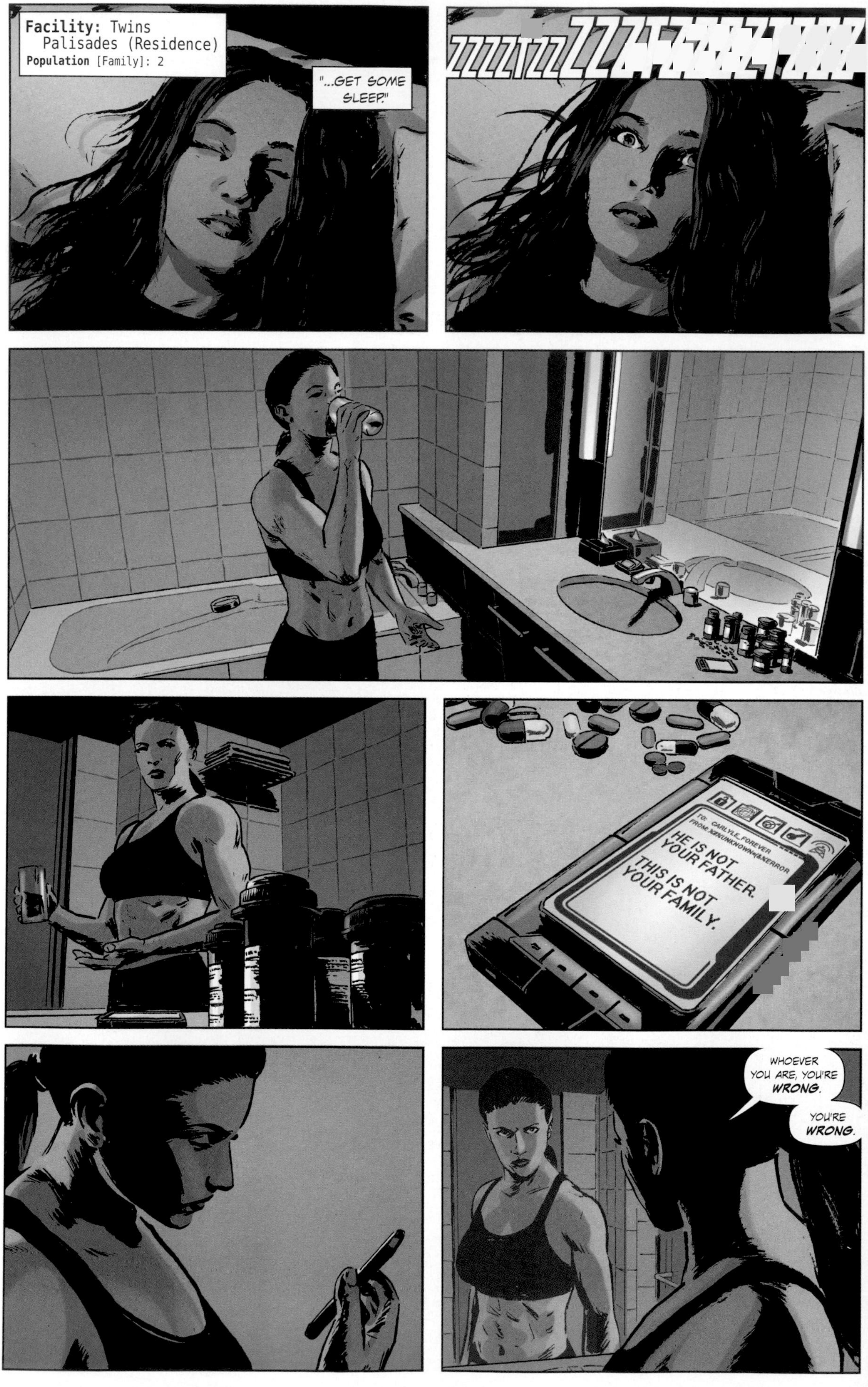
Facility: Twins Palisades (Residence)
Population [Family]: 2
"...GET SOME SLEEP."
HE IS NOT YOUR FATHER.
THIS IS NOT YOUR FAMILY.
WHOEVER YOU ARE, YOU'RE WRONG.
YOU'RE WRONG.

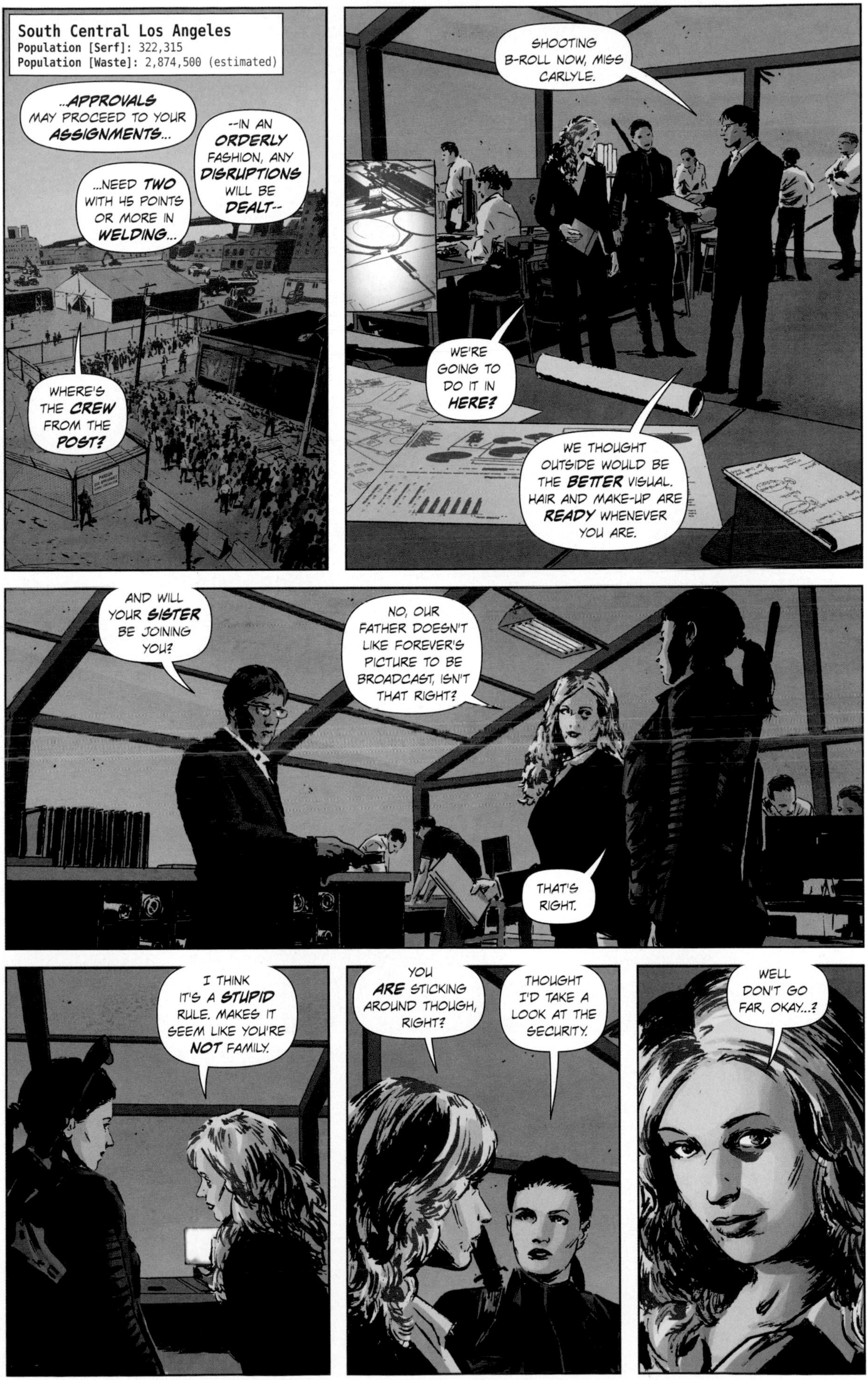
South Central Los Angeles
Population [Serf]: 322,315
Population [Waste]: 2,874,500 (estimated)
...APPROVALS MAY PROCEED TO YOUR ASSIGNMENTS...
...NEED TWO WITH 45 POINTS OR MORE IN WELDING...
--IN AN ORDERLY FASHION, ANY DISRUPTIONS WILL BE DEALT--
WHERE'S THE CREW FROM THE POST?
SHOOTING B-ROLL NOW, MISS CARLYLE.
WE'RE GOING TO DO IT IN HERE?
WE THOUGHT OUTSIDE WOULD BE THE BETTER VISUAL. HAIR AND MAKE-UP ARE READY WHENEVER YOU ARE.
AND WILL YOUR SISTER BE JOINING YOU?
NO, OUR FATHER DOESN'T LIKE FOREVER'S PICTURE TO BE BROADCAST, ISN'T THAT RIGHT?
THAT'S RIGHT.
I THINK IT'S A STUPID RULE. MAKES IT SEEM LIKE YOU'RE NOT FAMILY.
YOU ARE STICKING AROUND THOUGH, RIGHT?
THOUGHT I'D TAKE A LOOK AT THE SECURITY.
WELL DON'T GO FAR, OKAY...?

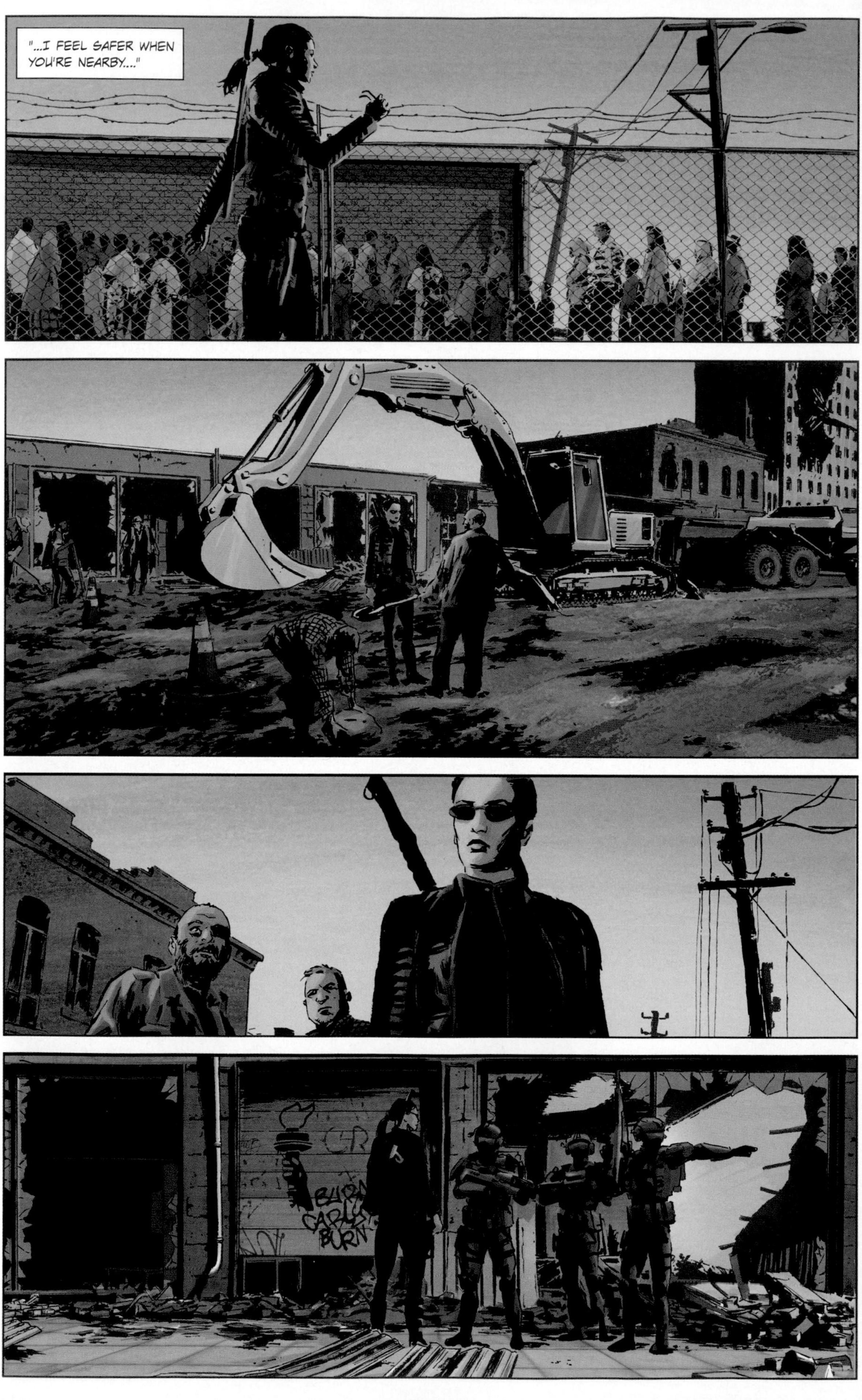
"...I FEEL SAFER WHEN YOU'RE NEARBY..."

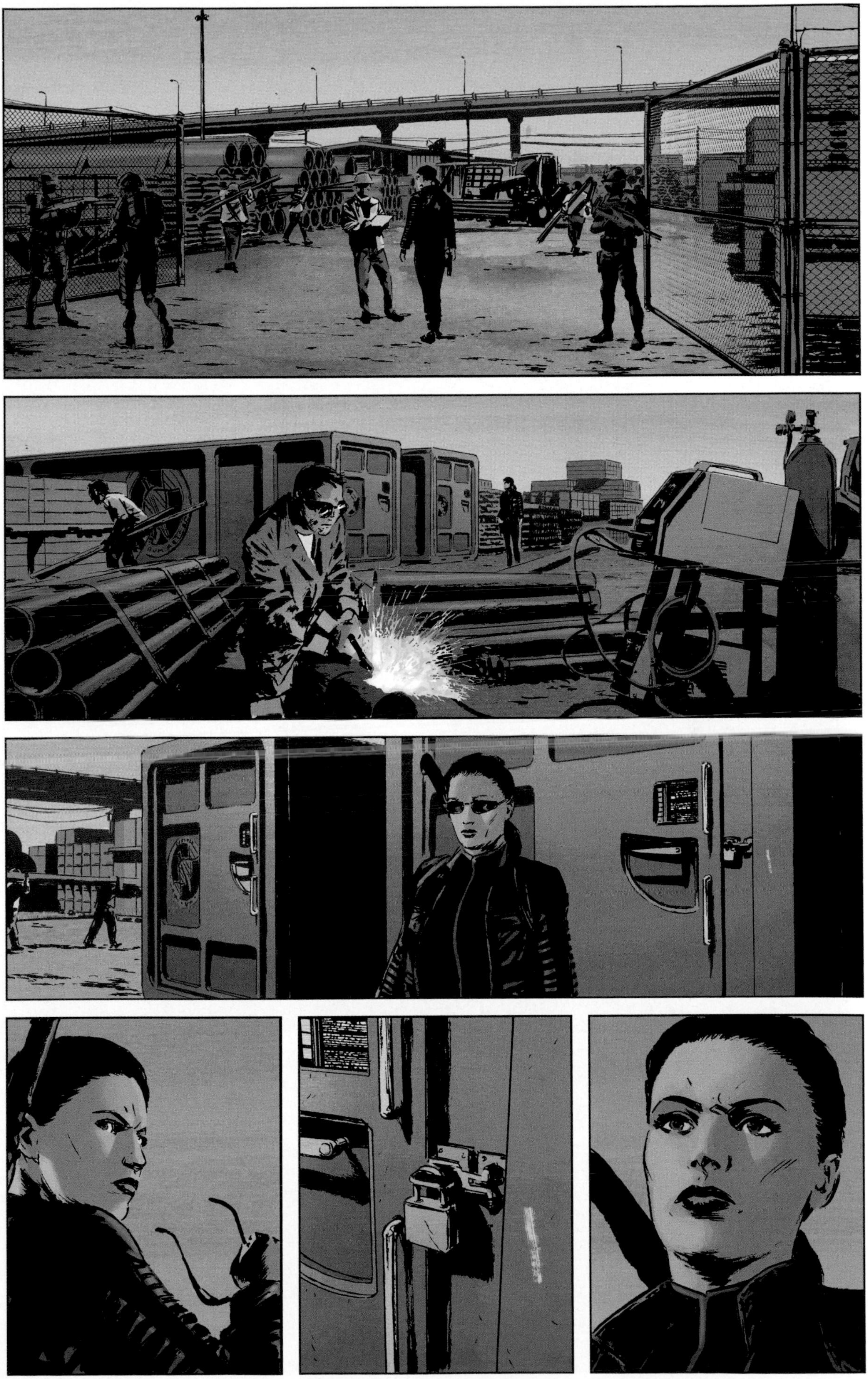

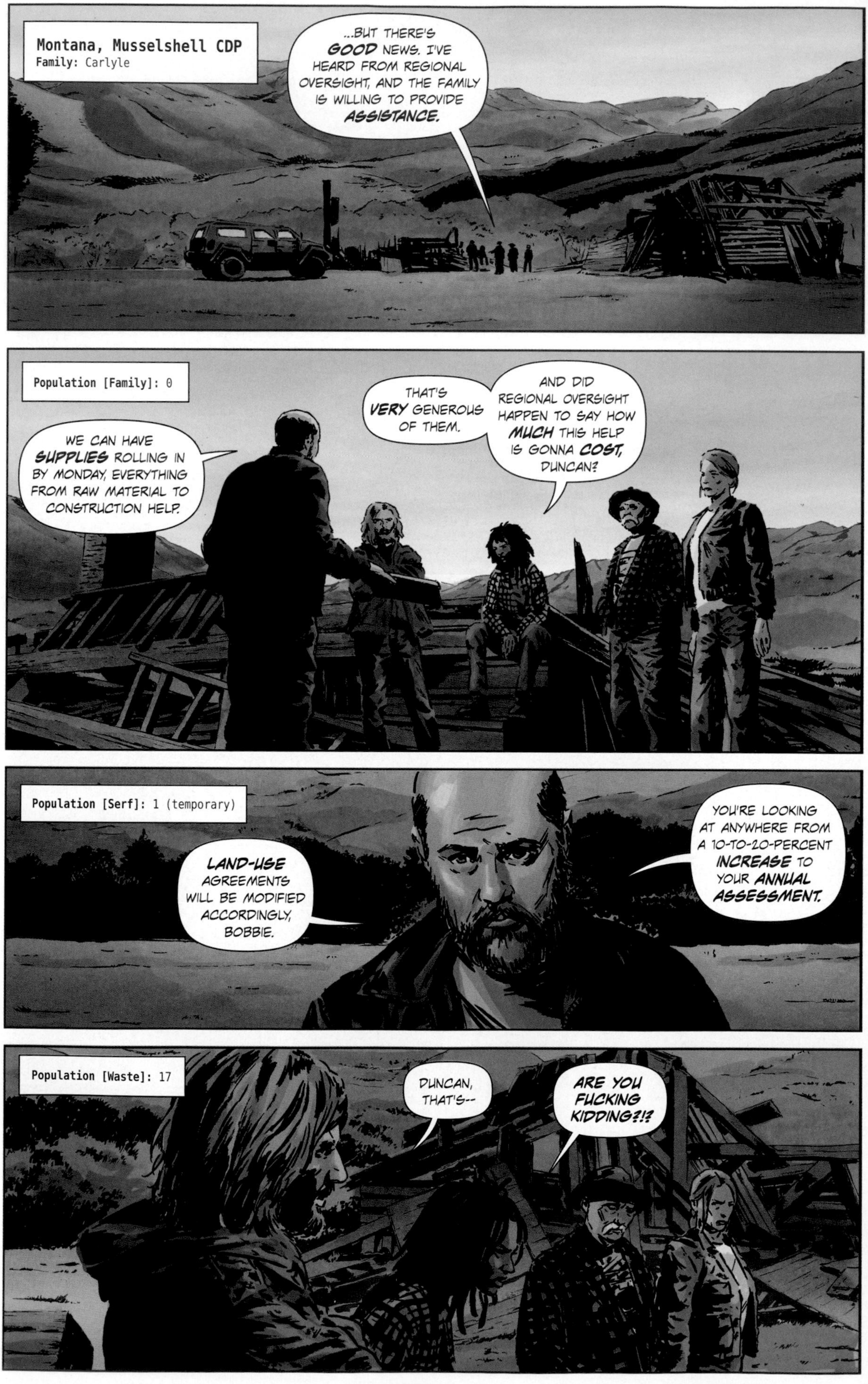
Montana, Musselshell CDP
Family: Carlyle
...BUT THERE'S GOOD NEWS. I'VE HEARD FROM REGIONAL OVERSIGHT, AND THE FAMILY IS WILLING TO PROVIDE ASSISTANCE.
Population [Family]: 0
WE CAN HAVE SUPPLIES ROLLING IN BY MONDAY, EVERYTHING FROM RAW MATERIAL TO CONSTRUCTION HELP.
THAT'S VERY GENEROUS OF THEM.
AND DID REGIONAL OVERSIGHT HAPPEN TO SAY HOW MUCH THIS HELP IS GONNA COST, DUNCAN?
Population [Serf]: 1 (temporary)
LAND-USE AGREEMENTS WILL BE MODIFIED ACCORDINGLY, BOBBIE.
YOU'RE LOOKING AT ANYWHERE FROM A 10-TO-20-PERCENT INCREASE TO YOUR ANNUAL ASSESSMENT.
Population [Waste]: 17
DUNCAN, THAT'S--
ARE YOU FUCKING KIDDING?!?

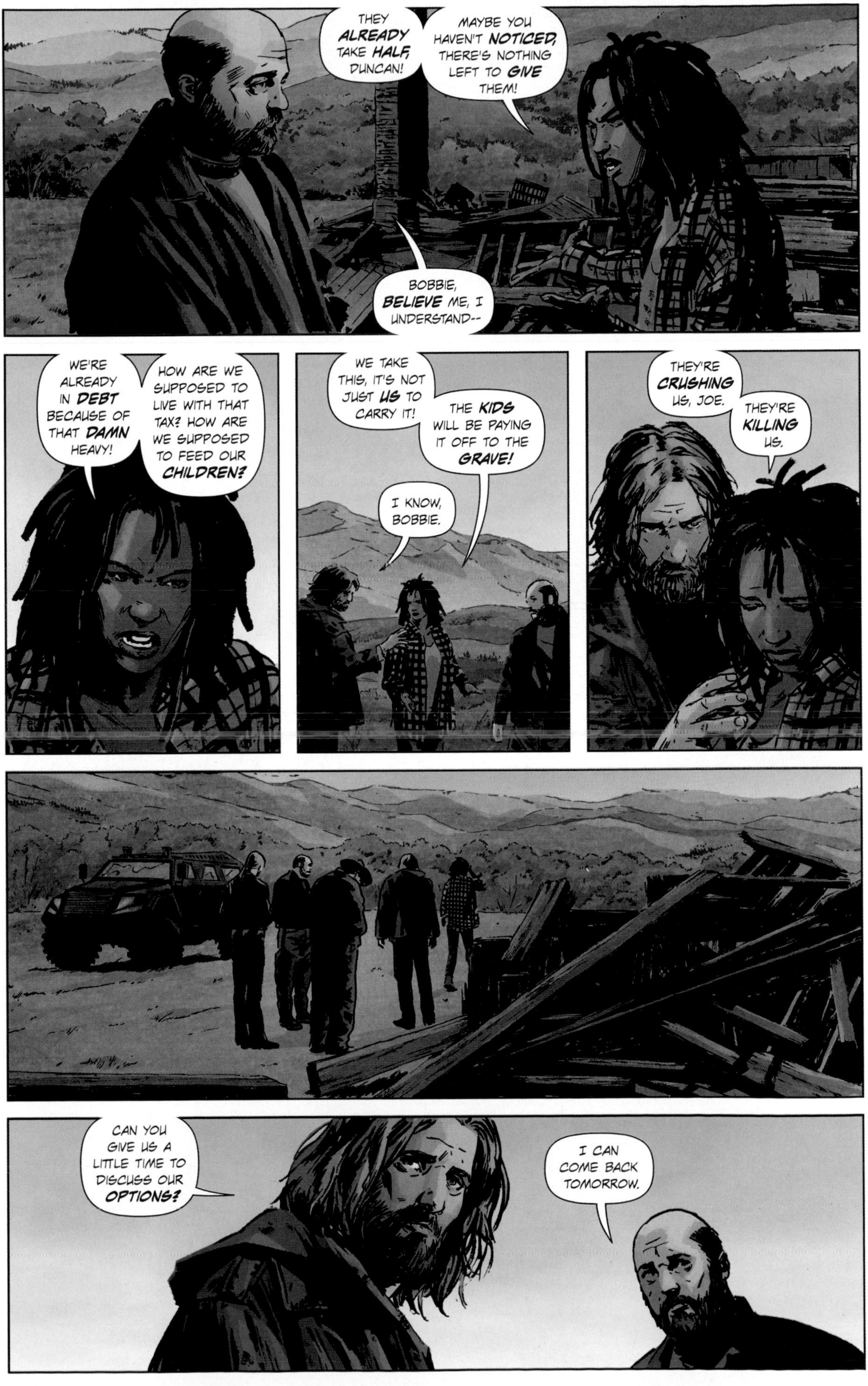
THEY ALREADY TAKE HALF, DUNCAN!
MAYBE YOU HAVEN'T NOTICED, THERE'S NOTHING LEFT TO GIVE THEM!
BOBBIE, BELIEVE ME, I UNDERSTAND--
WE'RE ALREADY IN DEBT BECAUSE OF THAT DAMN HEAVY!
HOW ARE WE SUPPOSED TO LIVE WITH THAT TAX? HOW ARE WE SUPPOSED TO FEED OUR CHILDREN?
WE TAKE THIS, IT'S NOT JUST US TO CARRY IT!
THE KIDS WILL BE PAYING IT OFF TO THE GRAVE!
I KNOW, BOBBIE.
THEY'RE CRUSHING US, JOE.
THEY'RE KILLING US.
CAN YOU GIVE US A LITTLE TIME TO DISCUSS OUR OPTIONS?
I CAN COME BACK TOMORROW.

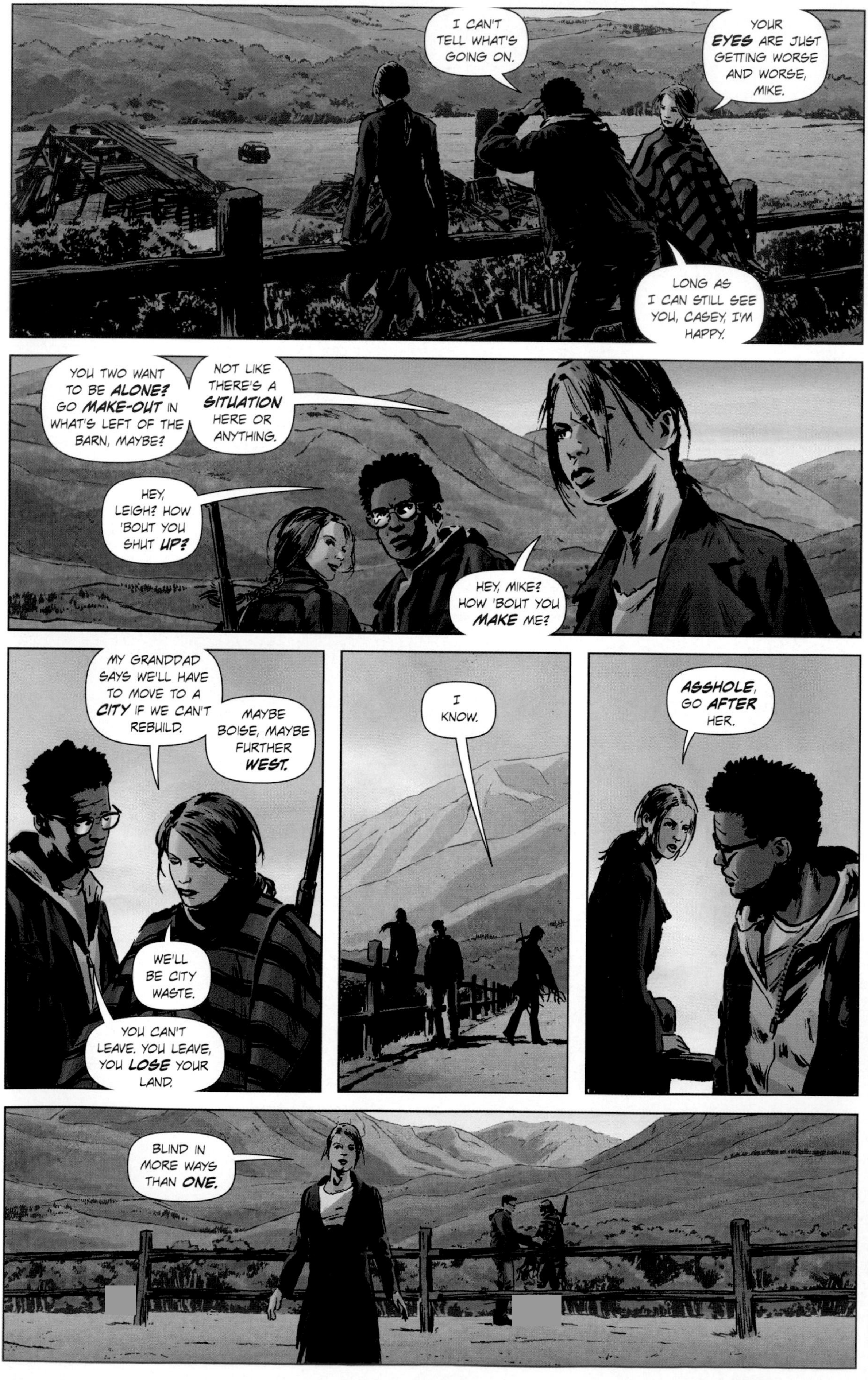
I CAN'T TELL WHAT'S GOING ON.
YOUR EYES ARE JUST GETTING WORSE AND WORSE, MIKE.
LONG AS I CAN STILL SEE YOU, CASEY, I'M HAPPY.
YOU TWO WANT TO BE ALONE? GO MAKE-OUT IN WHAT'S LEFT OF THE BARN, MAYBE?
NOT LIKE THERE'S A SITUATION HERE OR ANYTHING.
HEY, LEIGH? HOW 'BOUT YOU SHUT UP?
HEY, MIKE? HOW 'BOUT YOU MAKE ME?
MY GRANDDAD SAYS WE'LL HAVE TO MOVE TO A CITY IF WE CAN'T REBUILD.
MAYBE BOISE, MAYBE FURTHER WEST.
WE'LL BE CITY WASTE.
YOU CAN'T LEAVE. YOU LEAVE, YOU LOSE YOUR LAND.
I KNOW.
ASSHOLE, GO AFTER HER.
BLIND IN MORE WAYS THAN ONE.

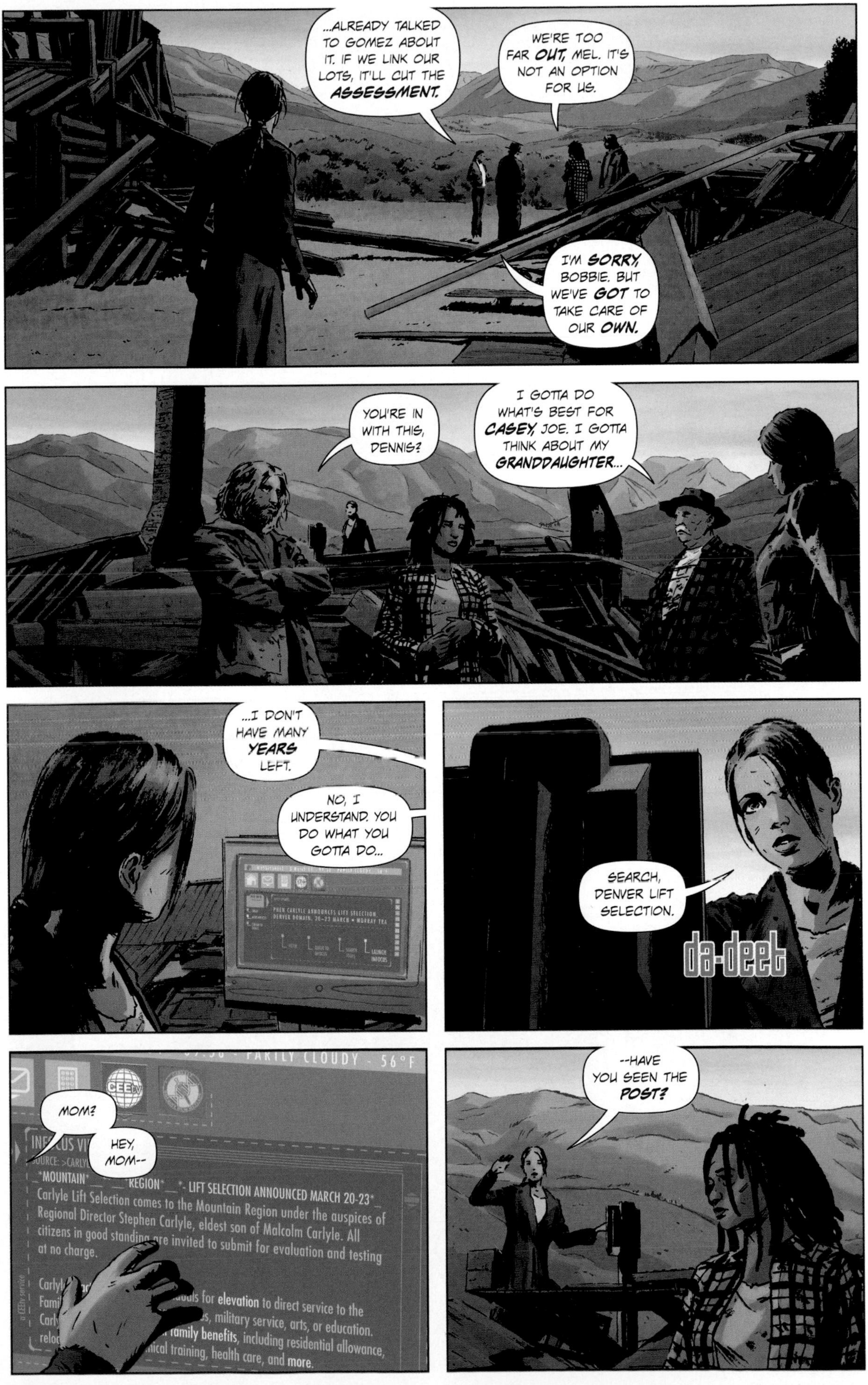
...ALREADY TALKED TO GOMEZ ABOUT IT. IF WE LINK OUR LOTS, IT'LL CUT THE ASSESSMENT.
WE'RE TOO FAR OUT, MEL. IT'S NOT AN OPTION FOR US.
I'M SORRY, BOBBIE. BUT WE'VE GOT TO TAKE CARE OF OUR OWN.
YOU'RE IN WITH THIS, DENNIS?
I GOTTA DO WHAT'S BEST FOR CASEY, JOE. I GOTTA THINK ABOUT MY GRANDDAUGHTER...
...I DON'T HAVE MANY YEARS LEFT.
NO, I UNDERSTAND. YOU DO WHAT YOU GOTTA DO...
SEARCH, DENVER LIFT SELECTION.
da-deet
PARTLY CLOUDY - 56°F
MOM?
HEY, MOM--
_*MOUNTAIN*_ _*REGION*_*- LIFT SELECTION ANNOUNCED MARCH 20-23*_
Carlyle Lift Selection comes to the Mountain Region under the auspices of Regional Director Stephen Carlyle, eldest son of Malcolm Carlyle. All citizens in good standing are invited to submit for evaluation and testing at no charge.
family benefits, including residential allowance,
--HAVE YOU SEEN THE POST?

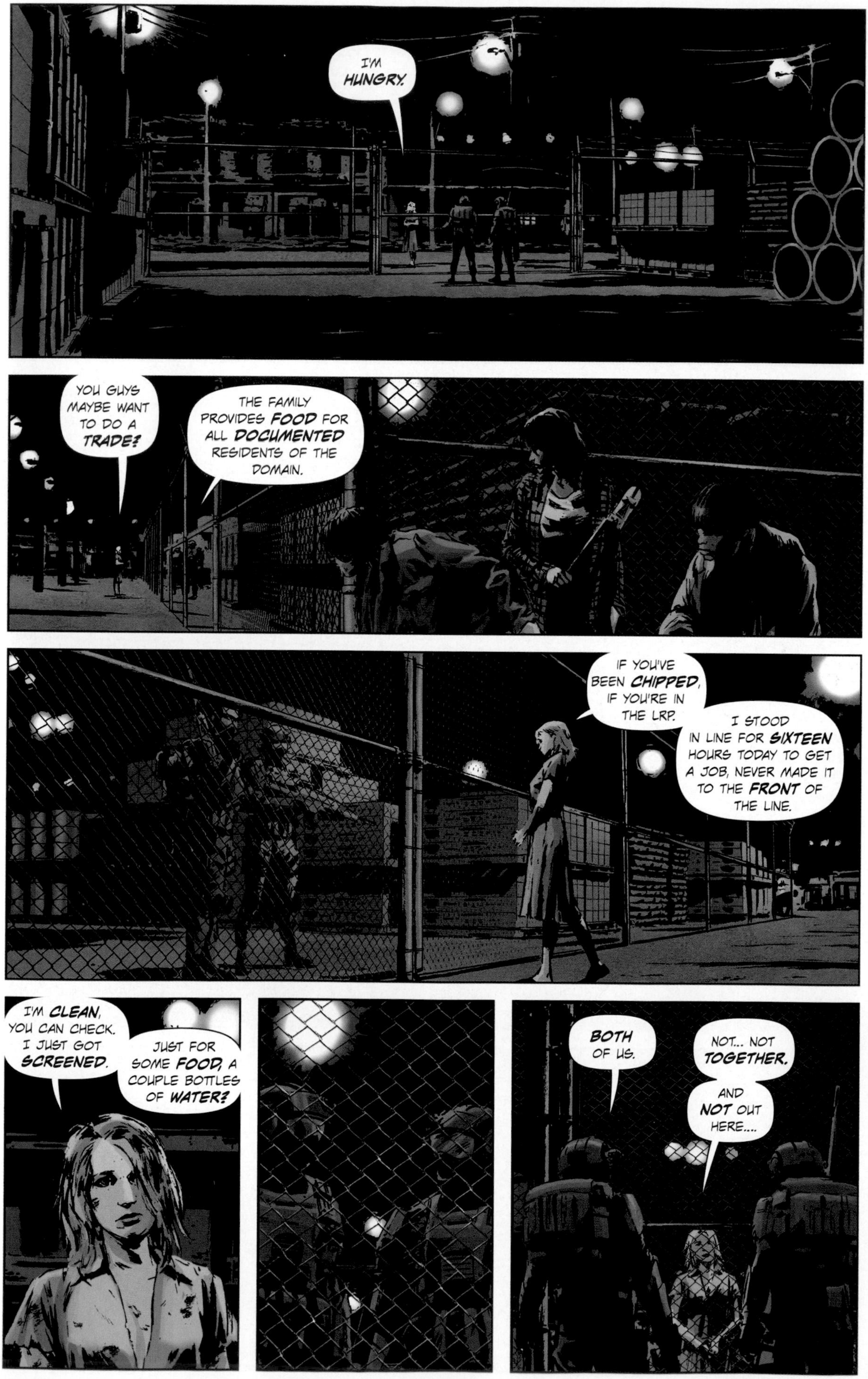
I'M HUNGRY.
YOU GUYS MAYBE WANT TO DO A TRADE?
THE FAMILY PROVIDES FOOD FOR ALL DOCUMENTED RESIDENTS OF THE DOMAIN.
IF YOU'VE BEEN CHIPPED, IF YOU'RE IN THE LRP.
I STOOD IN LINE FOR SIXTEEN HOURS TODAY TO GET A JOB, NEVER MADE IT TO THE FRONT OF THE LINE.
I'M CLEAN, YOU CAN CHECK. I JUST GOT SCREENED.
JUST FOR SOME FOOD, A COUPLE BOTTLES OF WATER?
BOTH OF US.
NOT... NOT TOGETHER.
AND NOT OUT HERE....

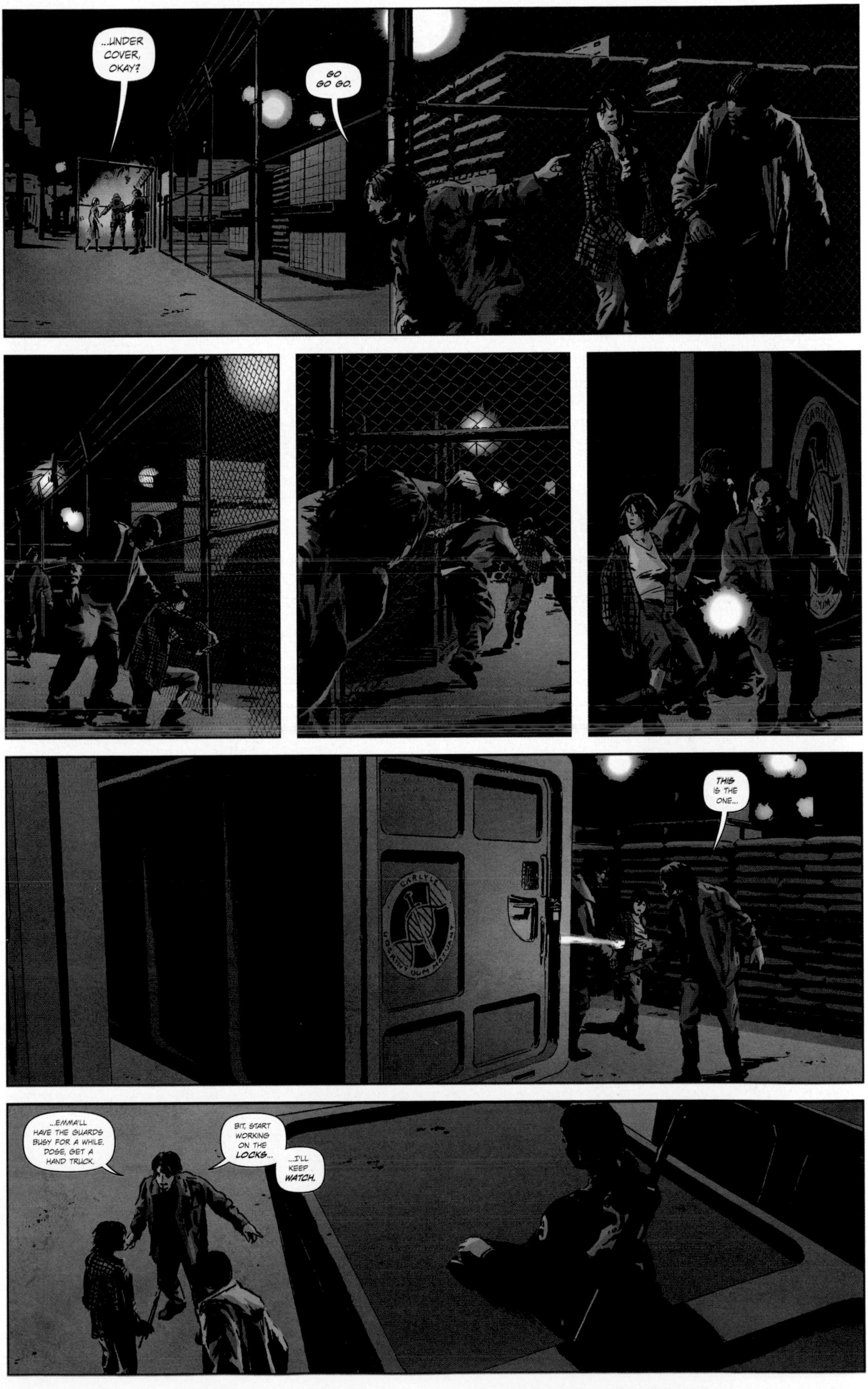
...UNDER COVER, OKAY?
GO GO GO.
THIS IS THE ONE...
...EMMA'LL HAVE THE GUARDS BUSY FOR A WHILE. DOSE, GET A HAND TRUCK.
BIT, START WORKING ON THE LOCKS...
...I'LL KEEP WATCH.

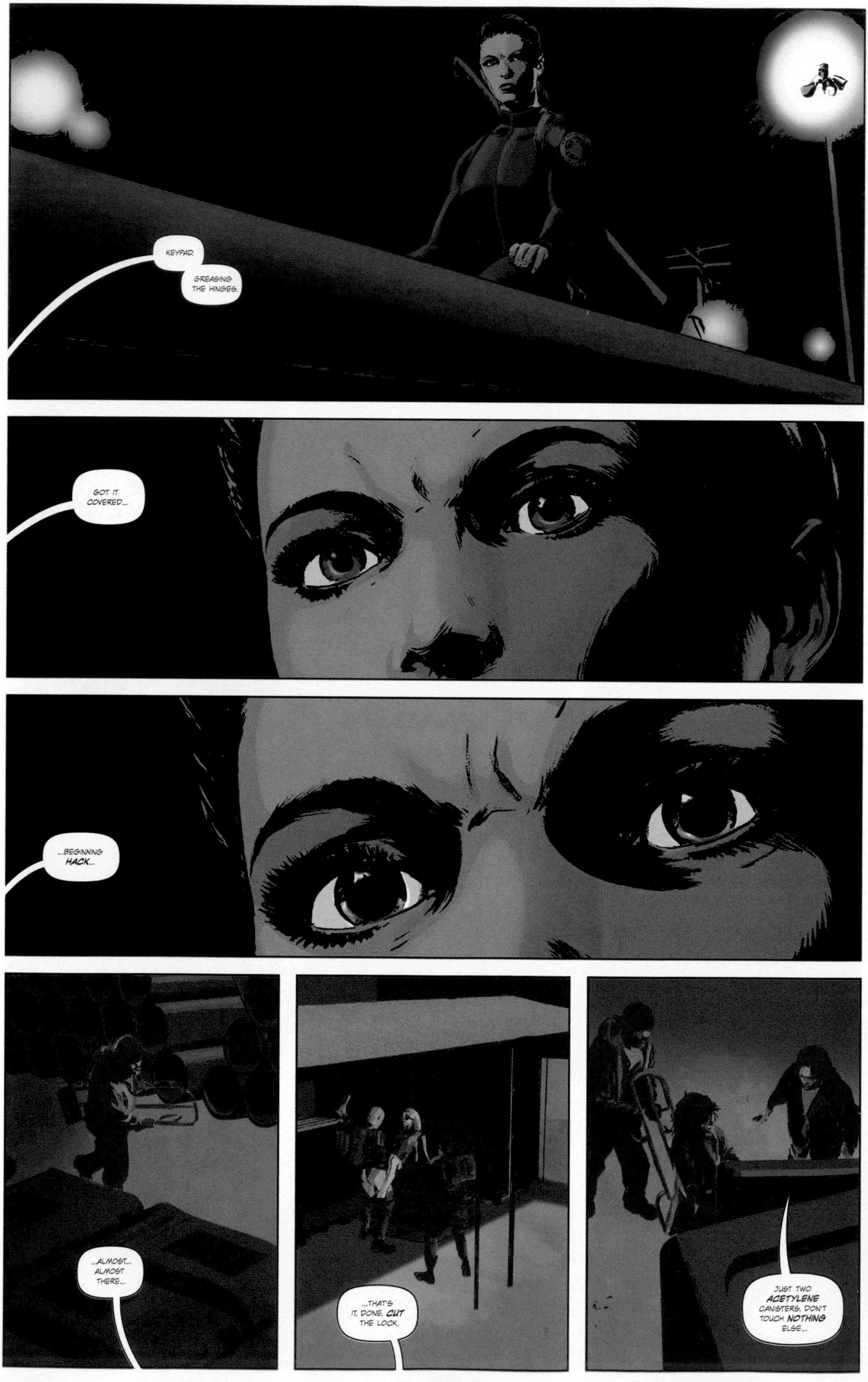
KEYPAD.
GREASING THE HINGES.
GOT IT COVERED...
...BEGINNING HACK...
...ALMOST... ALMOST THERE...
...THAT'S IT, DONE, CUT THE LOCK.
JUST TWO ACETYLENE CANISTERS, DON'T TOUCH NOTHING ELSE...

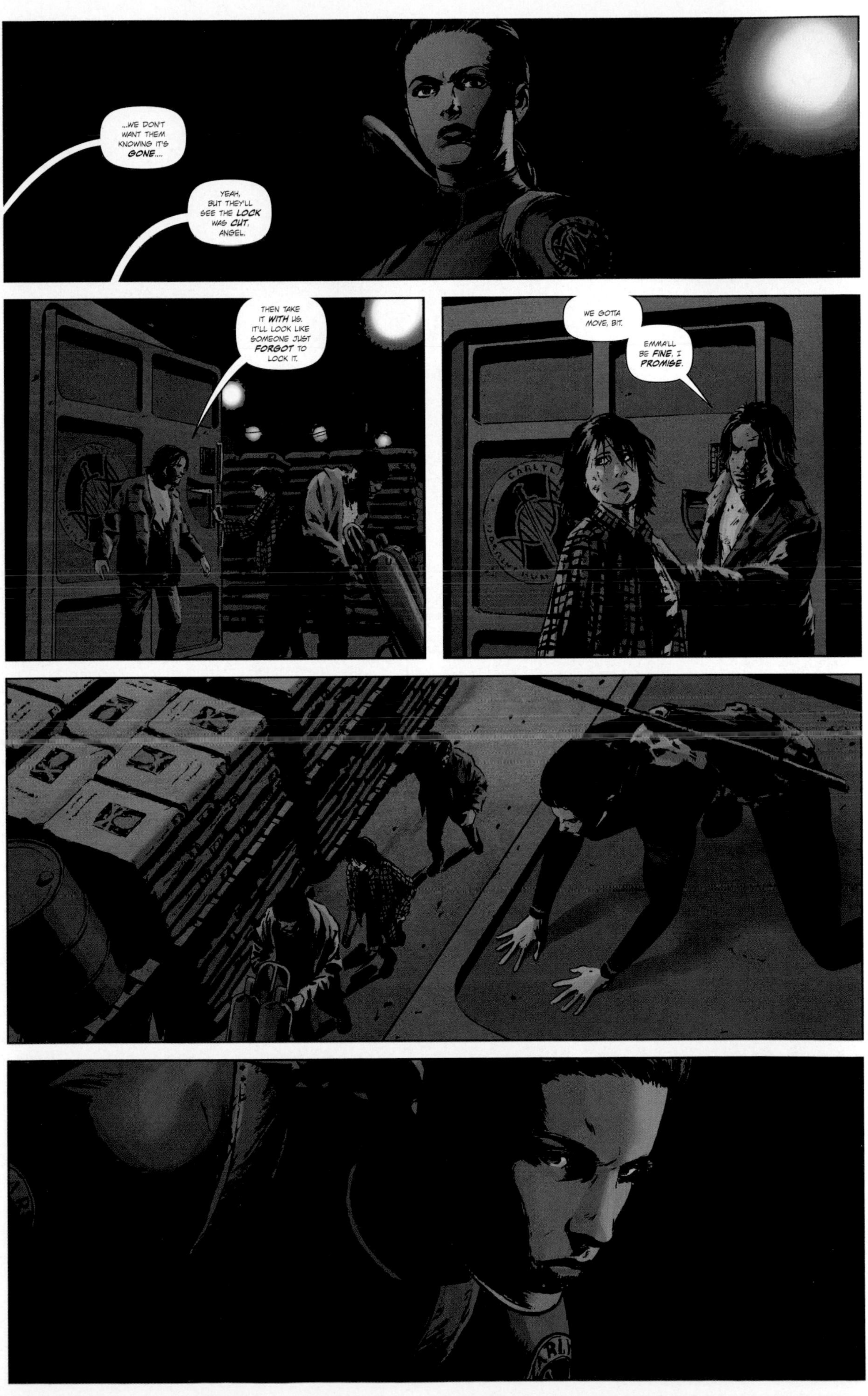
...WE DON'T WANT THEM KNOWING IT'S GONE....
YEAH, BUT THEY'LL SEE THE LOCK WAS CUT, ANGEL.
THEN TAKE IT WITH US. IT'LL LOOK LIKE SOMEONE JUST FORGOT TO LOCK IT.
WE GOTTA MOVE, BIT.
EMMA'LL BE FINE, I PROMISE.

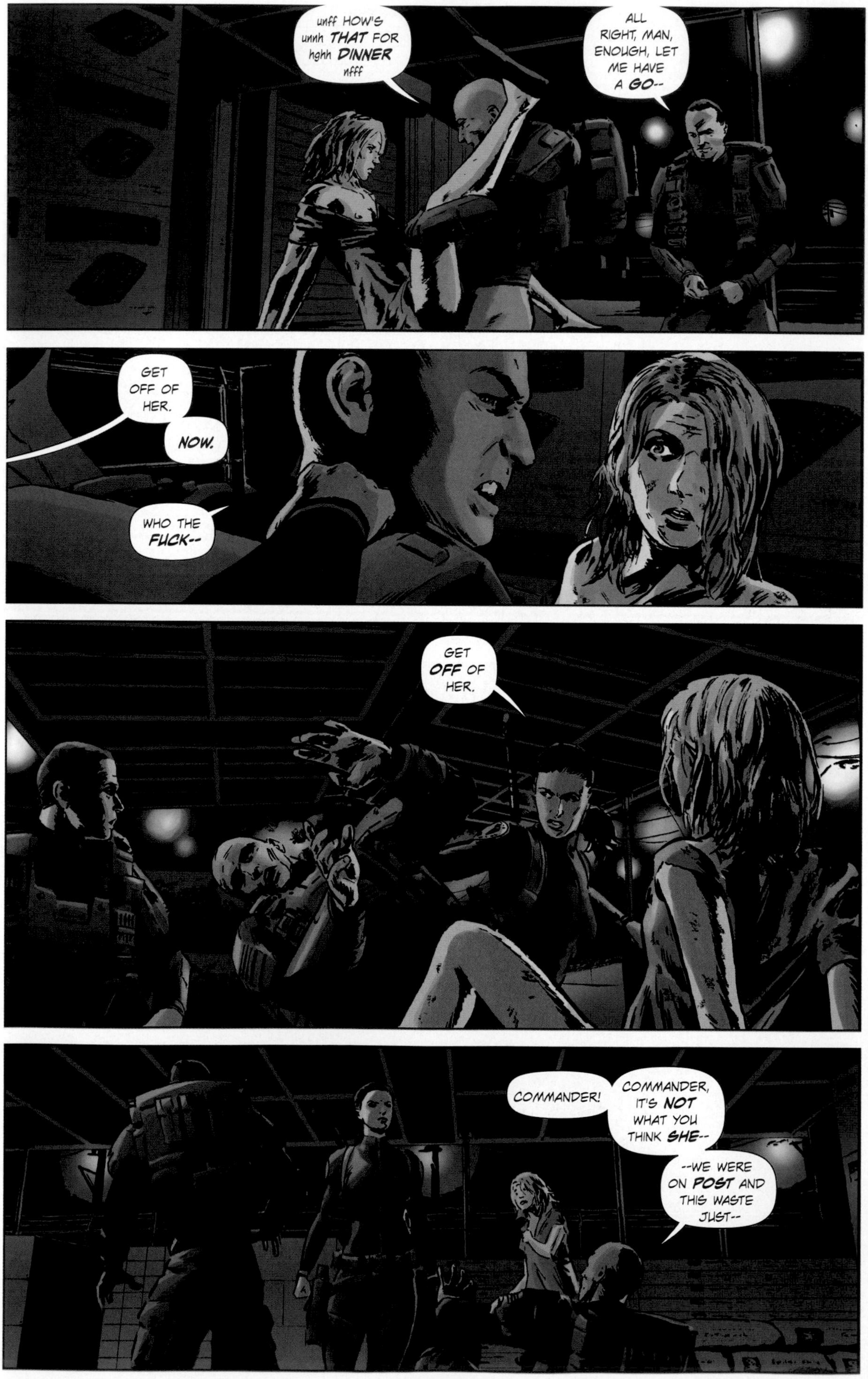
unff HOW'S unnh THAT FOR hghh DINNER nfff
ALL RIGHT, MAN, ENOUGH, LET ME HAVE A GO--
GET OFF OF HER.
NOW.
WHO THE FUCK--
GET OFF OF HER.
COMMANDER!
COMMANDER, IT'S NOT WHAT YOU THINK SHE--
--WE WERE ON POST AND THIS WASTE JUST--

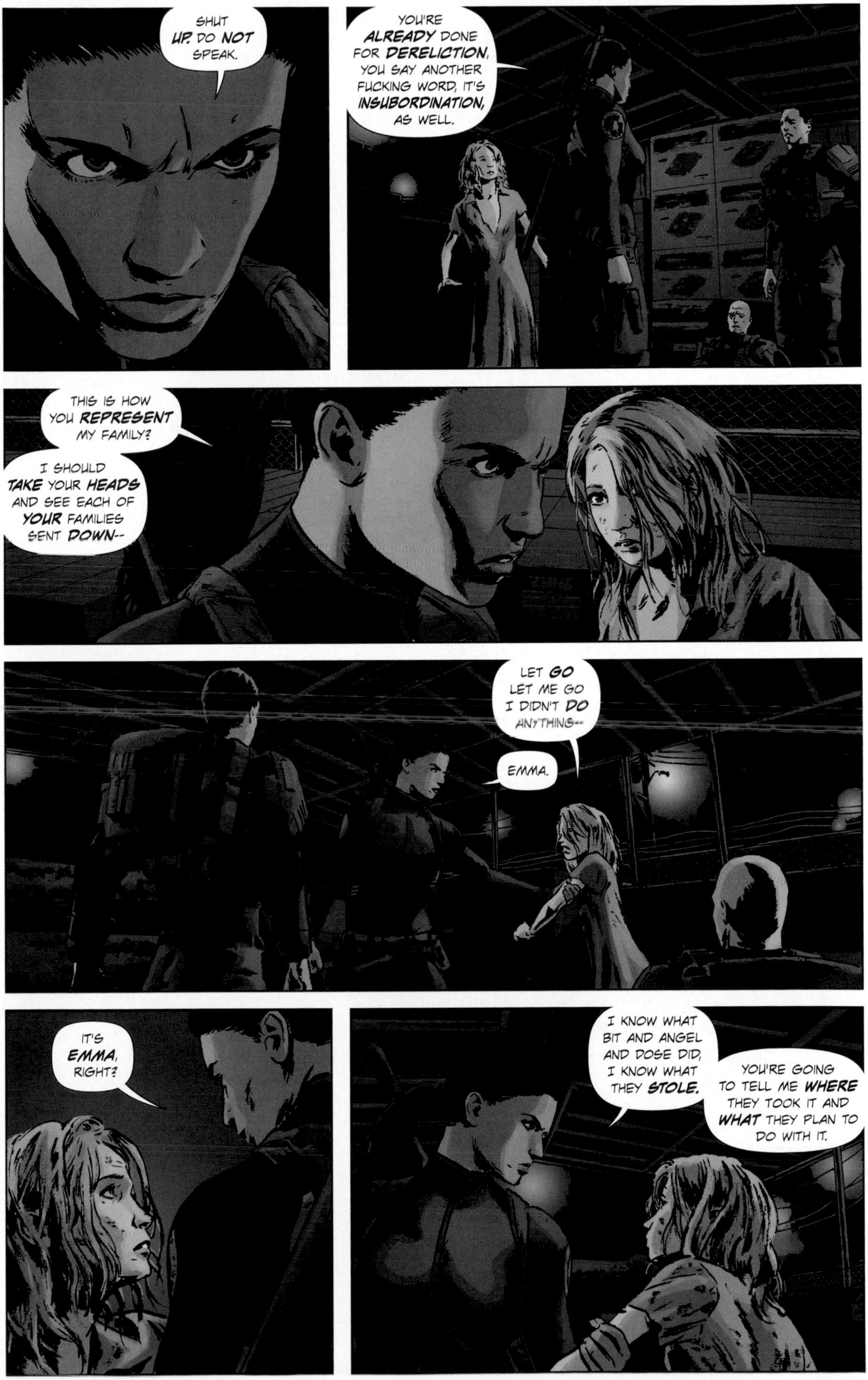

SHUT UP. DO NOT SPEAK.
YOU'RE ALREADY DONE FOR DERELICTION, YOU SAY ANOTHER FUCKING WORD, IT'S INSUBORDINATION, AS WELL.
THIS IS HOW YOU REPRESENT MY FAMILY?
I SHOULD TAKE YOUR HEADS AND SEE EACH OF YOUR FAMILIES SENT DOWN--
LET GO LET ME GO I DIDN'T DO ANYTHING--
EMMA.
IT'S EMMA, RIGHT?
I KNOW WHAT BIT AND ANGEL AND DOSE DID, I KNOW WHAT THEY STOLE.
YOU'RE GOING TO TELL ME WHERE THEY TOOK IT AND WHAT THEY PLAN TO DO WITH IT.

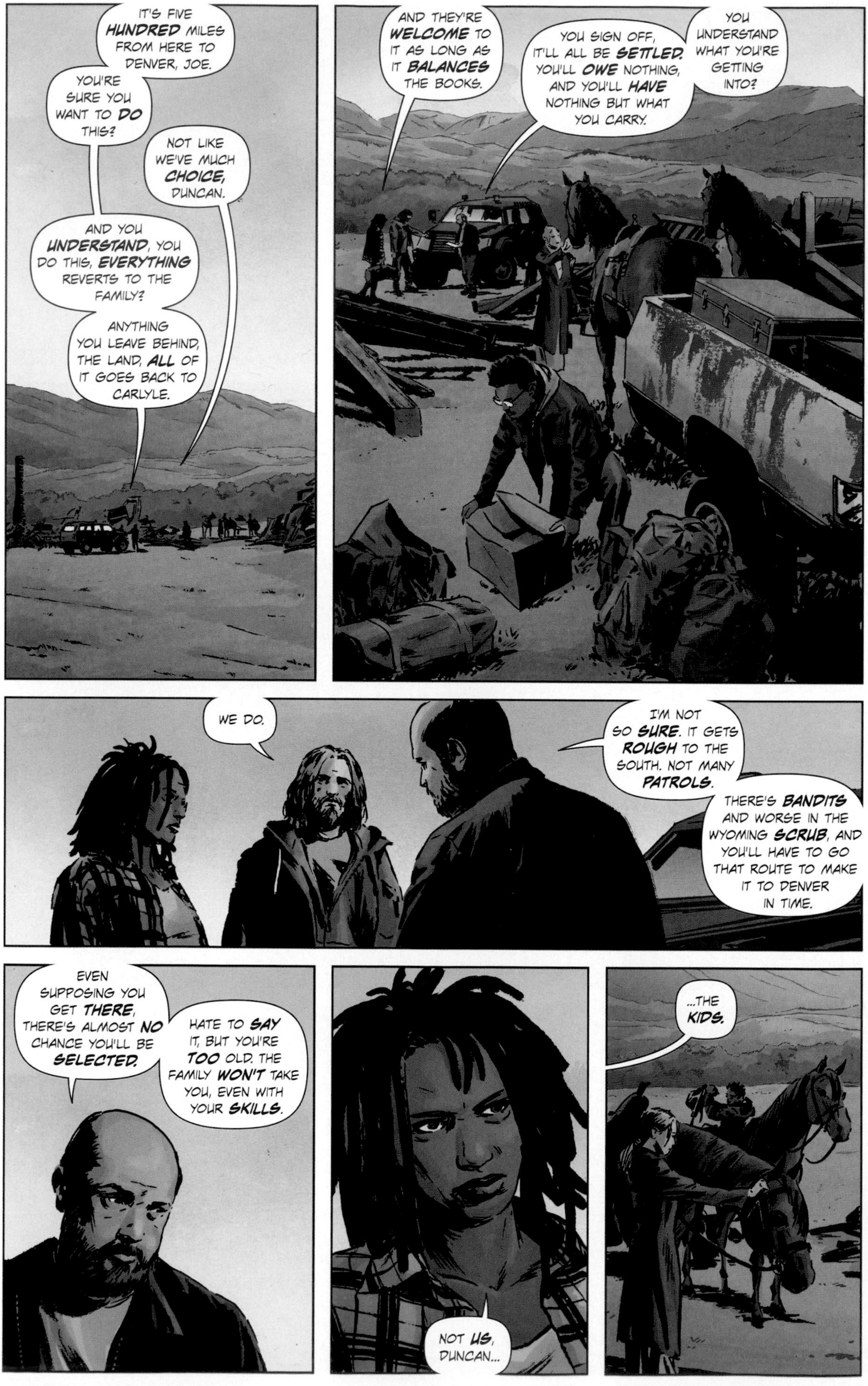
IT'S FIVE HUNDRED MILES FROM HERE TO DENVER, JOE.
YOU'RE SURE YOU WANT TO DO THIS?
NOT LIKE WE'VE MUCH CHOICE, DUNCAN.
AND YOU UNDERSTAND, YOU DO THIS, EVERYTHING REVERTS TO THE FAMILY?
ANYTHING YOU LEAVE BEHIND, THE LAND, ALL OF IT GOES BACK TO CARLYLE.
AND THEY'RE WELCOME TO IT AS LONG AS IT BALANCES THE BOOKS.
YOU SIGN OFF, IT'LL ALL BE SETTLED. YOU'LL OWE NOTHING, AND YOU'LL HAVE NOTHING BUT WHAT YOU CARRY.
YOU UNDERSTAND WHAT YOU'RE GETTING INTO?
WE DO.
I'M NOT SO SURE. IT GETS ROUGH TO THE SOUTH. NOT MANY PATROLS.
THERE'S BANDITS AND WORSE IN THE WYOMING SCRUB, AND YOU'LL HAVE TO GO THAT ROUTE TO MAKE IT TO DENVER IN TIME.
EVEN SUPPOSING YOU GET THERE, THERE'S ALMOST NO CHANCE YOU'LL BE SELECTED.
HATE TO SAY IT, BUT YOU'RE TOO OLD. THE FAMILY WON'T TAKE YOU, EVEN WITH YOUR SKILLS.
NOT US, DUNCAN...
...THE KIDS.

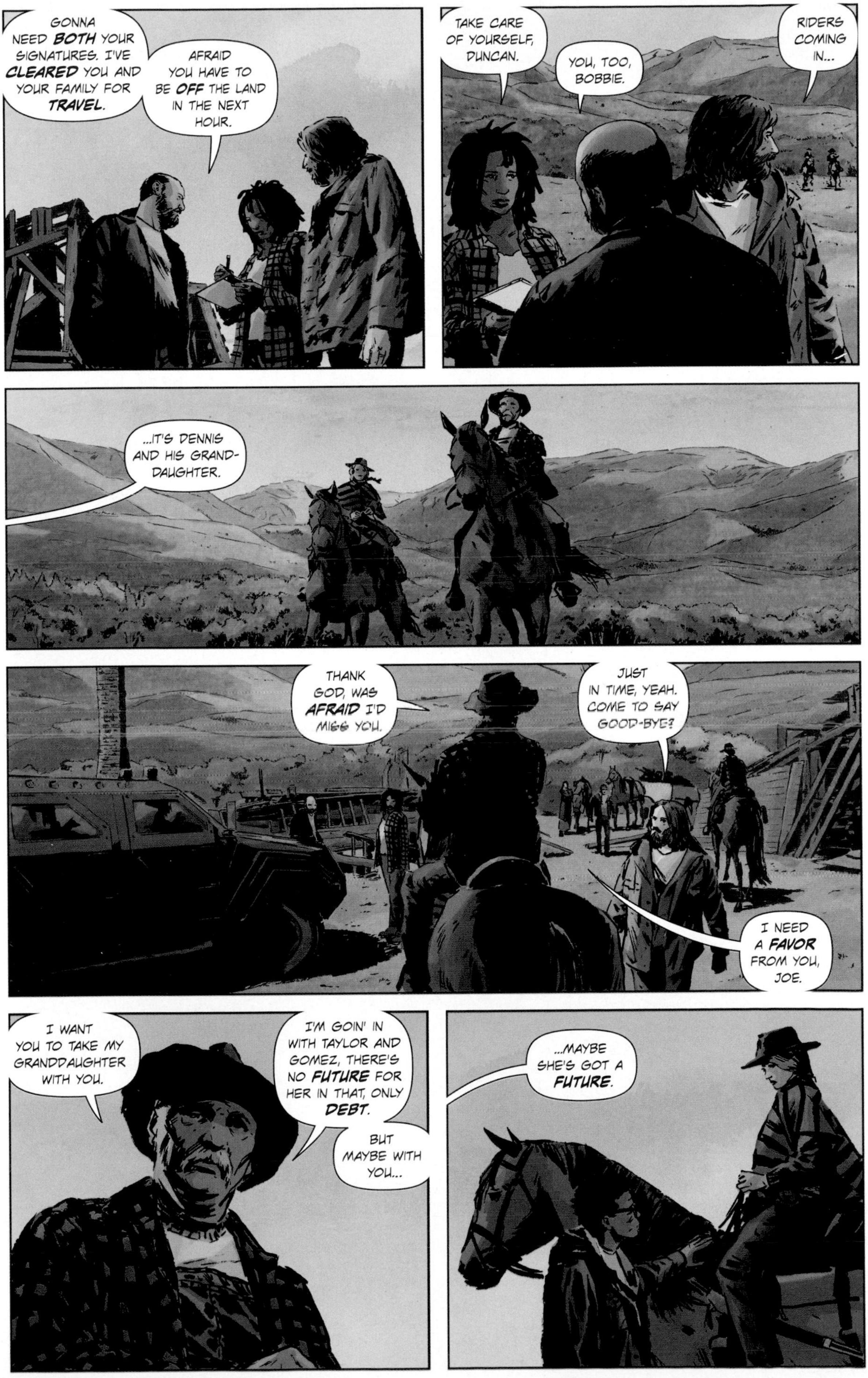
GONNA NEED BOTH YOUR SIGNATURES. I'VE CLEARED YOU AND YOUR FAMILY FOR TRAVEL.
AFRAID YOU HAVE TO BE OFF THE LAND IN THE NEXT HOUR.
TAKE CARE OF YOURSELF, DUNCAN.
YOU, TOO, BOBBIE.
RIDERS COMING IN...
...IT'S DENNIS AND HIS GRAND-DAUGHTER.
THANK GOD, WAS AFRAID I'D MISS YOU.
JUST IN TIME, YEAH. COME TO SAY GOOD-BYE?
I NEED A FAVOR FROM YOU, JOE.
I WANT YOU TO TAKE MY GRANDDAUGHTER WITH YOU.
I'M GOIN' IN WITH TAYLOR AND GOMEZ, THERE'S NO FUTURE FOR HER IN THAT, ONLY DEBT.
BUT MAYBE WITH YOU...
...MAYBE SHE'S GOT A FUTURE.

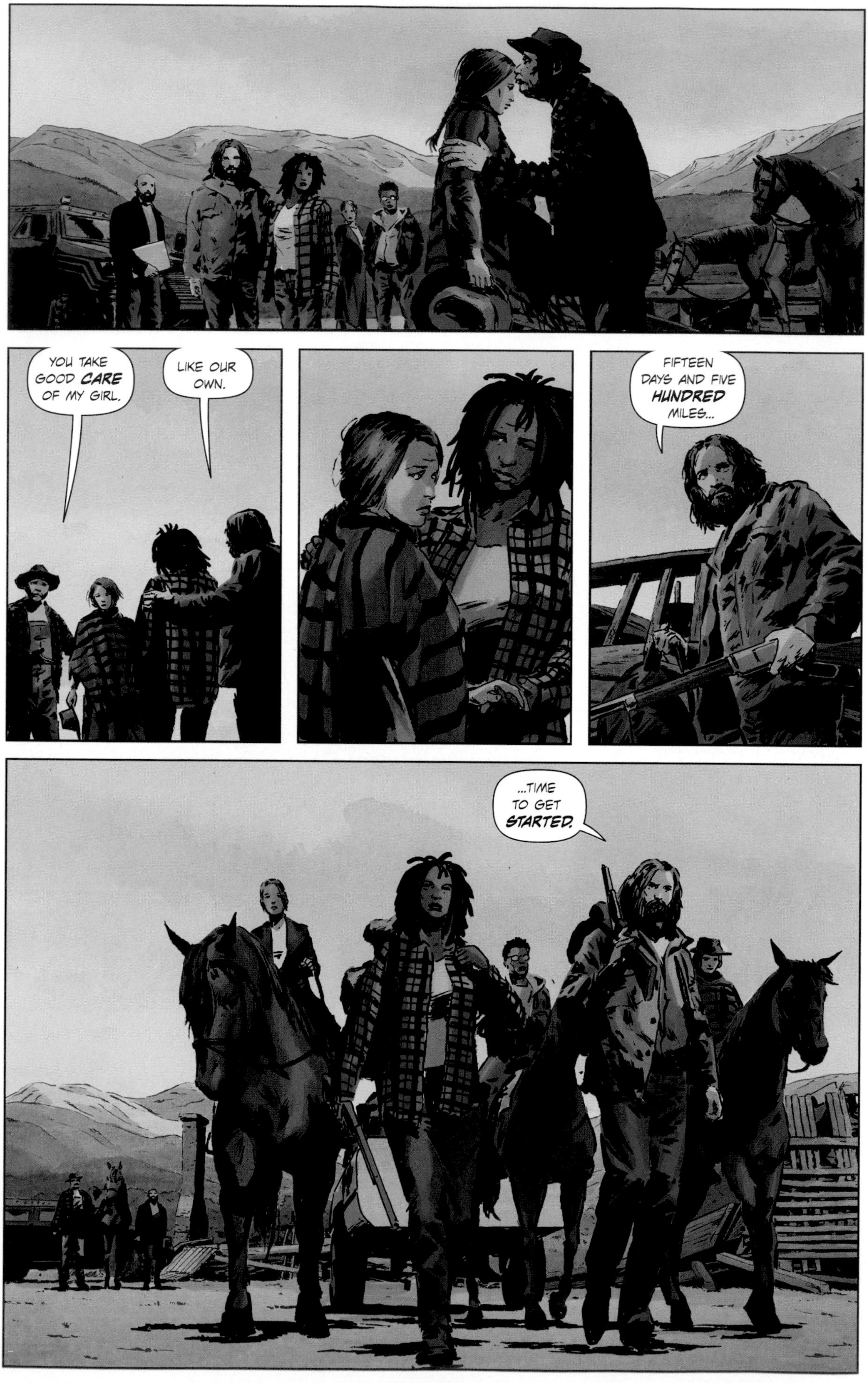

YOU TAKE GOOD CARE OF MY GIRL.
LIKE OUR OWN.
FIFTEEN DAYS AND FIVE HUNDRED MILES...
...TIME TO GET STARTED.

CARLYLE

ODERINT DUM METUANT

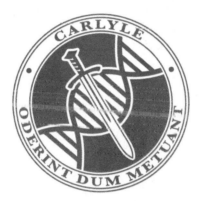

LIFT
CHAPTER THREE

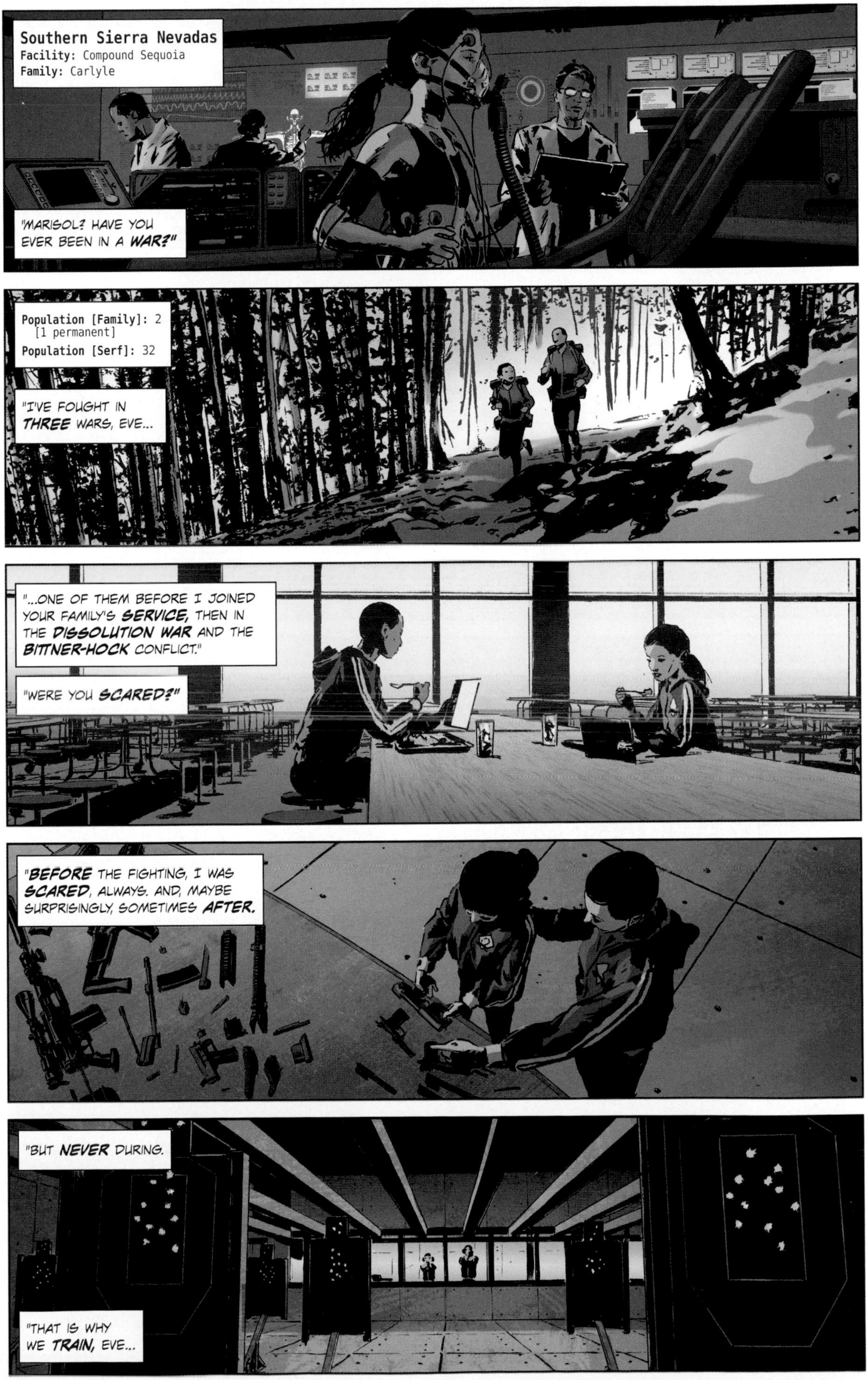
Southern Sierra Nevadas
Facility: Compound Sequoia
Family: Carlyle
"MARISOL? HAVE YOU EVER BEEN IN A WAR?"
Population [Family]: 2 [1 permanent]
Population [Serf]: 32
"I'VE FOUGHT IN THREE WARS, EVE...
"...ONE OF THEM BEFORE I JOINED YOUR FAMILY'S SERVICE, THEN IN THE DISSOLUTION WAR AND THE BITTNER-HOCK CONFLICT."
"WERE YOU SCARED?"
"BEFORE THE FIGHTING, I WAS SCARED, ALWAYS. AND, MAYBE SURPRISINGLY, SOMETIMES AFTER.
"BUT NEVER DURING.
"THAT IS WHY WE TRAIN, EVE...

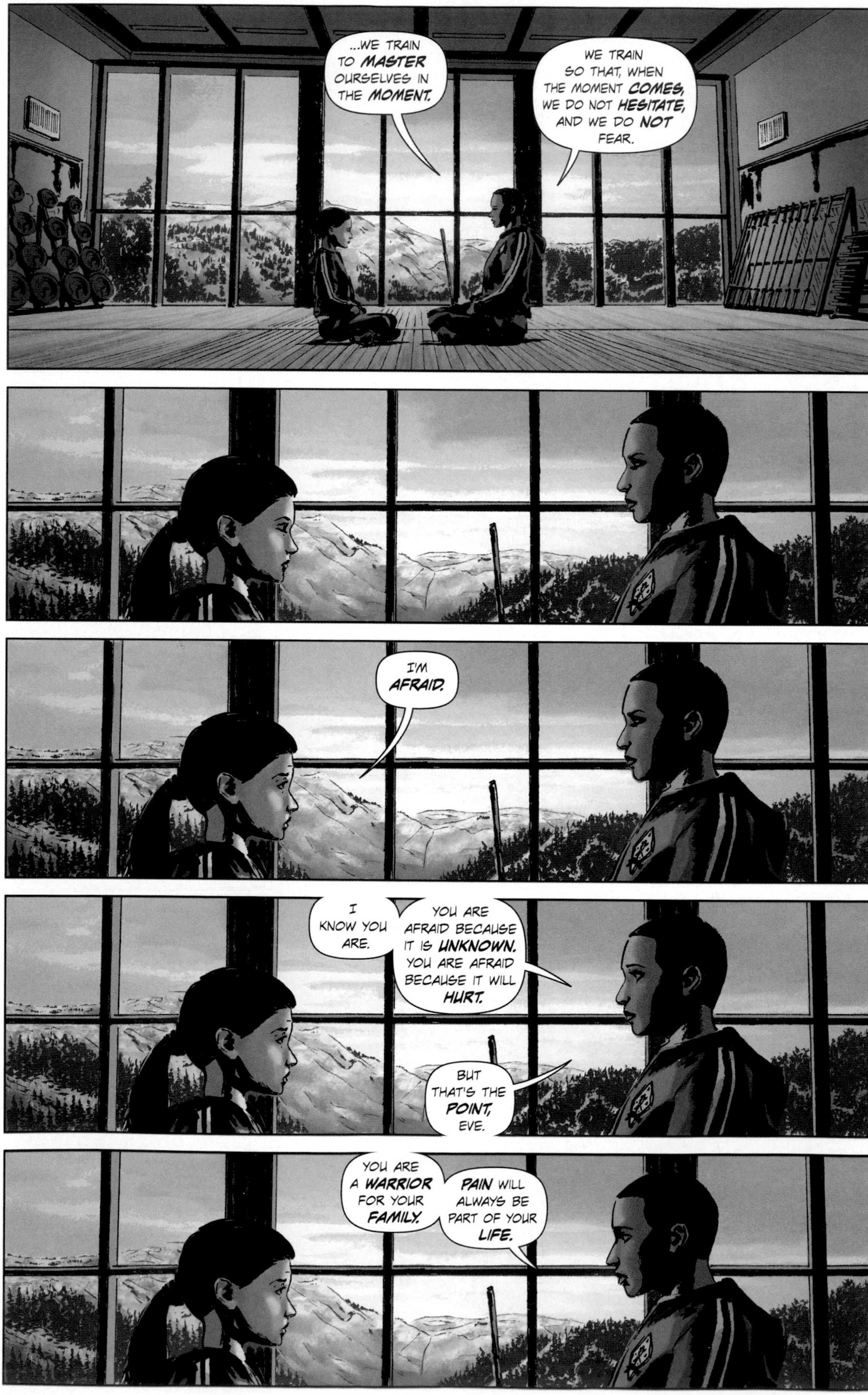
...WE TRAIN TO MASTER OURSELVES IN THE MOMENT.
WE TRAIN SO THAT, WHEN THE MOMENT COMES, WE DO NOT HESITATE, AND WE DO NOT FEAR.
I'M AFRAID.
I KNOW YOU ARE.
YOU ARE AFRAID BECAUSE IT IS UNKNOWN. YOU ARE AFRAID BECAUSE IT WILL HURT.
BUT THAT'S THE POINT, EVE.
YOU ARE A WARRIOR FOR YOUR FAMILY.
PAIN WILL ALWAYS BE PART OF YOUR LIFE.

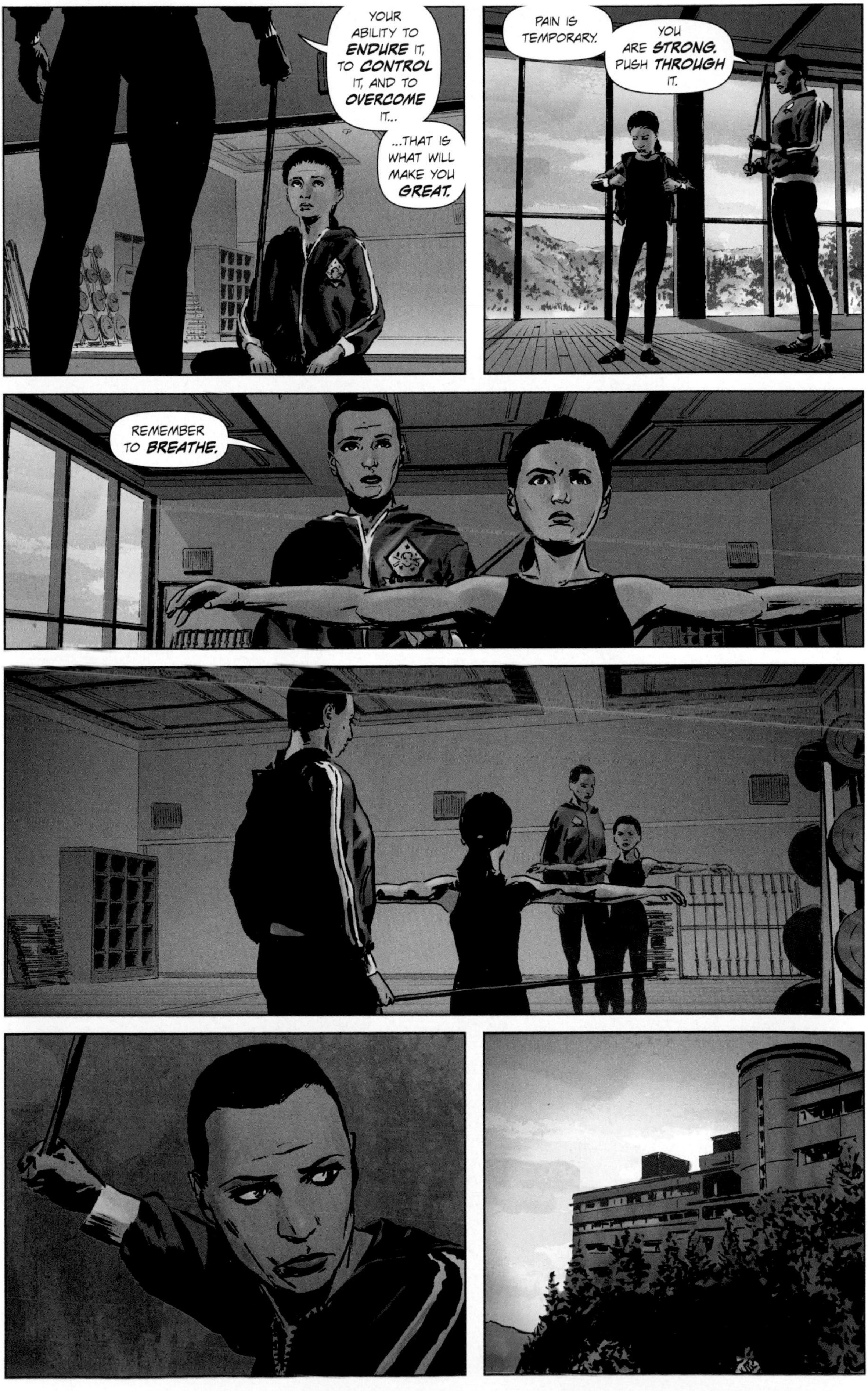
YOUR ABILITY TO ENDURE IT, TO CONTROL IT, AND TO OVERCOME IT...
...THAT IS WHAT WILL MAKE YOU GREAT.
PAIN IS TEMPORARY.
YOU ARE STRONG. PUSH THROUGH IT.
REMEMBER TO BREATHE.

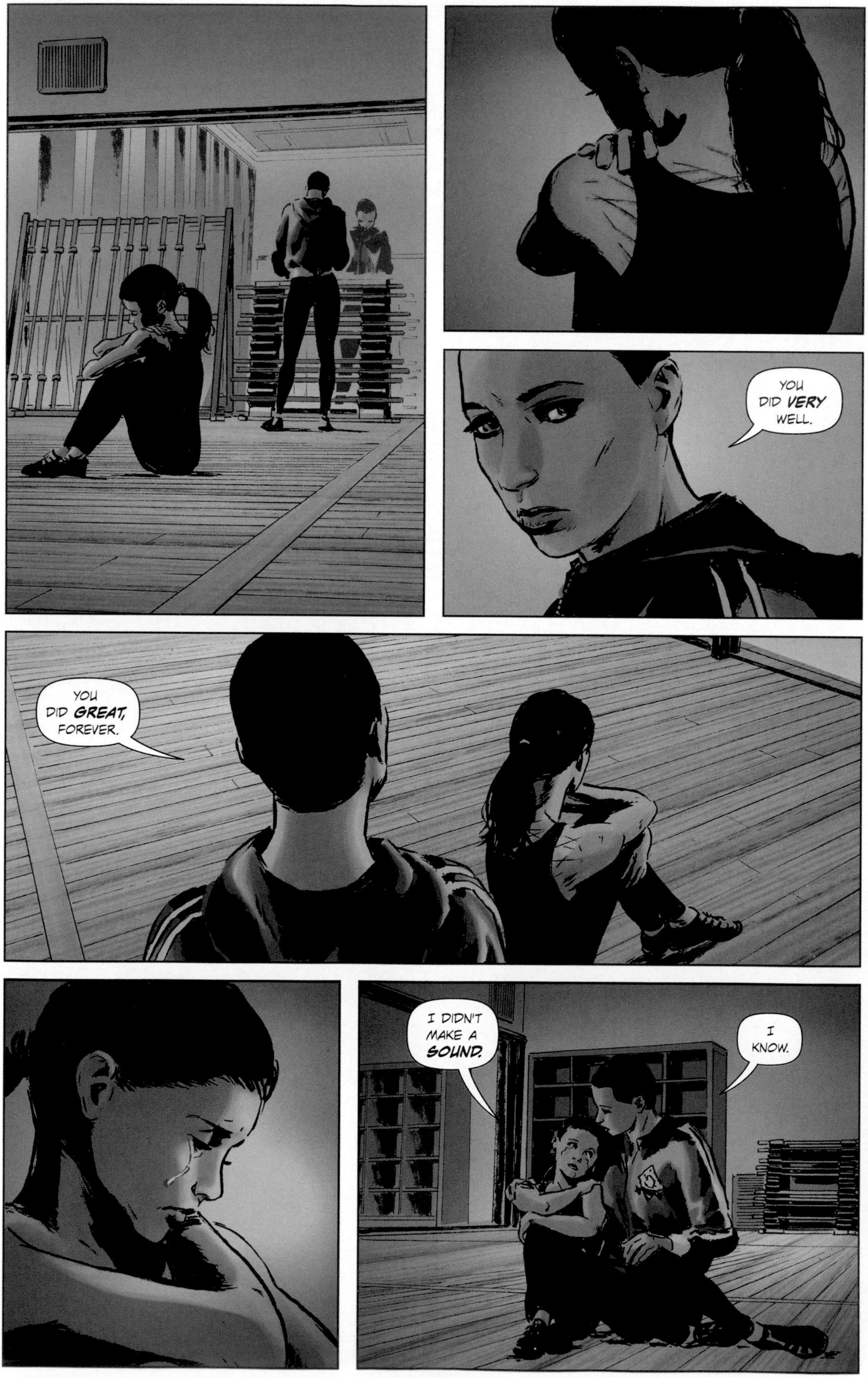
YOU DID VERY WELL.
YOU DID GREAT, FOREVER.
I DIDN'T MAKE A SOUND.
I KNOW.

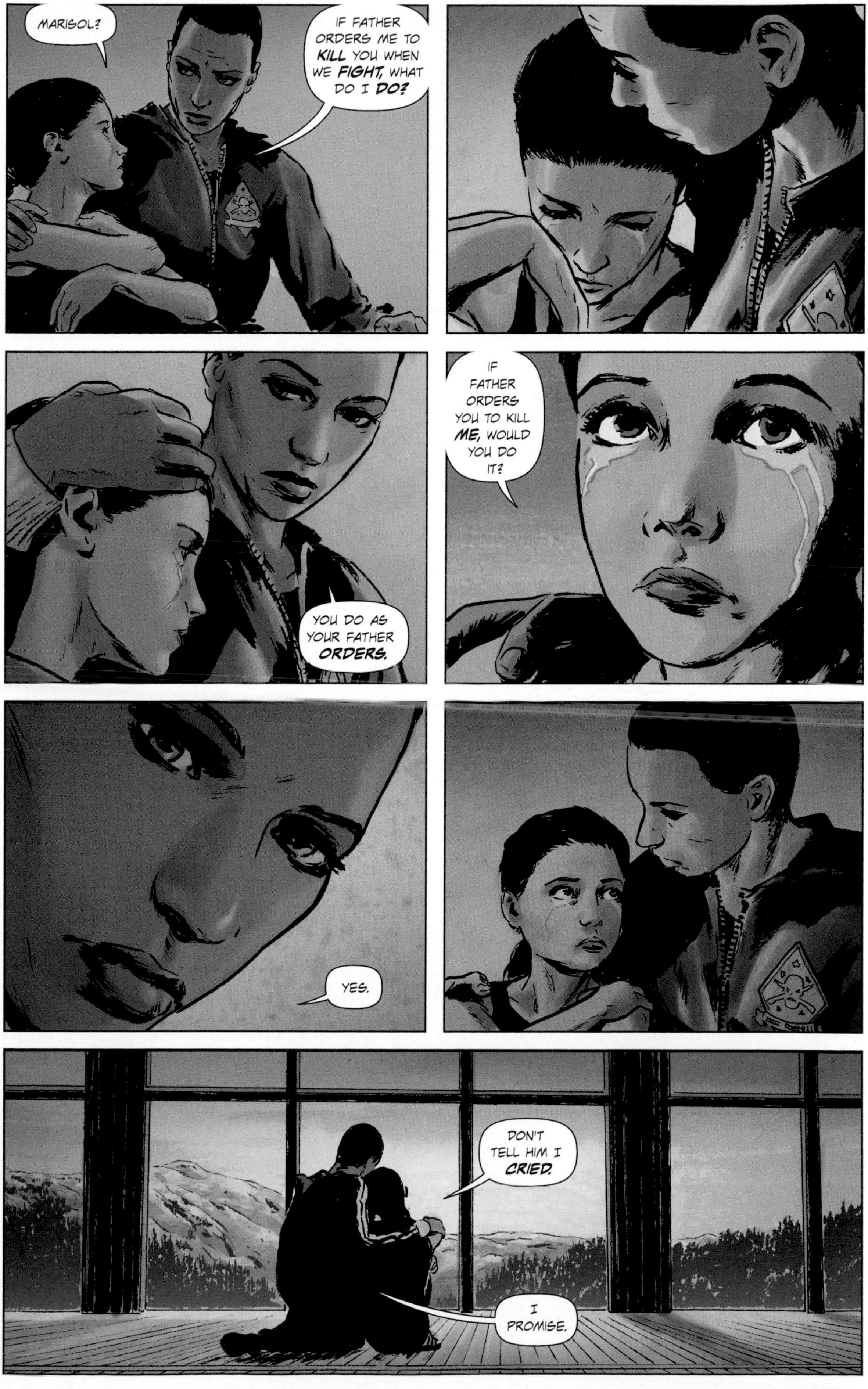
MARISOL?
IF FATHER ORDERS ME TO KILL YOU WHEN WE FIGHT, WHAT DO I DO?
YOU DO AS YOUR FATHER ORDERS.
IF FATHER ORDERS YOU TO KILL ME, WOULD YOU DO IT?
YES.
DON'T TELL HIM I CRIED.
I PROMISE.

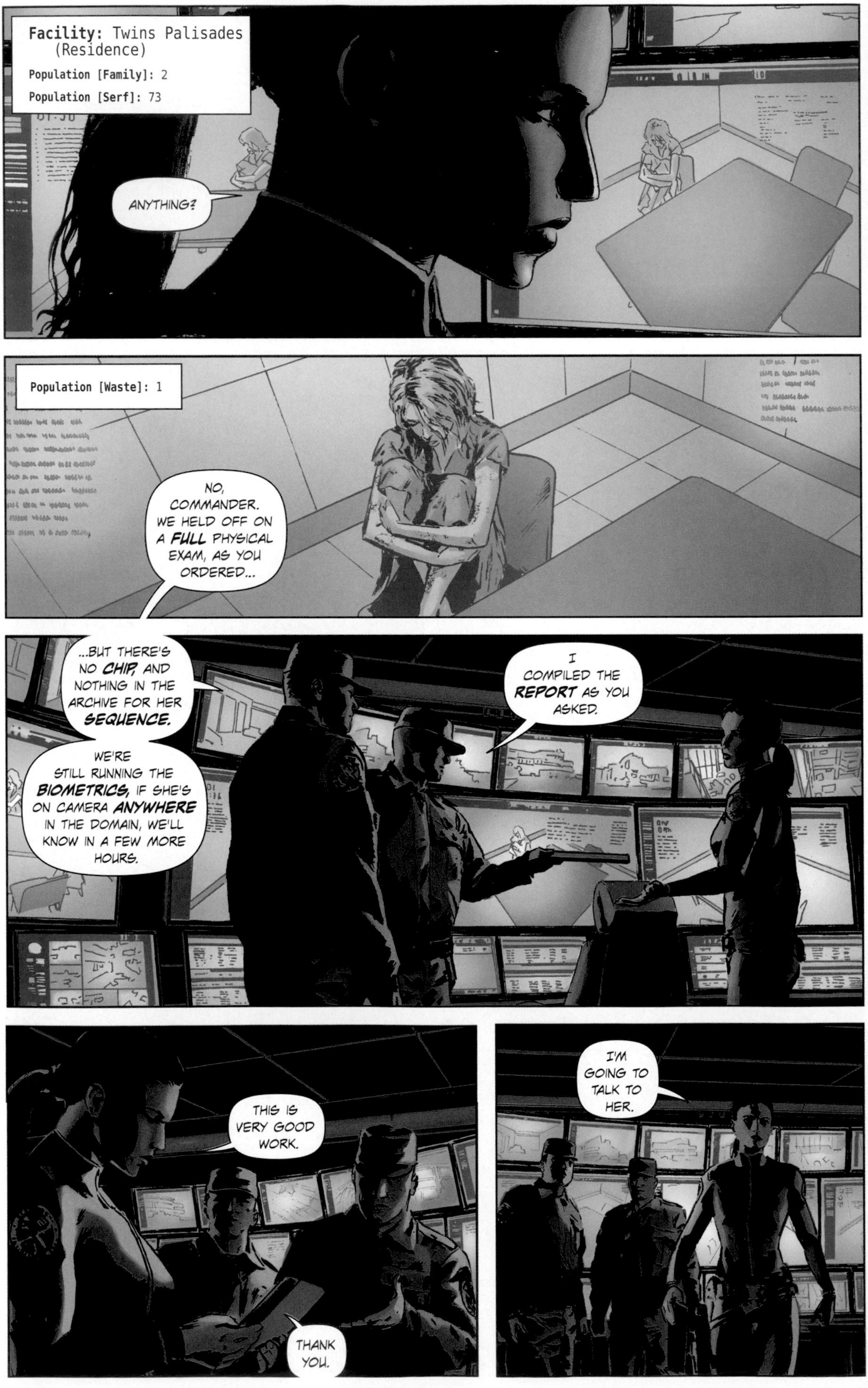
Facility: Twins Palisades (Residence)
Population [Family]: 2
Population [Serf]: 73
ANYTHING?
Population [Waste]: 1
NO, COMMANDER. WE HELD OFF ON A FULL PHYSICAL EXAM, AS YOU ORDERED...
...BUT THERE'S NO CHIP, AND NOTHING IN THE ARCHIVE FOR HER SEQUENCE.
WE'RE STILL RUNNING THE BIOMETRICS, IF SHE'S ON CAMERA ANYWHERE IN THE DOMAIN, WE'LL KNOW IN A FEW MORE HOURS.
I COMPILED THE REPORT AS YOU ASKED.
THIS IS VERY GOOD WORK.
THANK YOU.
I'M GOING TO TALK TO HER.

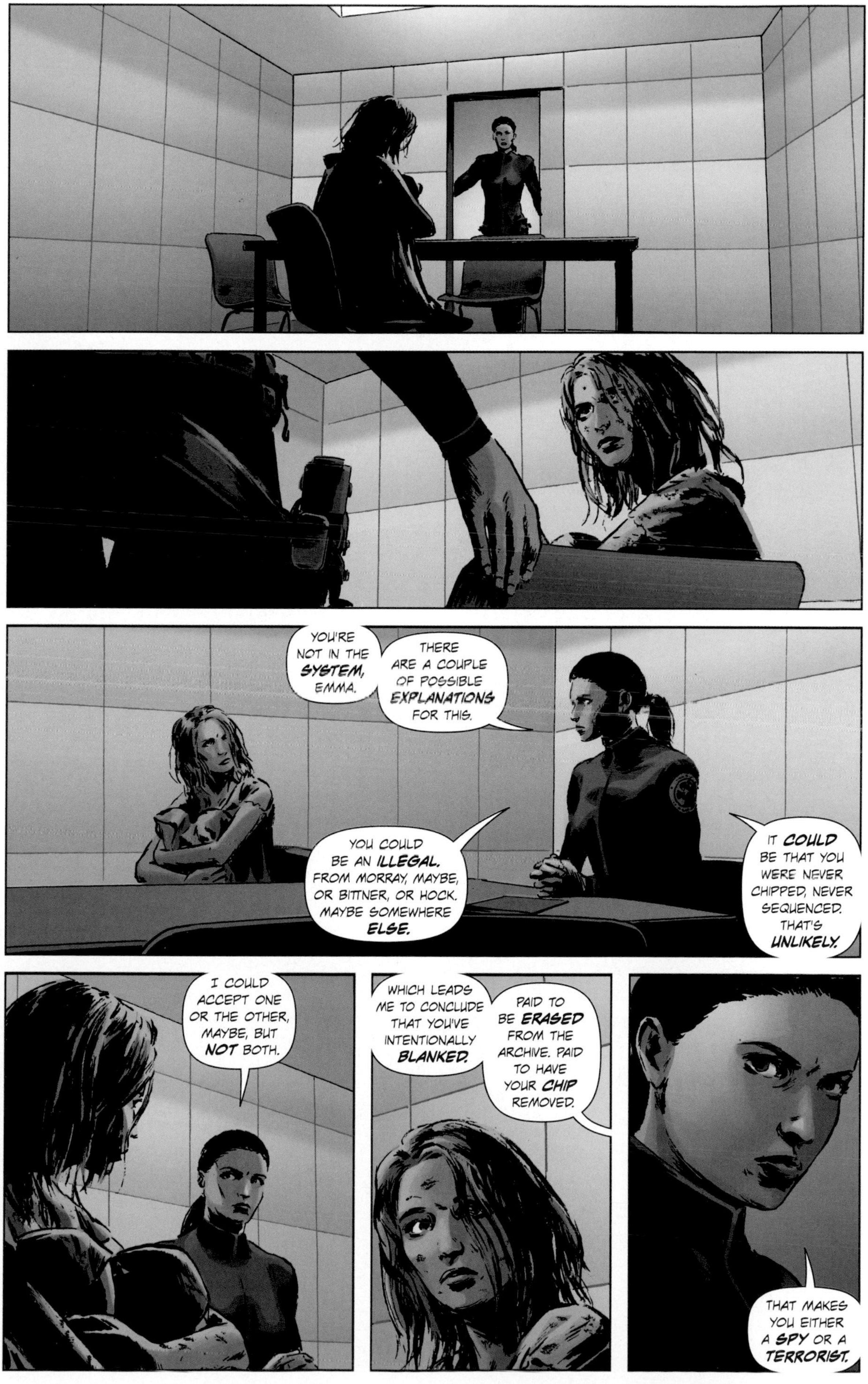
YOU'RE NOT IN THE SYSTEM, EMMA.
THERE ARE A COUPLE OF POSSIBLE EXPLANATIONS FOR THIS.
YOU COULD BE AN ILLEGAL. FROM MORRAY, MAYBE, OR BITTNER, OR HOCK. MAYBE SOMEWHERE ELSE.
IT COULD BE THAT YOU WERE NEVER CHIPPED, NEVER SEQUENCED. THAT'S UNLIKELY.
I COULD ACCEPT ONE OR THE OTHER, MAYBE, BUT NOT BOTH.
WHICH LEADS ME TO CONCLUDE THAT YOU'VE INTENTIONALLY BLANKED.
PAID TO BE ERASED FROM THE ARCHIVE. PAID TO HAVE YOUR CHIP REMOVED.
THAT MAKES YOU EITHER A SPY OR A TERRORIST.

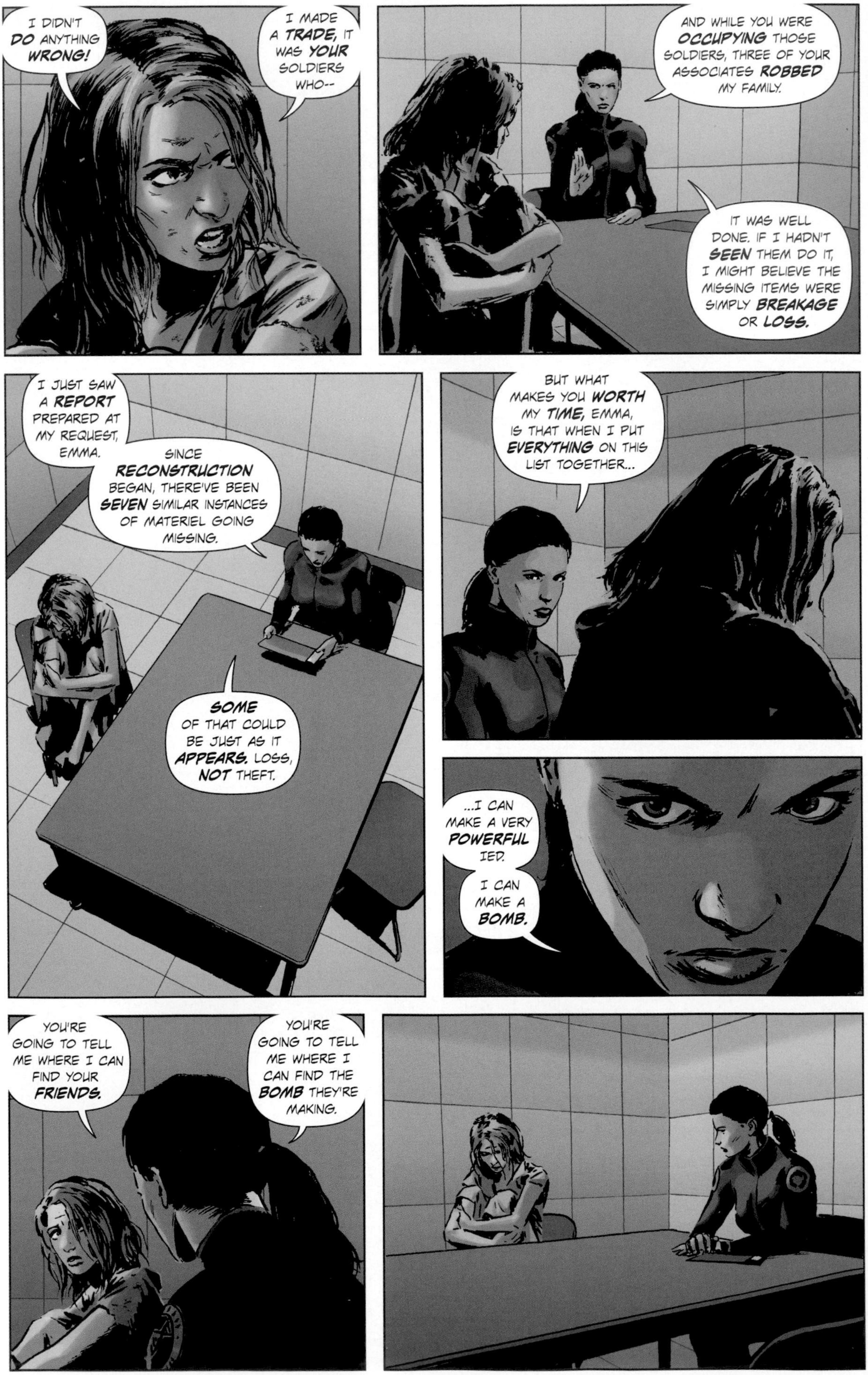
I DIDN'T DO ANYTHING WRONG!
I MADE A TRADE, IT WAS YOUR SOLDIERS WHO--
AND WHILE YOU WERE OCCUPYING THOSE SOLDIERS, THREE OF YOUR ASSOCIATES ROBBED MY FAMILY.
IT WAS WELL DONE. IF I HADN'T SEEN THEM DO IT, I MIGHT BELIEVE THE MISSING ITEMS WERE SIMPLY BREAKAGE OR LOSS.
I JUST SAW A REPORT PREPARED AT MY REQUEST, EMMA.
SINCE RECONSTRUCTION BEGAN, THERE'VE BEEN SEVEN SIMILAR INSTANCES OF MATERIEL GOING MISSING.
SOME OF THAT COULD BE JUST AS IT APPEARS. LOSS, NOT THEFT.
BUT WHAT MAKES YOU WORTH MY TIME, EMMA, IS THAT WHEN I PUT EVERYTHING ON THIS LIST TOGETHER...
...I CAN MAKE A VERY POWERFUL IED.
I CAN MAKE A BOMB.
YOU'RE GOING TO TELL ME WHERE I CAN FIND YOUR FRIENDS.
YOU'RE GOING TO TELL ME WHERE I CAN FIND THE BOMB THEY'RE MAKING.

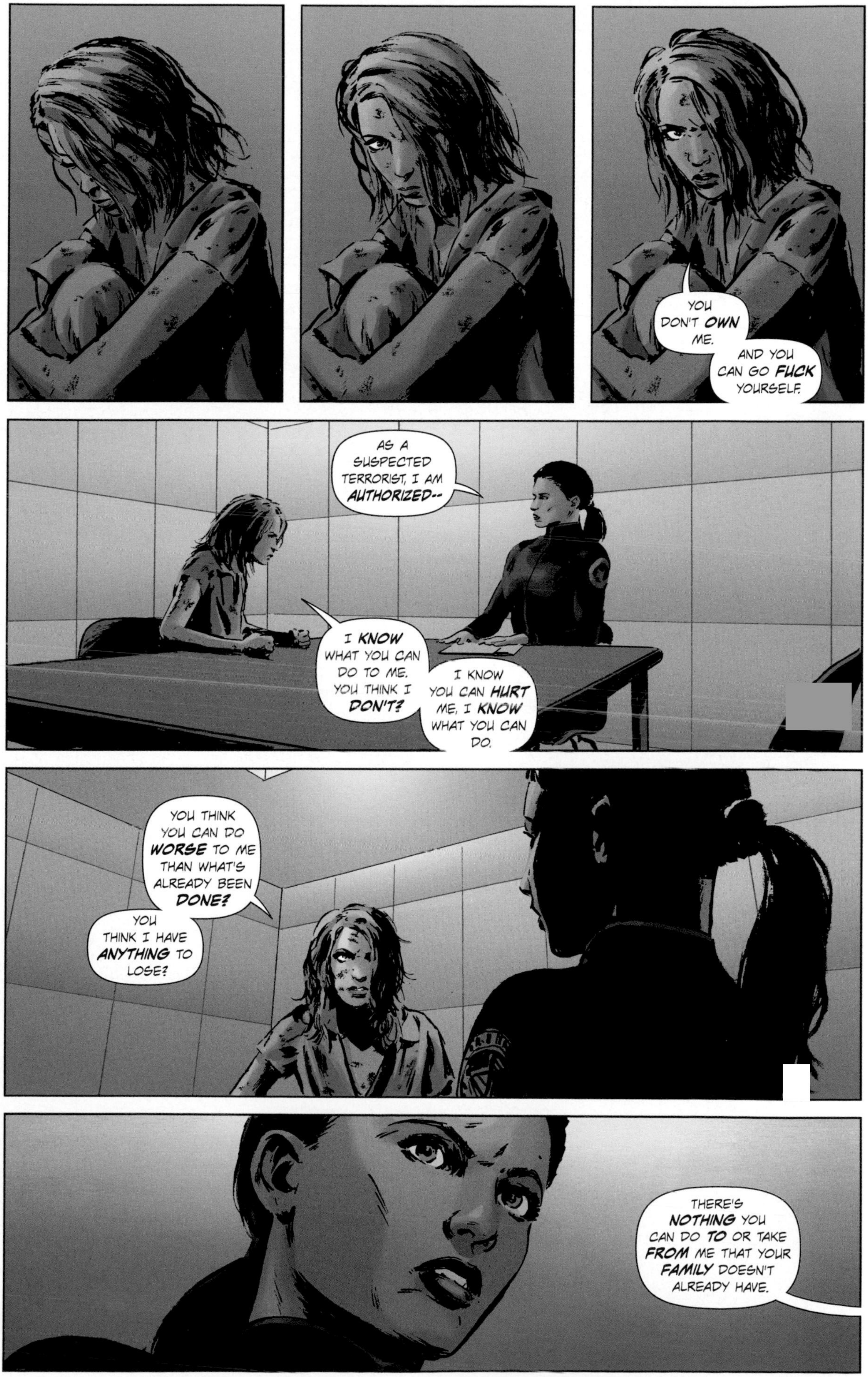
YOU DON'T OWN ME.
AND YOU CAN GO FUCK YOURSELF.
AS A SUSPECTED TERRORIST, I AM AUTHORIZED--
I KNOW WHAT YOU CAN DO TO ME. YOU THINK I DON'T?
I KNOW YOU CAN HURT ME, I KNOW WHAT YOU CAN DO.
YOU THINK YOU CAN DO WORSE TO ME THAN WHAT'S ALREADY BEEN DONE?
YOU THINK I HAVE ANYTHING TO LOSE?
THERE'S NOTHING YOU CAN DO TO OR TAKE FROM ME THAT YOUR FAMILY DOESN'T ALREADY HAVE.

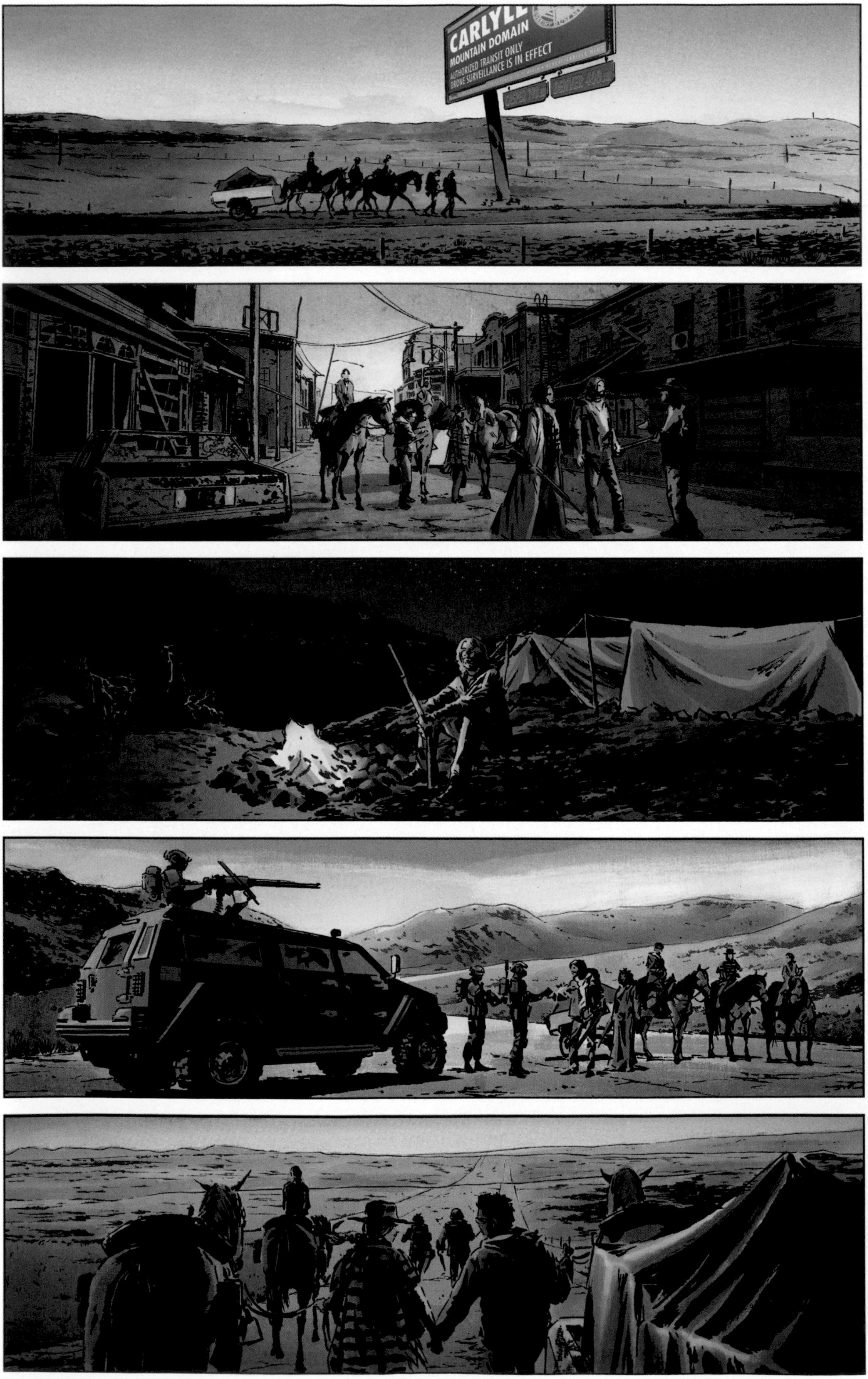
CARLYLE
MOUNTAIN DOMAIN
AUTHORIZED TRANSIT ONLY
DRONE SURVEILLANCE IS IN EFFECT

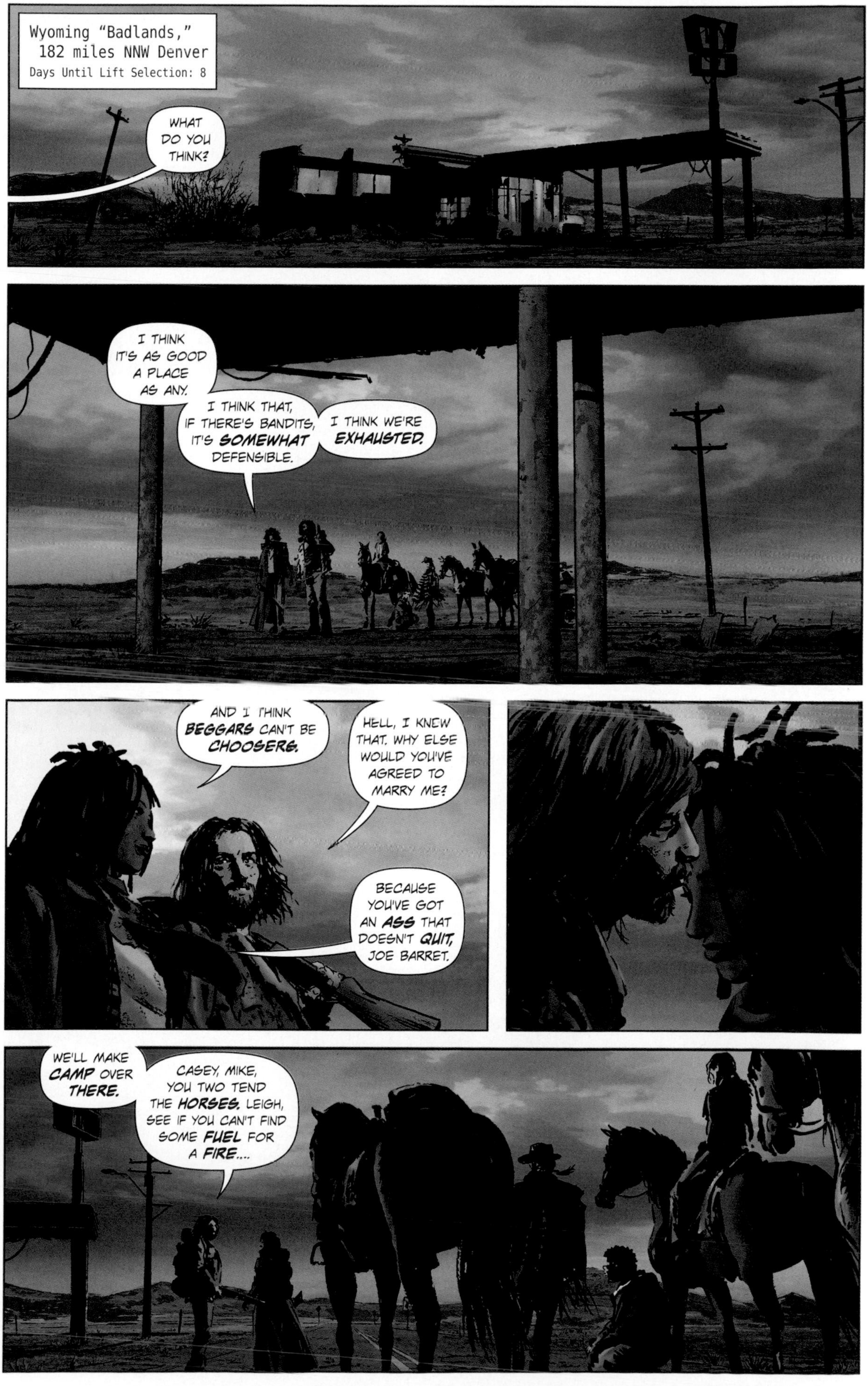
Wyoming "Badlands," 182 miles NNW Denver
Days Until Lift Selection: 8
WHAT DO YOU THINK?
I THINK IT'S AS GOOD A PLACE AS ANY.
I THINK THAT, IF THERE'S BANDITS, IT'S SOMEWHAT DEFENSIBLE.
I THINK WE'RE EXHAUSTED.
AND I THINK BEGGARS CAN'T BE CHOOSERS.
HELL, I KNEW THAT. WHY ELSE WOULD YOU'VE AGREED TO MARRY ME?
BECAUSE YOU'VE GOT AN ASS THAT DOESN'T QUIT, JOE BARRET.
WE'LL MAKE CAMP OVER THERE.
CASEY, MIKE, YOU TWO TEND THE HORSES. LEIGH, SEE IF YOU CAN'T FIND SOME FUEL FOR A FIRE....

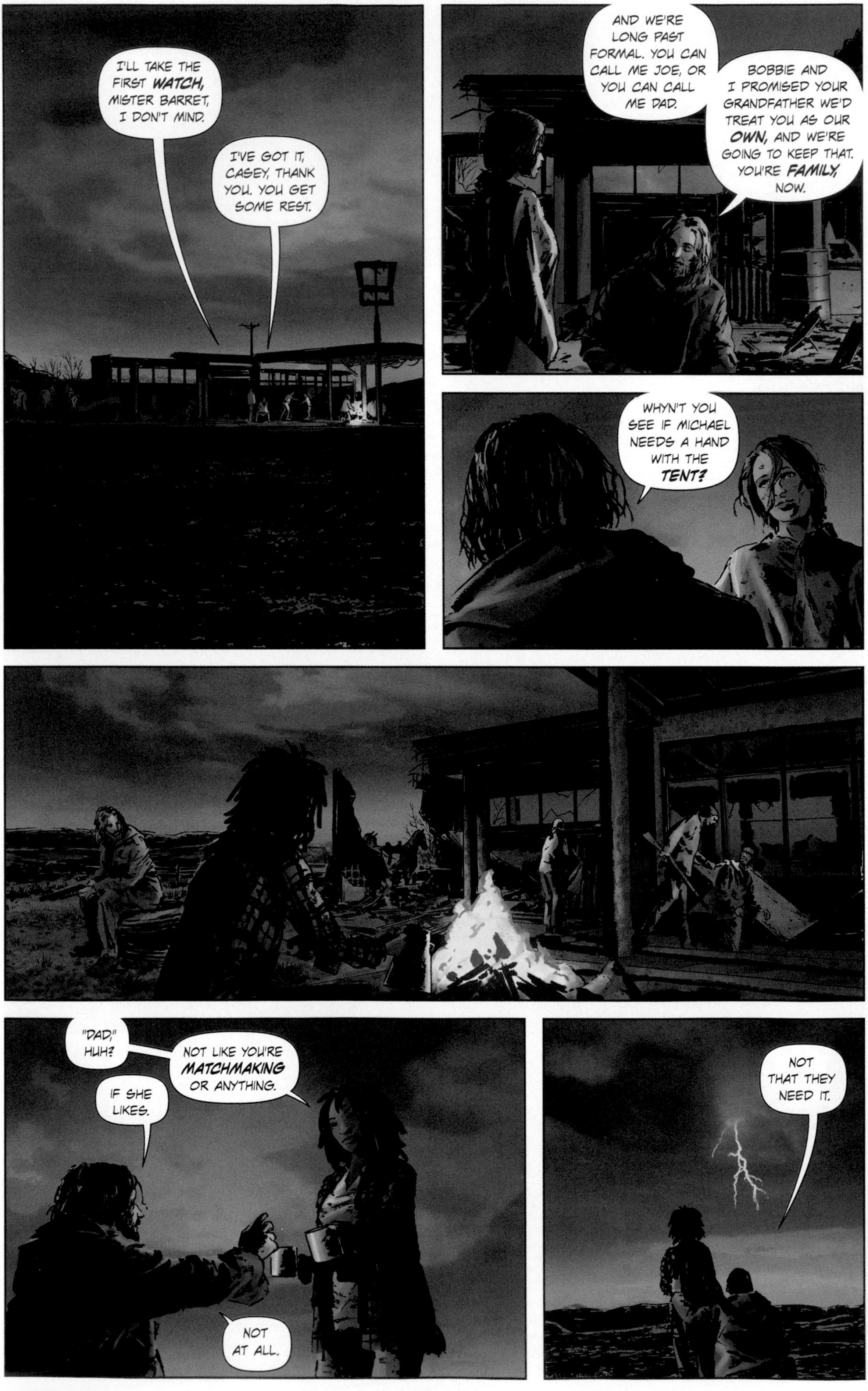
I'LL TAKE THE FIRST WATCH, MISTER BARRET, I DON'T MIND.
I'VE GOT IT, CASEY, THANK YOU. YOU GET SOME REST.
AND WE'RE LONG PAST FORMAL. YOU CAN CALL ME JOE, OR YOU CAN CALL ME DAD.
BOBBIE AND I PROMISED YOUR GRANDFATHER WE'D TREAT YOU AS OUR OWN, AND WE'RE GOING TO KEEP THAT. YOU'RE FAMILY, NOW.
WHYN'T YOU SEE IF MICHAEL NEEDS A HAND WITH THE TENT?
"DAD," HUH?
NOT LIKE YOU'RE MATCHMAKING OR ANYTHING.
IF SHE LIKES.
NOT AT ALL.
NOT THAT THEY NEED IT.

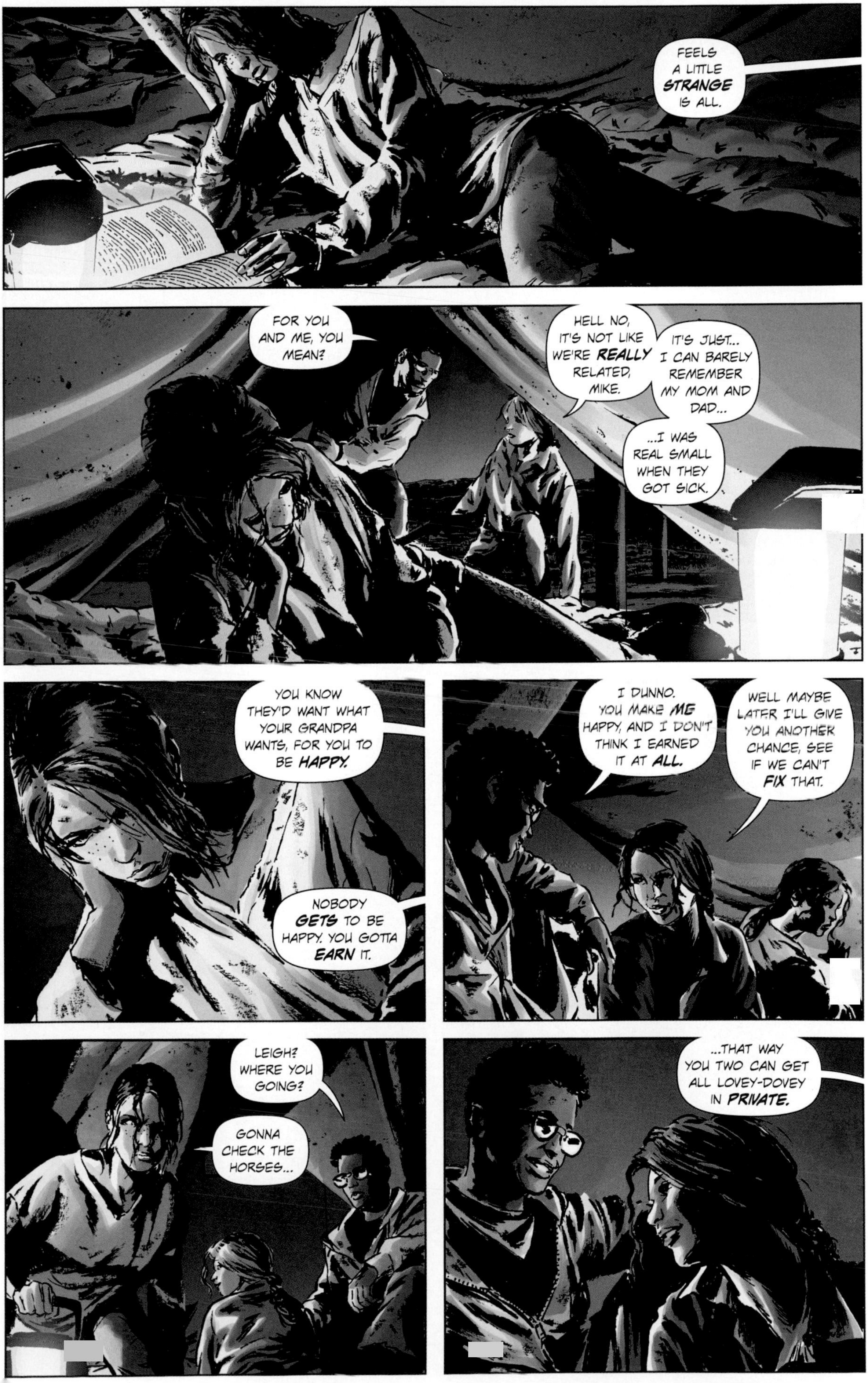
FEELS A LITTLE STRANGE IS ALL.
FOR YOU AND ME, YOU MEAN?
HELL NO, IT'S NOT LIKE WE'RE REALLY RELATED, MIKE.
IT'S JUST... I CAN BARELY REMEMBER MY MOM AND DAD...
...I WAS REAL SMALL WHEN THEY GOT SICK.
YOU KNOW THEY'D WANT WHAT YOUR GRANDPA WANTS, FOR YOU TO BE HAPPY.
NOBODY GETS TO BE HAPPY. YOU GOTTA EARN IT.
I DUNNO. YOU MAKE ME HAPPY, AND I DON'T THINK I EARNED IT AT ALL.
WELL MAYBE LATER I'LL GIVE YOU ANOTHER CHANCE, SEE IF WE CAN'T FIX THAT.
LEIGH? WHERE YOU GOING?
GONNA CHECK THE HORSES...
...THAT WAY YOU TWO CAN GET ALL LOVEY-DOVEY IN PRIVATE.

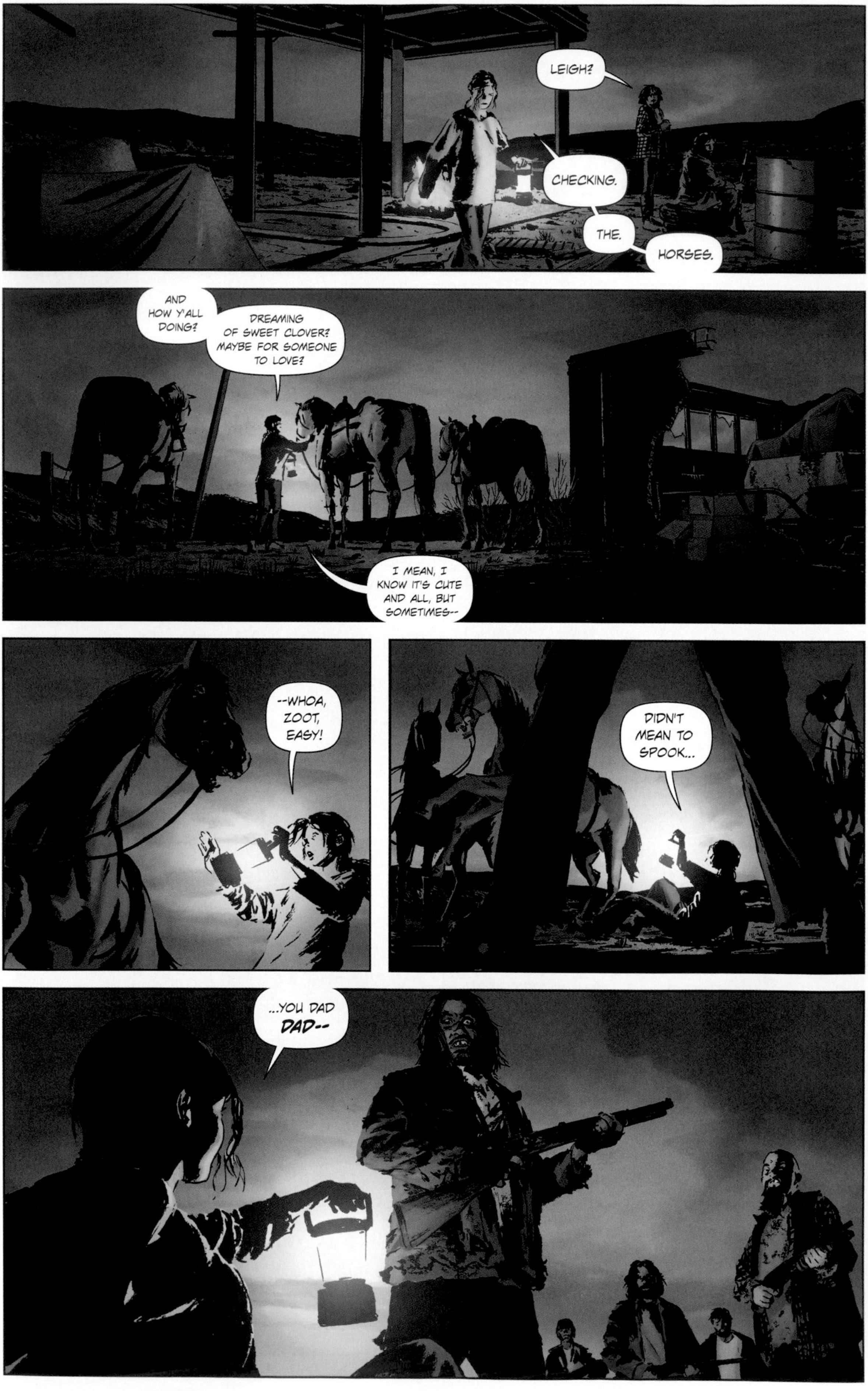

LEIGH?
CHECKING.
THE.
HORSES.
AND HOW Y'ALL DOING?
DREAMING OF SWEET CLOVER? MAYBE FOR SOMEONE TO LOVE?
I MEAN, I KNOW IT'S CUTE AND ALL, BUT SOMETIMES--
--WHOA, ZOOT, EASY!
DIDN'T MEAN TO SPOOK...
...YOU DAD
DAD--

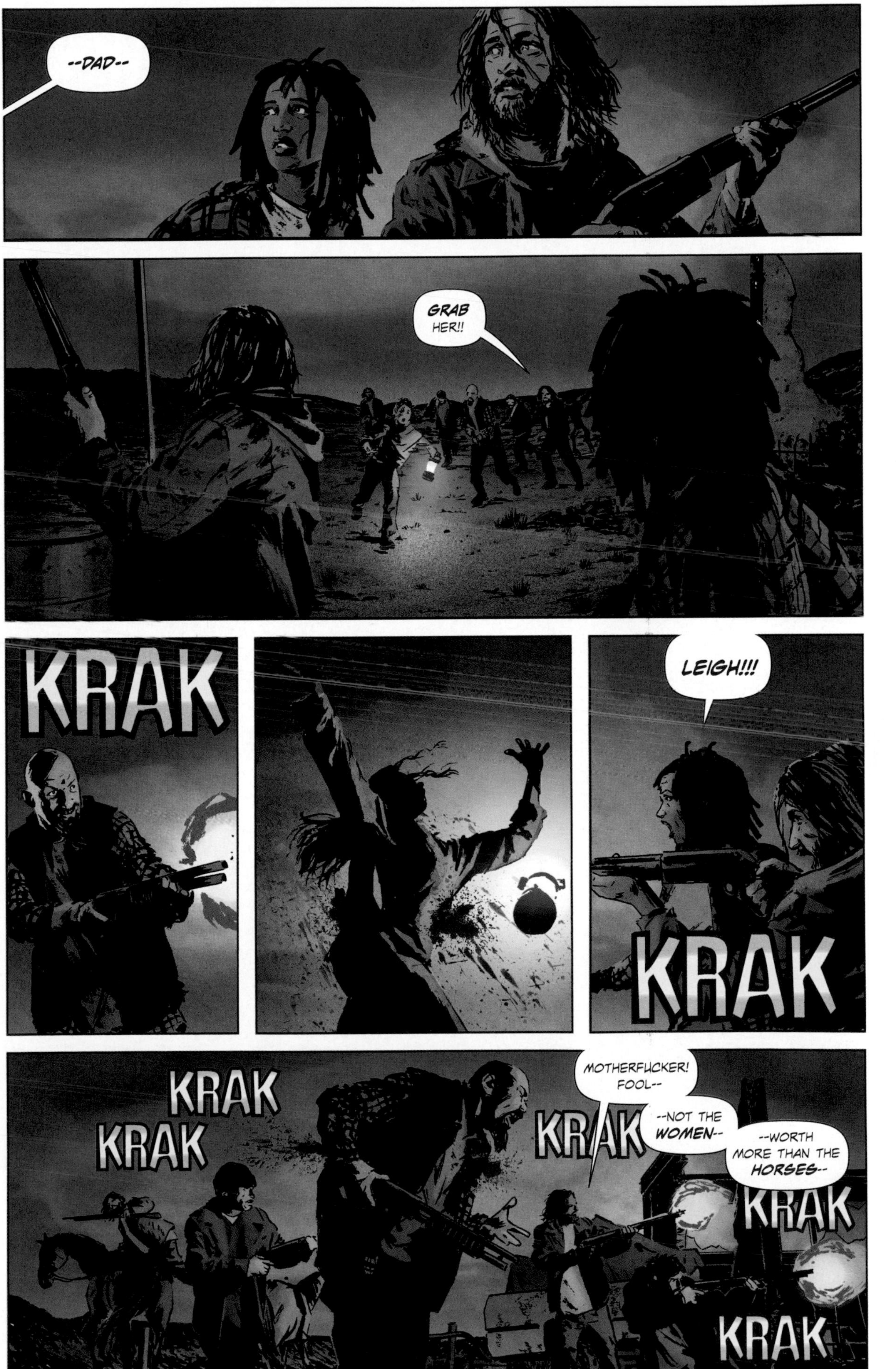
--DAD--
GRAB HER!!
KRAK
LEIGH!!!
KRAK
KRAK
KRAK
MOTHERFUCKER! FOOL--
KRAK
--NOT THE WOMEN--
--WORTH MORE THAN THE HORSES--
KRAK
KRAK

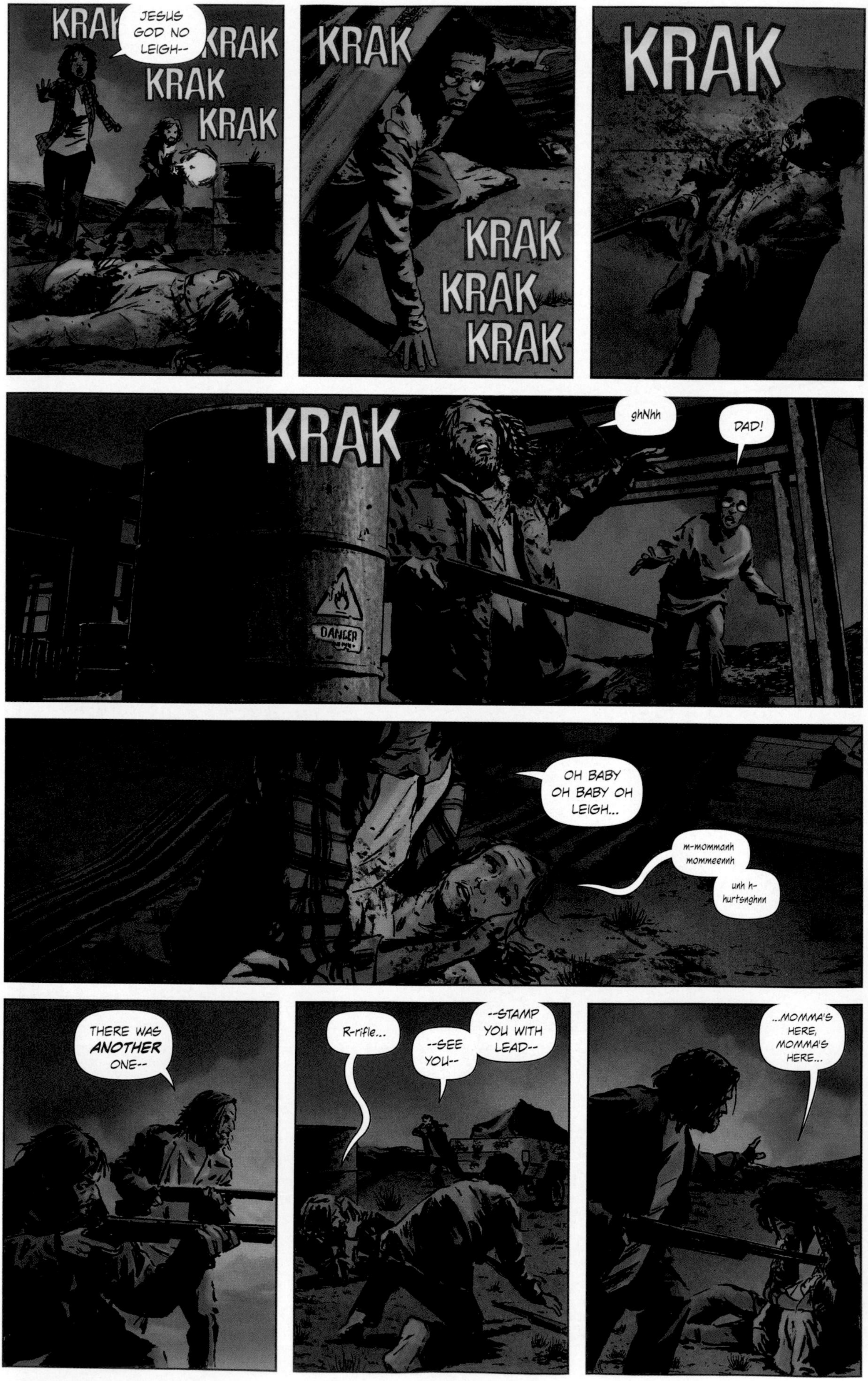
KRAK
JESUS GOD NO LEIGH--
KRAK
KRAK
KRAK
KRAK
KRAK
KRAK
KRAK
KRAK
KRAK
ghNhh
DAD!
OH BABY OH BABY OH LEIGH...
m-mommanh mommeennh
unh h-hurtsnghnn
THERE WAS ***ANOTHER*** ONE--
R-rifle...
--SEE YOU--
--STAMP YOU WITH LEAD--
...MOMMA'S HERE, MOMMA'S HERE...

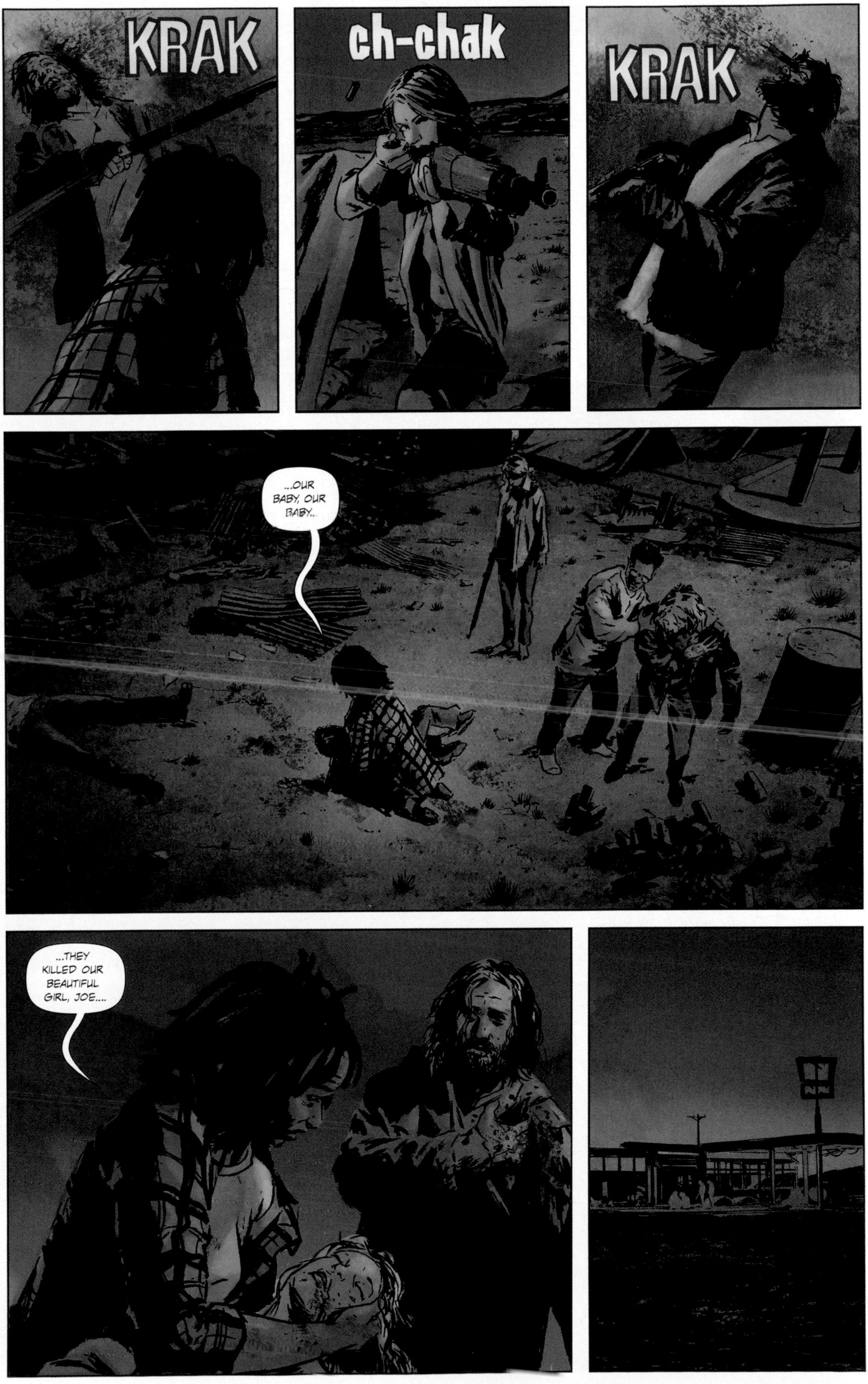
KRAK
ch-chak
KRAK
...OUR BABY, OUR BABY...
...THEY KILLED OUR BEAUTIFUL GIRL, JOE....

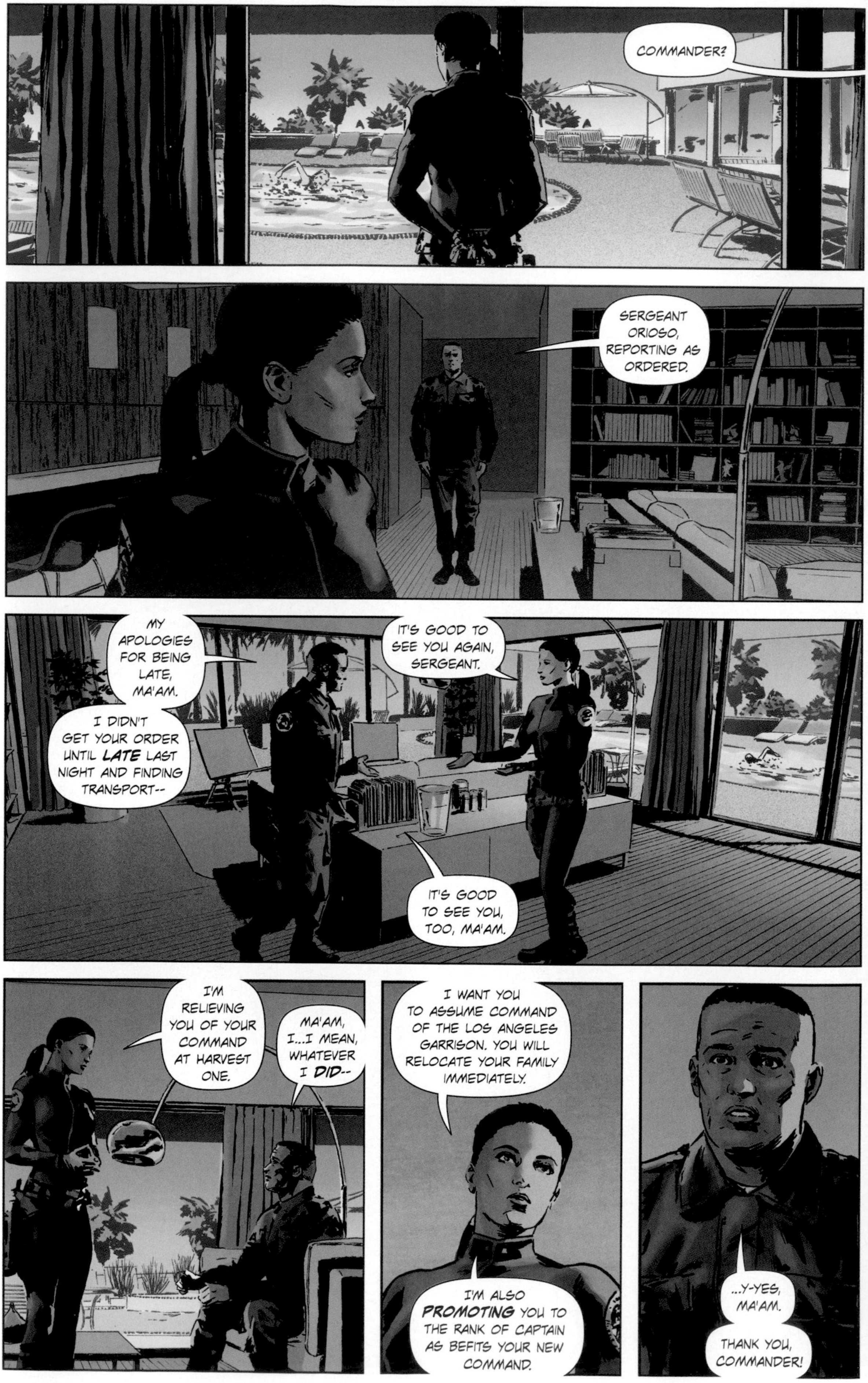
COMMANDER?
SERGEANT ORIOSO, REPORTING AS ORDERED.
MY APOLOGIES FOR BEING LATE, MA'AM.
I DIDN'T GET YOUR ORDER UNTIL **LATE** LAST NIGHT AND FINDING TRANSPORT--
IT'S GOOD TO SEE YOU AGAIN, SERGEANT.
IT'S GOOD TO SEE YOU, TOO, MA'AM.
I'M RELIEVING YOU OF YOUR COMMAND AT HARVEST ONE.
MA'AM, I...I MEAN, WHATEVER I **DID**--
I WANT YOU TO ASSUME COMMAND OF THE LOS ANGELES GARRISON. YOU WILL RELOCATE YOUR FAMILY IMMEDIATELY.
I'M ALSO **PROMOTING** YOU TO THE RANK OF CAPTAIN AS BEFITS YOUR NEW COMMAND.
...Y-YES, MA'AM.
THANK YOU, COMMANDER!

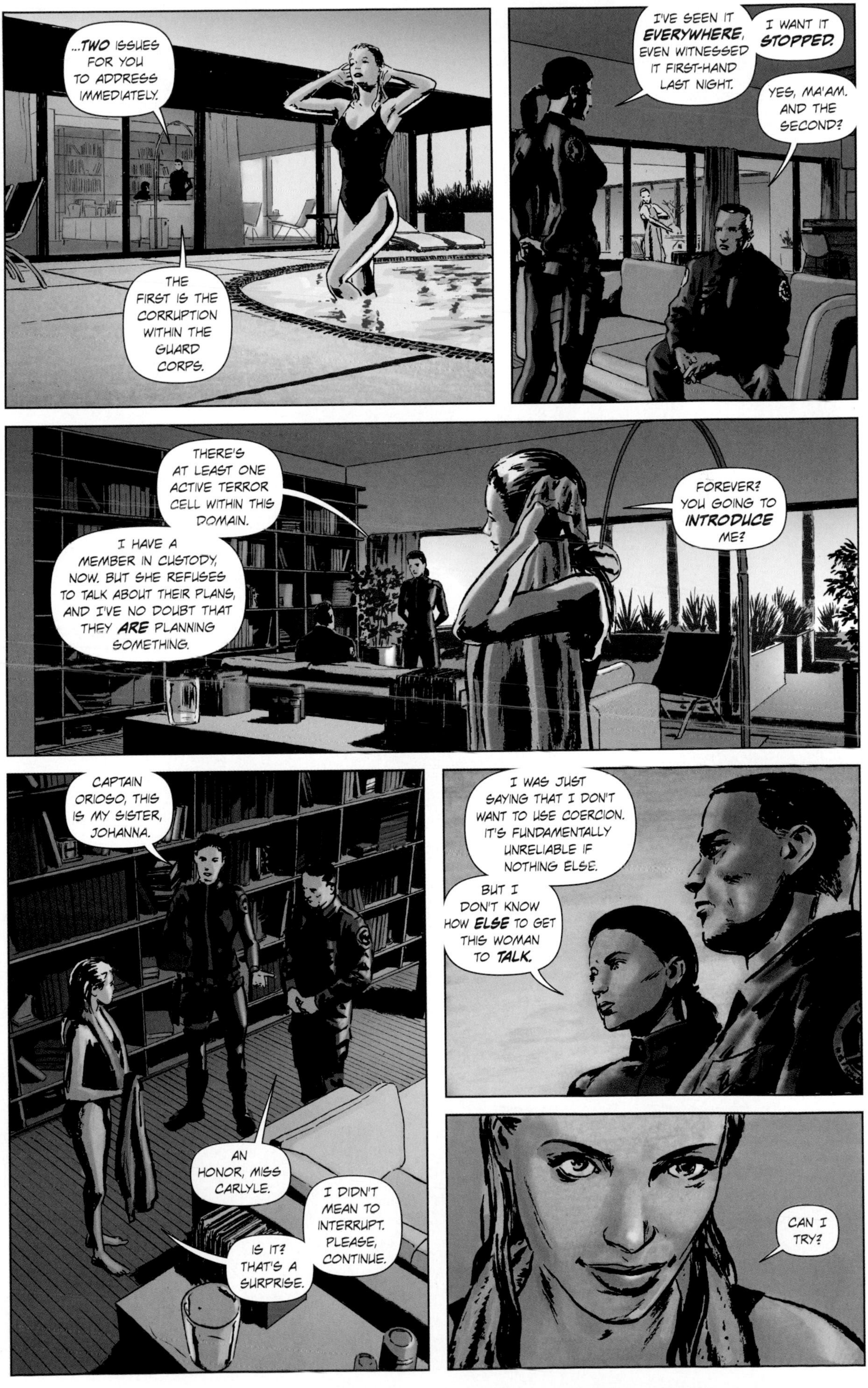
...TWO ISSUES FOR YOU TO ADDRESS IMMEDIATELY.
THE FIRST IS THE CORRUPTION WITHIN THE GUARD CORPS.
I'VE SEEN IT EVERYWHERE, EVEN WITNESSED IT FIRST-HAND LAST NIGHT.
I WANT IT STOPPED.
YES, MA'AM. AND THE SECOND?
THERE'S AT LEAST ONE ACTIVE TERROR CELL WITHIN THIS DOMAIN.
I HAVE A MEMBER IN CUSTODY, NOW. BUT SHE REFUSES TO TALK ABOUT THEIR PLANS, AND I'VE NO DOUBT THAT THEY ARE PLANNING SOMETHING.
FOREVER? YOU GOING TO INTRODUCE ME?
CAPTAIN ORIOSO, THIS IS MY SISTER, JOHANNA.
AN HONOR, MISS CARLYLE.
IS IT? THAT'S A SURPRISE.
I DIDN'T MEAN TO INTERRUPT. PLEASE, CONTINUE.
I WAS JUST SAYING THAT I DON'T WANT TO USE COERCION. IT'S FUNDAMENTALLY UNRELIABLE IF NOTHING ELSE.
BUT I DON'T KNOW HOW ELSE TO GET THIS WOMAN TO TALK.
CAN I TRY?

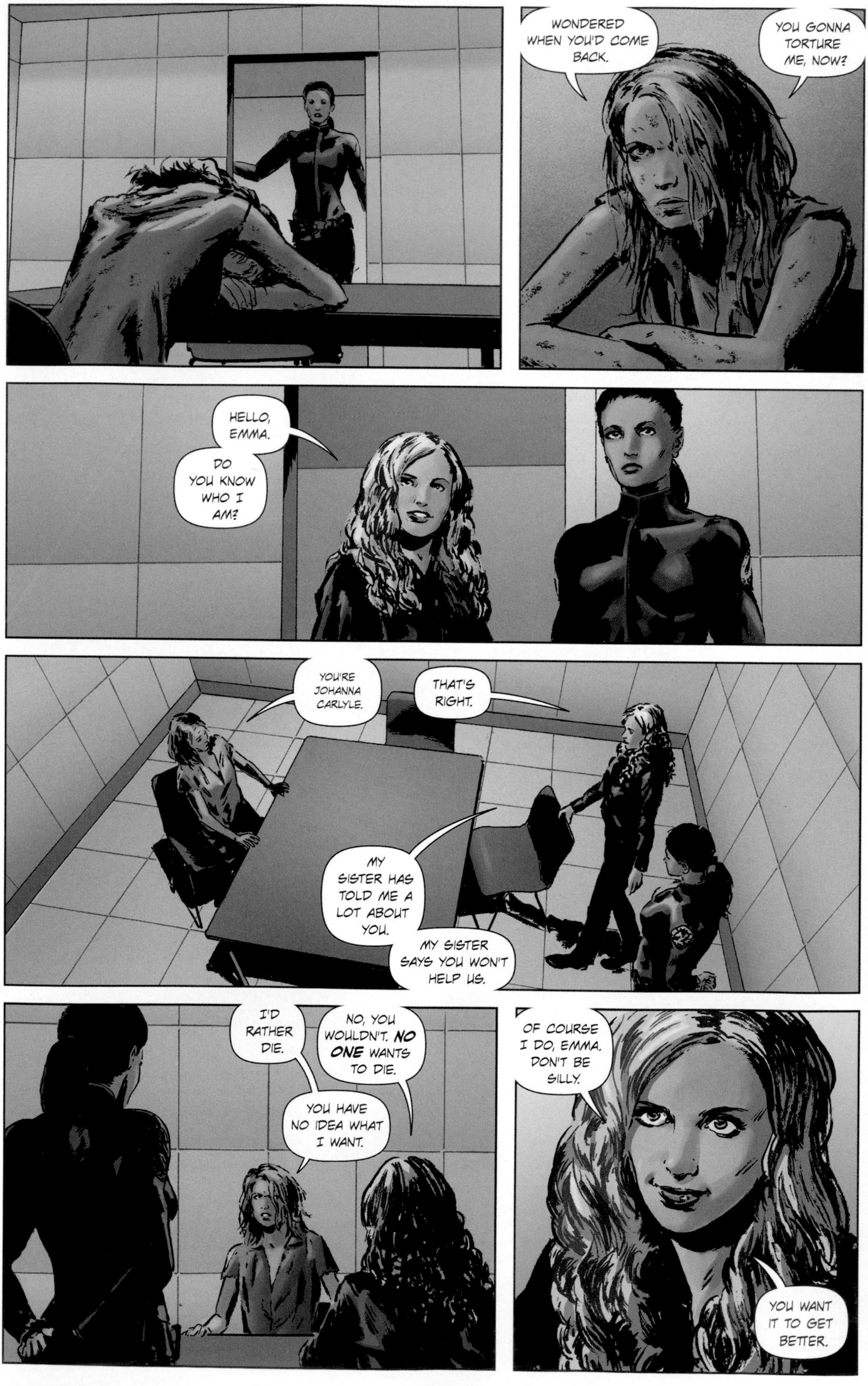
WONDERED WHEN YOU'D COME BACK.
YOU GONNA TORTURE ME, NOW?
HELLO, EMMA.
DO YOU KNOW WHO I AM?
YOU'RE JOHANNA CARLYLE.
THAT'S RIGHT.
MY SISTER HAS TOLD ME A LOT ABOUT YOU.
MY SISTER SAYS YOU WON'T HELP US.
I'D RATHER DIE.
NO, YOU WOULDN'T. NO ONE WANTS TO DIE.
YOU HAVE NO IDEA WHAT I WANT.
OF COURSE I DO, EMMA. DON'T BE SILLY.
YOU WANT IT TO GET BETTER.

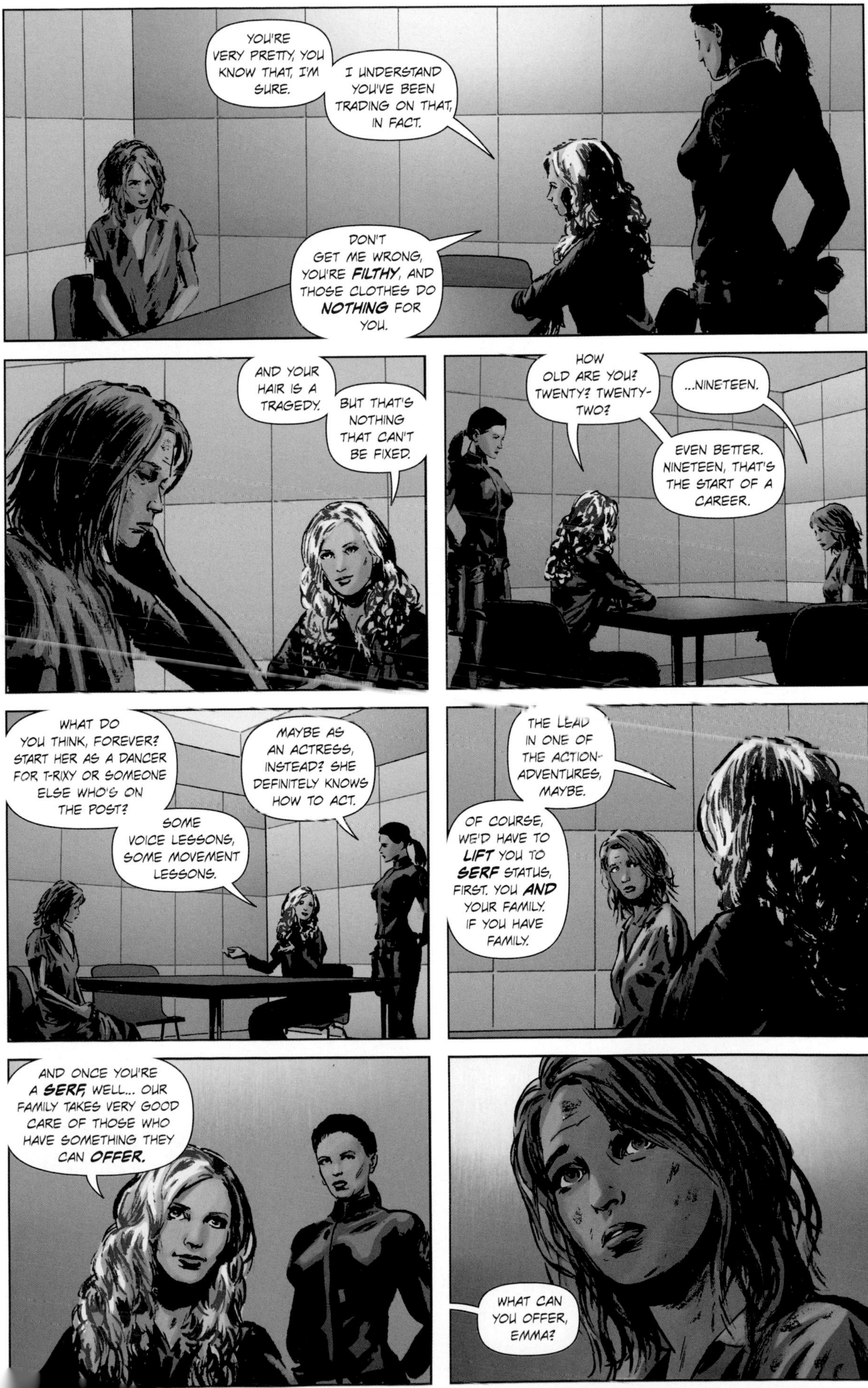
YOU'RE VERY PRETTY, YOU KNOW THAT, I'M SURE.
I UNDERSTAND YOU'VE BEEN TRADING ON THAT, IN FACT.
DON'T GET ME WRONG, YOU'RE FILTHY, AND THOSE CLOTHES DO NOTHING FOR YOU.
AND YOUR HAIR IS A TRAGEDY.
BUT THAT'S NOTHING THAT CAN'T BE FIXED.
HOW OLD ARE YOU? TWENTY? TWENTY-TWO?
...NINETEEN.
EVEN BETTER. NINETEEN, THAT'S THE START OF A CAREER.
WHAT DO YOU THINK, FOREVER? START HER AS A DANCER FOR T-RIXY OR SOMEONE ELSE WHO'S ON THE POST?
MAYBE AS AN ACTRESS, INSTEAD? SHE DEFINITELY KNOWS HOW TO ACT.
SOME VOICE LESSONS, SOME MOVEMENT LESSONS.
THE LEAD IN ONE OF THE ACTION-ADVENTURES, MAYBE.
OF COURSE, WE'D HAVE TO LIFT YOU TO SERF STATUS, FIRST. YOU AND YOUR FAMILY. IF YOU HAVE FAMILY.
AND ONCE YOU'RE A SERF, WELL... OUR FAMILY TAKES VERY GOOD CARE OF THOSE WHO HAVE SOMETHING THEY CAN OFFER.
WHAT CAN YOU OFFER, EMMA?

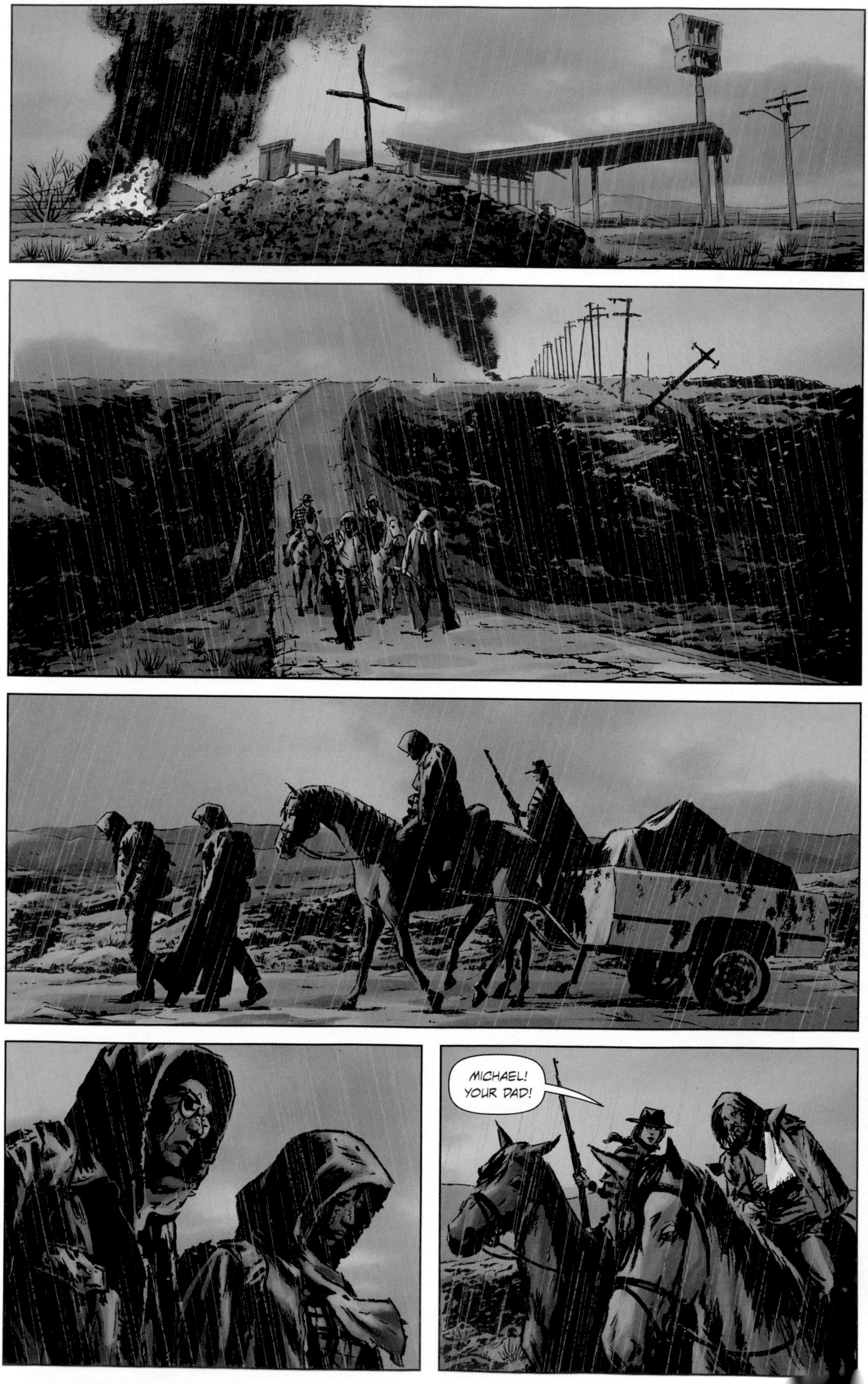
MICHAEL! YOUR DAD!

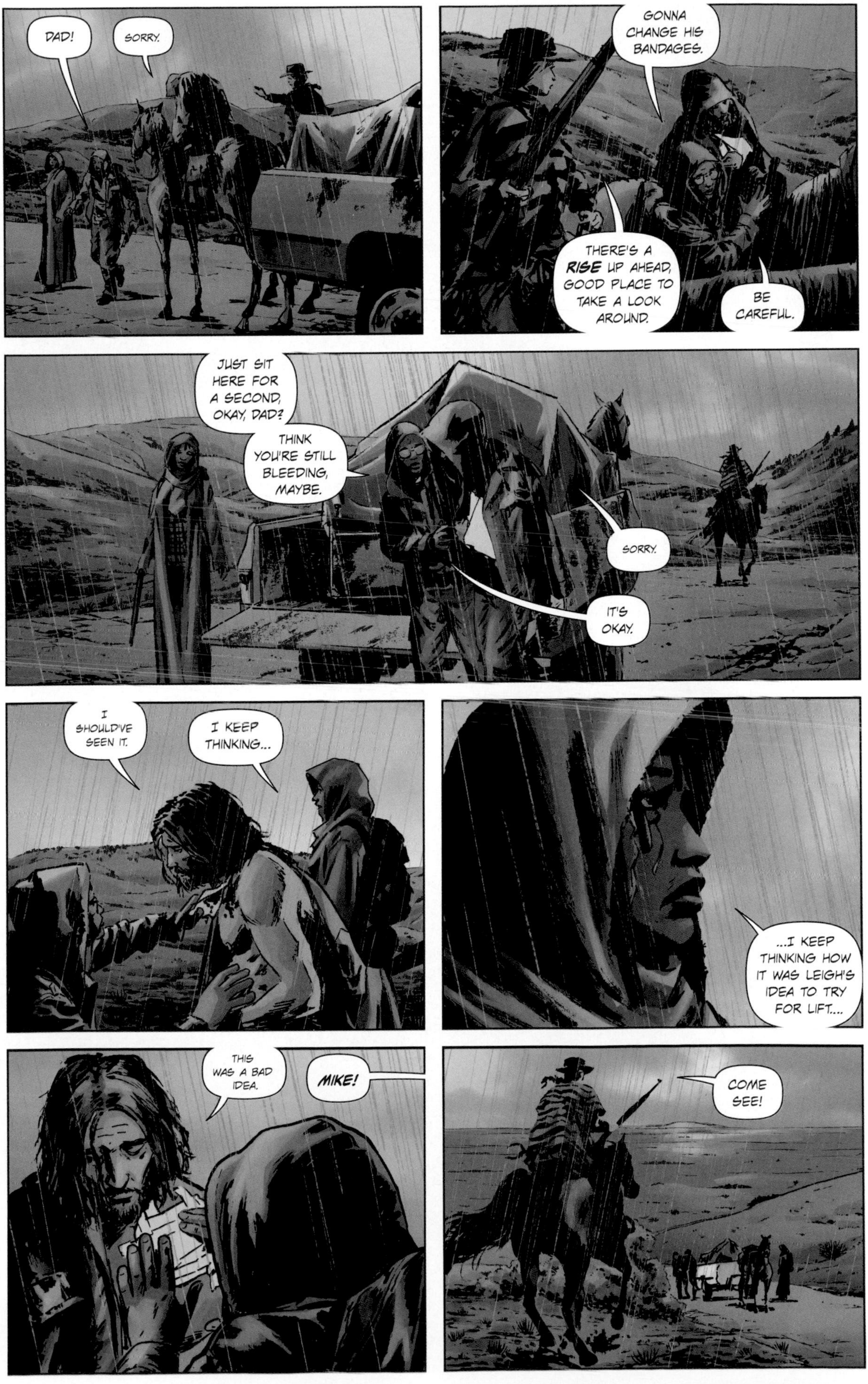
DAD!
SORRY.
GONNA CHANGE HIS BANDAGES.
THERE'S A RISE UP AHEAD, GOOD PLACE TO TAKE A LOOK AROUND.
BE CAREFUL.
JUST SIT HERE FOR A SECOND, OKAY, DAD?
THINK YOU'RE STILL BLEEDING, MAYBE.
SORRY.
IT'S OKAY.
I SHOULD'VE SEEN IT.
I KEEP THINKING...
...I KEEP THINKING HOW IT WAS LEIGH'S IDEA TO TRY FOR LIFT....
THIS WAS A BAD IDEA.
MIKE!
COME SEE!

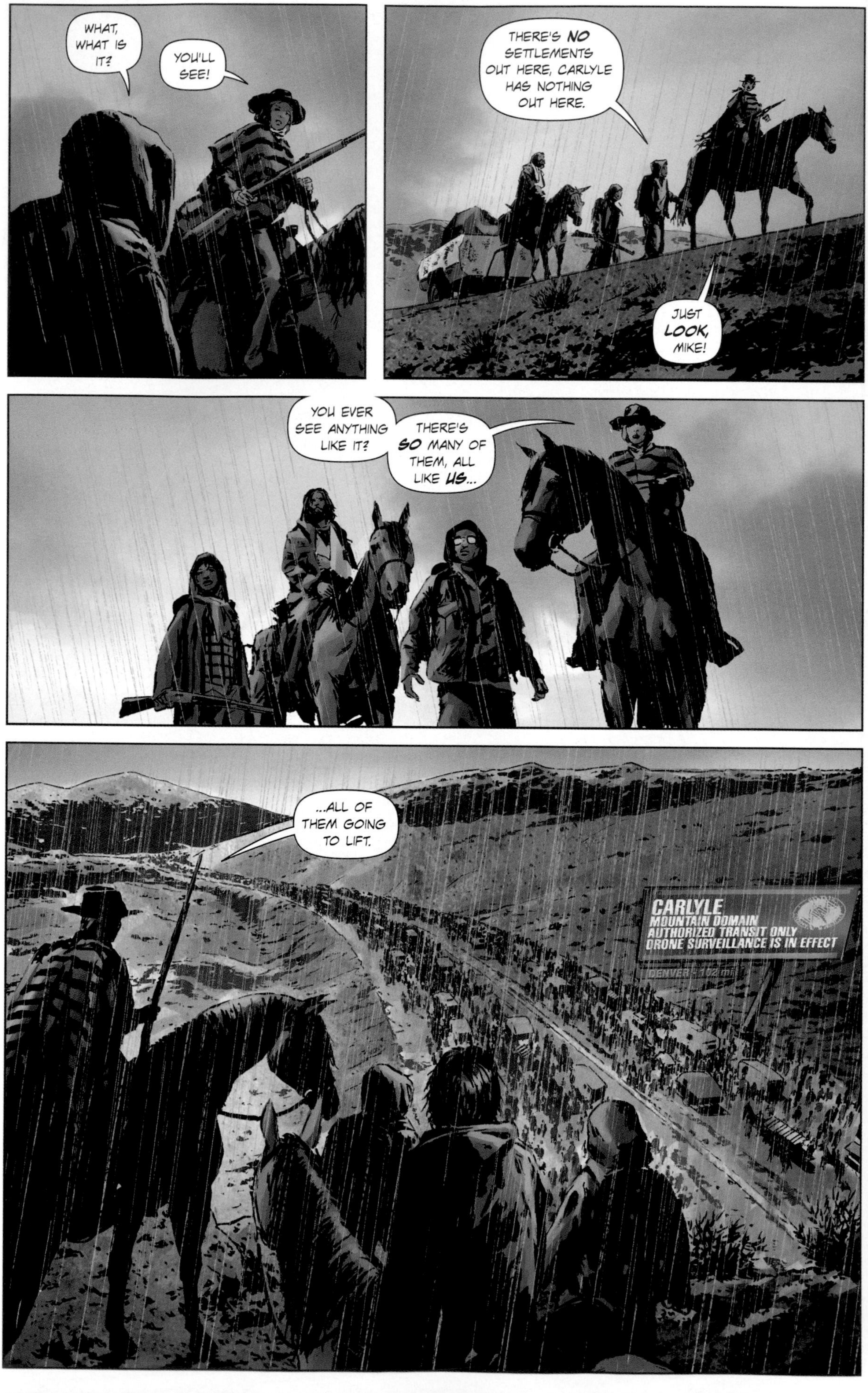
WHAT, WHAT IS IT?
YOU'LL SEE!
THERE'S NO SETTLEMENTS OUT HERE, CARLYLE HAS NOTHING OUT HERE.
JUST LOOK, MIKE!
YOU EVER SEE ANYTHING LIKE IT?
THERE'S SO MANY OF THEM, ALL LIKE US...
...ALL OF THEM GOING TO LIFT.
CARLYLE
MOUNTAIN DOMAIN
AUTHORIZED TRANSIT ONLY
DRONE SURVEILLANCE IS IN EFFECT
DENVER - 102 mi

ARE YOU THE ONE
WE'RE LOOKING FOR?
CARLYLE
ODERINT DUM METUANT
BETTER YOURSELF,
BETTER CARLYLE

# LIFT

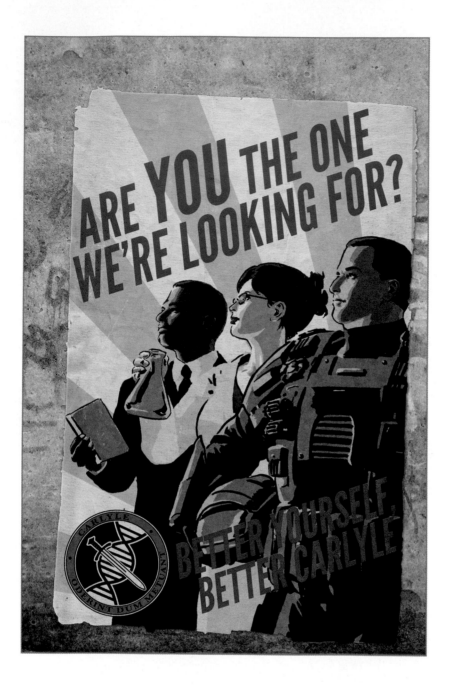

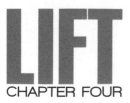

CHAPTER FOUR

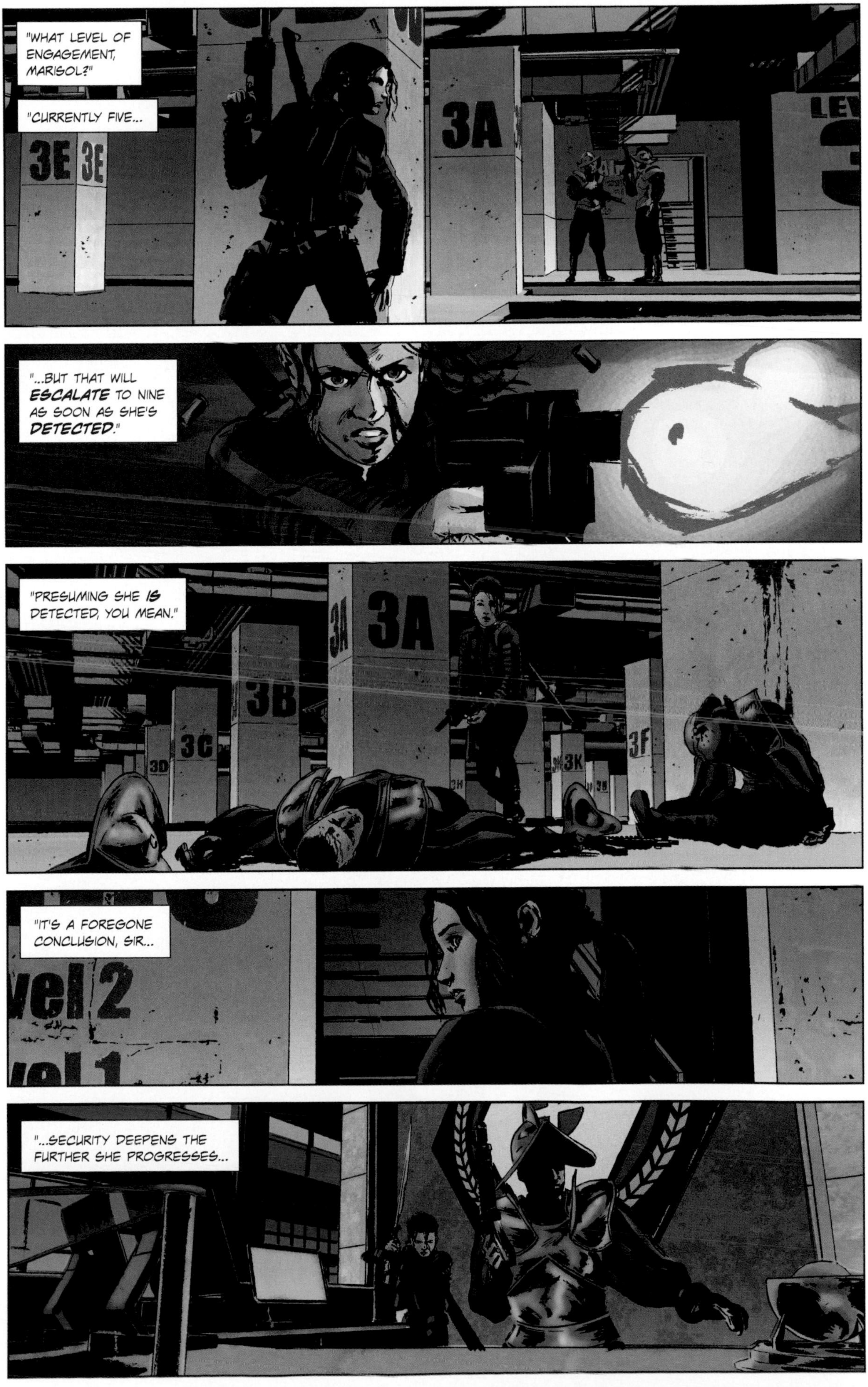
"WHAT LEVEL OF ENGAGEMENT, MARISOL?"
"CURRENTLY FIVE...
3E 3E
3A
"...BUT THAT WILL **ESCALATE** TO NINE AS SOON AS SHE'S **DETECTED**."
"PRESUMING SHE ***IS*** DETECTED, YOU MEAN."
3A 3A
3B
3C
3D
3F
3K
"IT'S A FOREGONE CONCLUSION, SIR...
vel 2
"...SECURITY DEEPENS THE FURTHER SHE PROGRESSES...

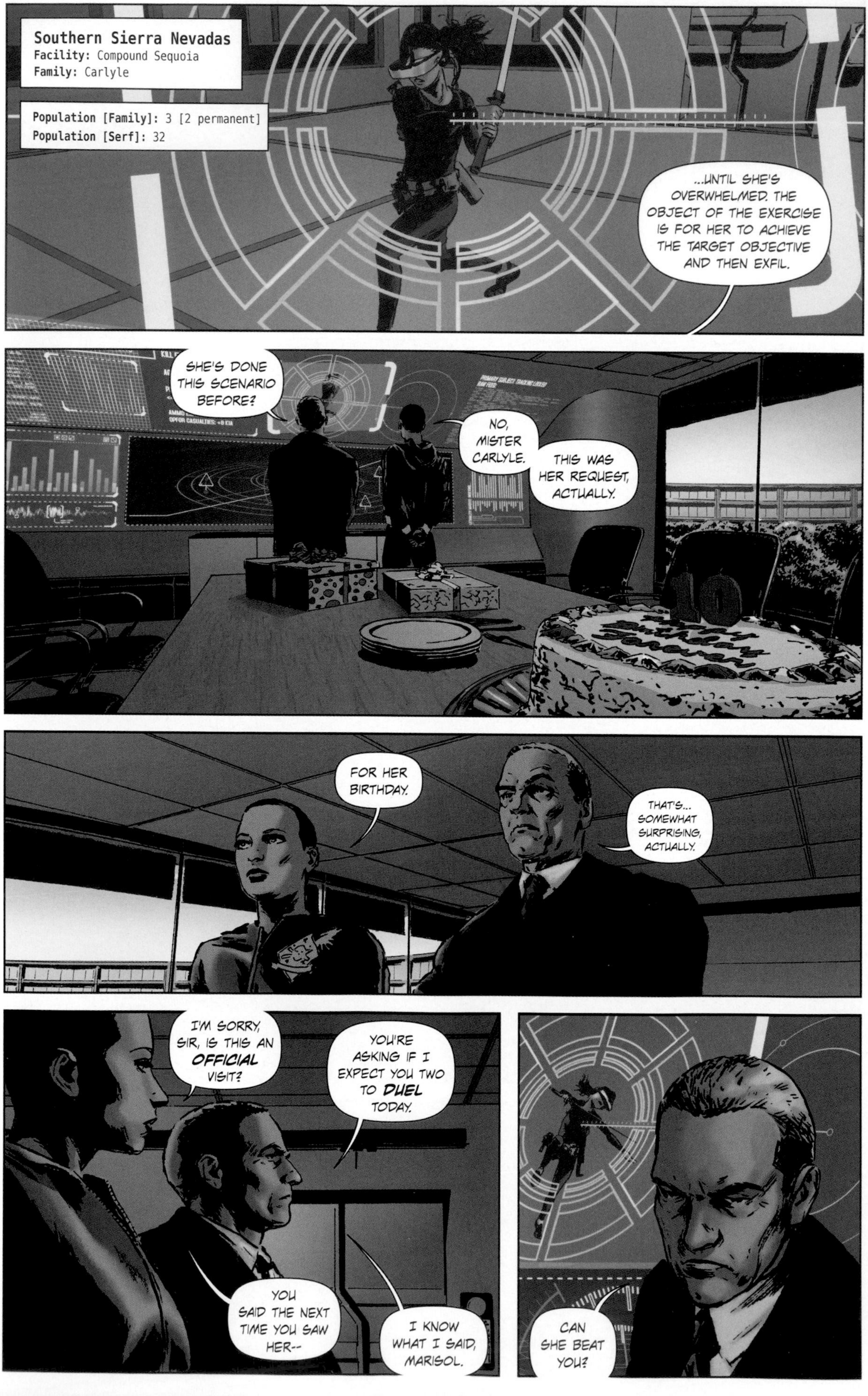
Southern Sierra Nevadas
Facility: Compound Sequoia
Family: Carlyle
Population [Family]: 3 [2 permanent]
Population [Serf]: 32
...UNTIL SHE'S OVERWHELMED. THE OBJECT OF THE EXERCISE IS FOR HER TO ACHIEVE THE TARGET OBJECTIVE AND THEN EXFIL.
SHE'S DONE THIS SCENARIO BEFORE?
NO, MISTER CARLYLE.
THIS WAS HER REQUEST, ACTUALLY.
FOR HER BIRTHDAY.
THAT'S... SOMEWHAT SURPRISING, ACTUALLY.
I'M SORRY, SIR, IS THIS AN OFFICIAL VISIT?
YOU'RE ASKING IF I EXPECT YOU TWO TO DUEL TODAY.
YOU SAID THE NEXT TIME YOU SAW HER--
I KNOW WHAT I SAID, MARISOL.
CAN SHE BEAT YOU?

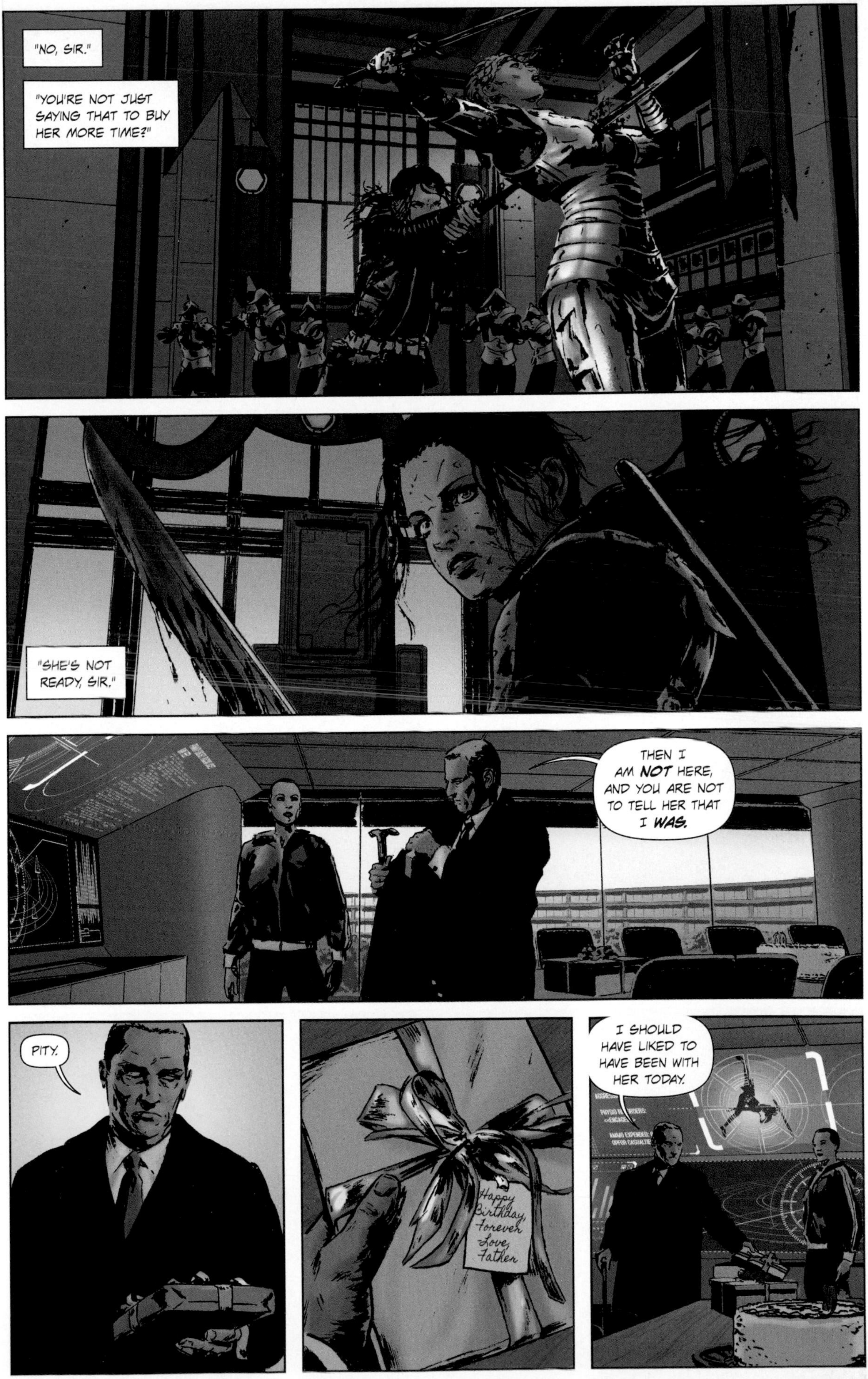
"NO, SIR."
"YOU'RE NOT JUST SAYING THAT TO BUY HER MORE TIME?"
"SHE'S NOT READY, SIR."
THEN I AM **NOT** HERE, AND YOU ARE NOT TO TELL HER THAT I ***WAS.***
PITY.
Happy Birthday, Forever Love, Father
I SHOULD HAVE LIKED TO HAVE BEEN WITH HER TODAY.

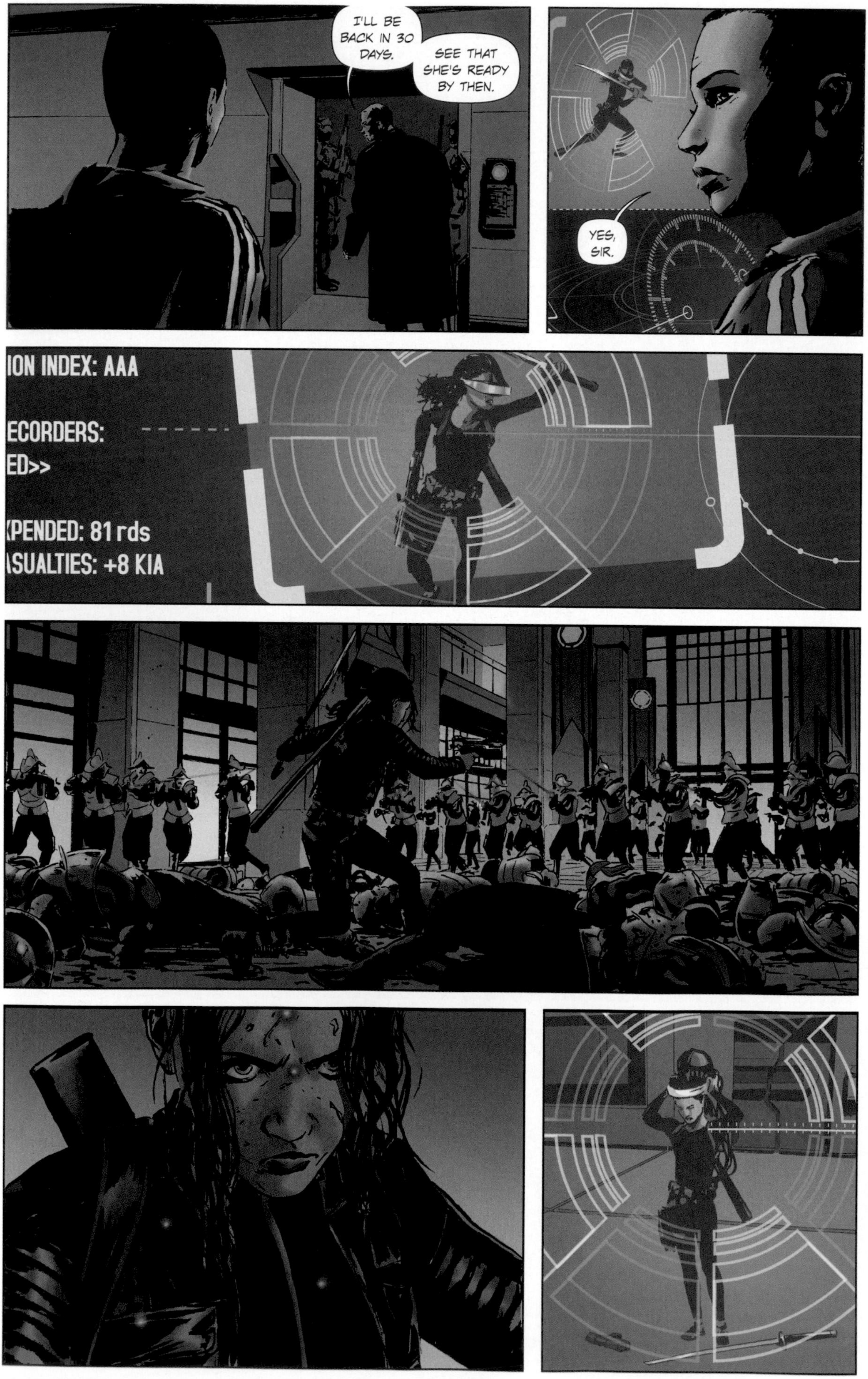
I'LL BE BACK IN 30 DAYS.
SEE THAT SHE'S READY BY THEN.
YES, SIR.
ION INDEX: AAA
ECORDERS:
ED>>
XPENDED: 81 rds
ASUALTIES: +8 KIA

--BUT I WENT FOR MY WEAPON THEN LIKE MARISOL TAUGHT ME--

--AND I KNOW I GOT MHFF *THREE* OF THEM AND THEN--

CHEW AND SWALLOW, FOREVER.

--YES, MS. KWAN, BUT *THREE* OF THEM, JAMES, ANDOHMYGODISTHATFROMDADDY--

--IT *IS!* HE *REMEMBERED,* HE REMEMBERED MY BIRTHDAY!

HE REMEMBERED...

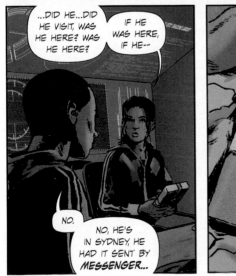

...DID HE...DID HE VISIT, WAS HE HERE? WAS HE HERE?

IF HE WAS HERE, IF HE--

NO.

NO, HE'S IN SYDNEY, HE HAD IT SENT BY *MESSENGER...*

...FOR YOUR BIRTHDAY...

THE ONCE & FUTURE KING
T. H. WHITE

...WITH HIS LOVE.

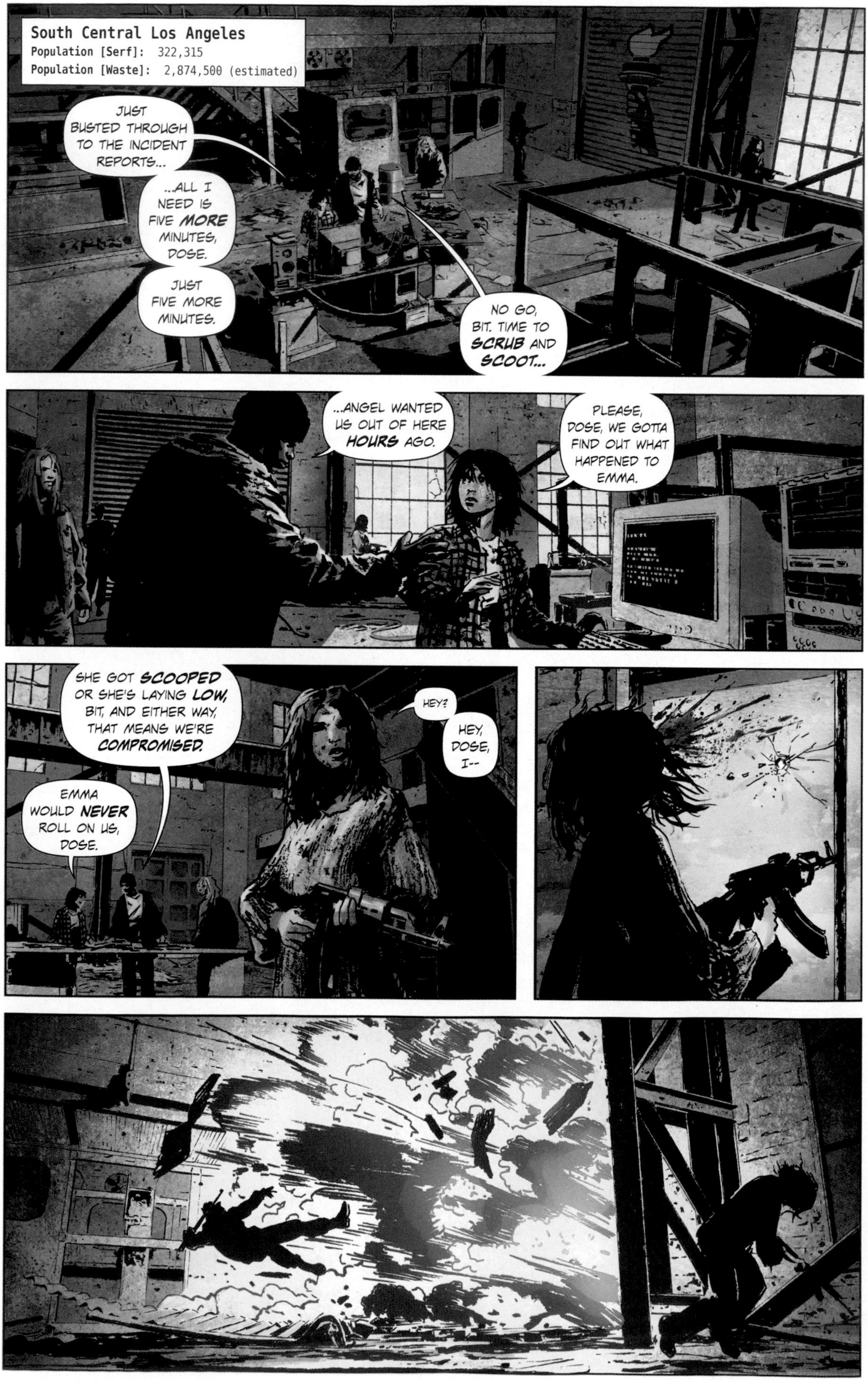
South Central Los Angeles
Population [Serf]: 322,315
Population [Waste]: 2,874,500 (estimated)
JUST BUSTED THROUGH TO THE INCIDENT REPORTS...
...ALL I NEED IS FIVE MORE MINUTES, DOSE.
JUST FIVE MORE MINUTES.
NO GO, BIT. TIME TO SCRUB AND SCOOT...
...ANGEL WANTED US OUT OF HERE HOURS AGO.
PLEASE, DOSE, WE GOTTA FIND OUT WHAT HAPPENED TO EMMA.
SHE GOT SCOOPED OR SHE'S LAYING LOW, BIT, AND EITHER WAY, THAT MEANS WE'RE COMPROMISED.
EMMA WOULD NEVER ROLL ON US, DOSE.
HEY?
HEY, DOSE, I--

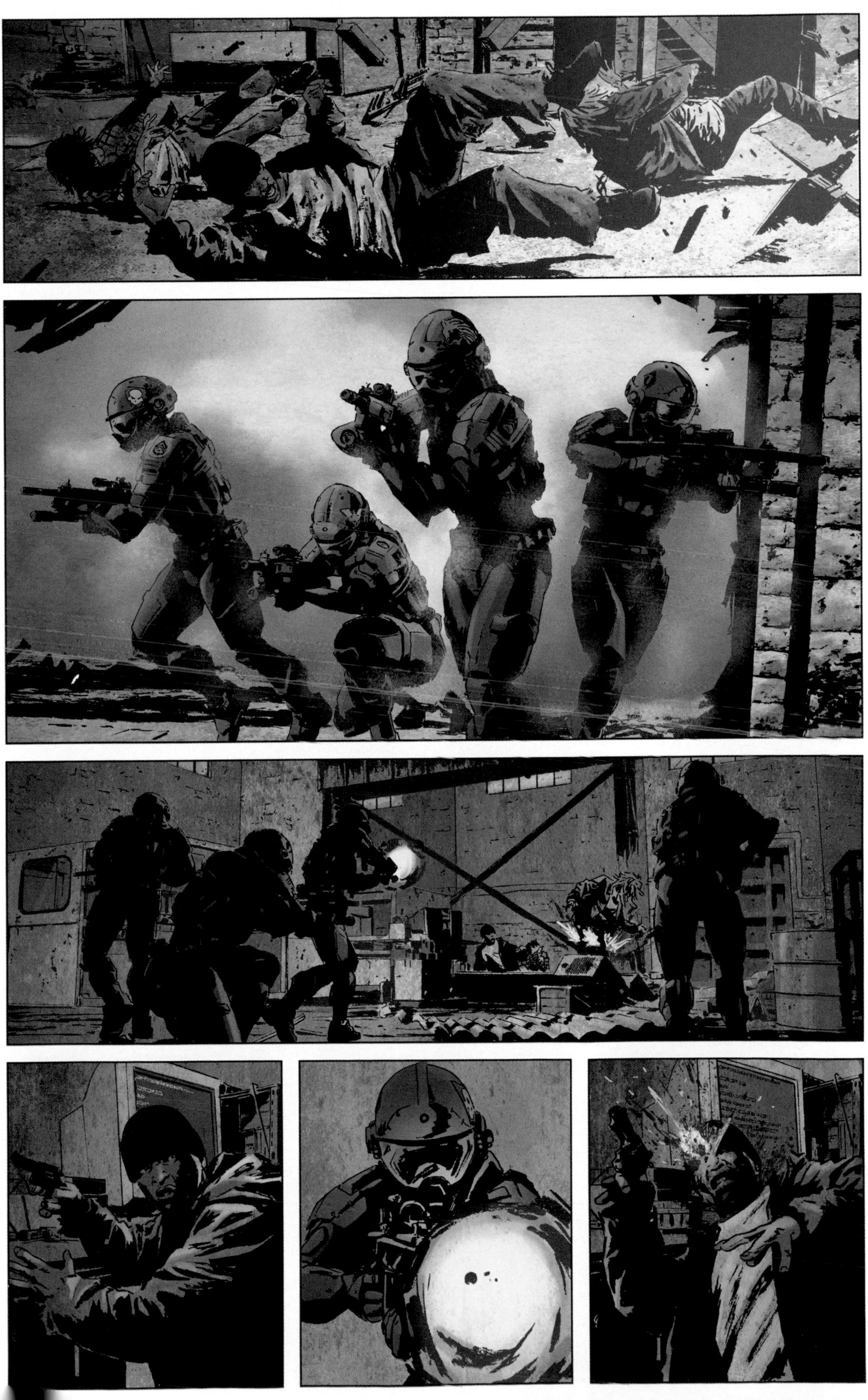

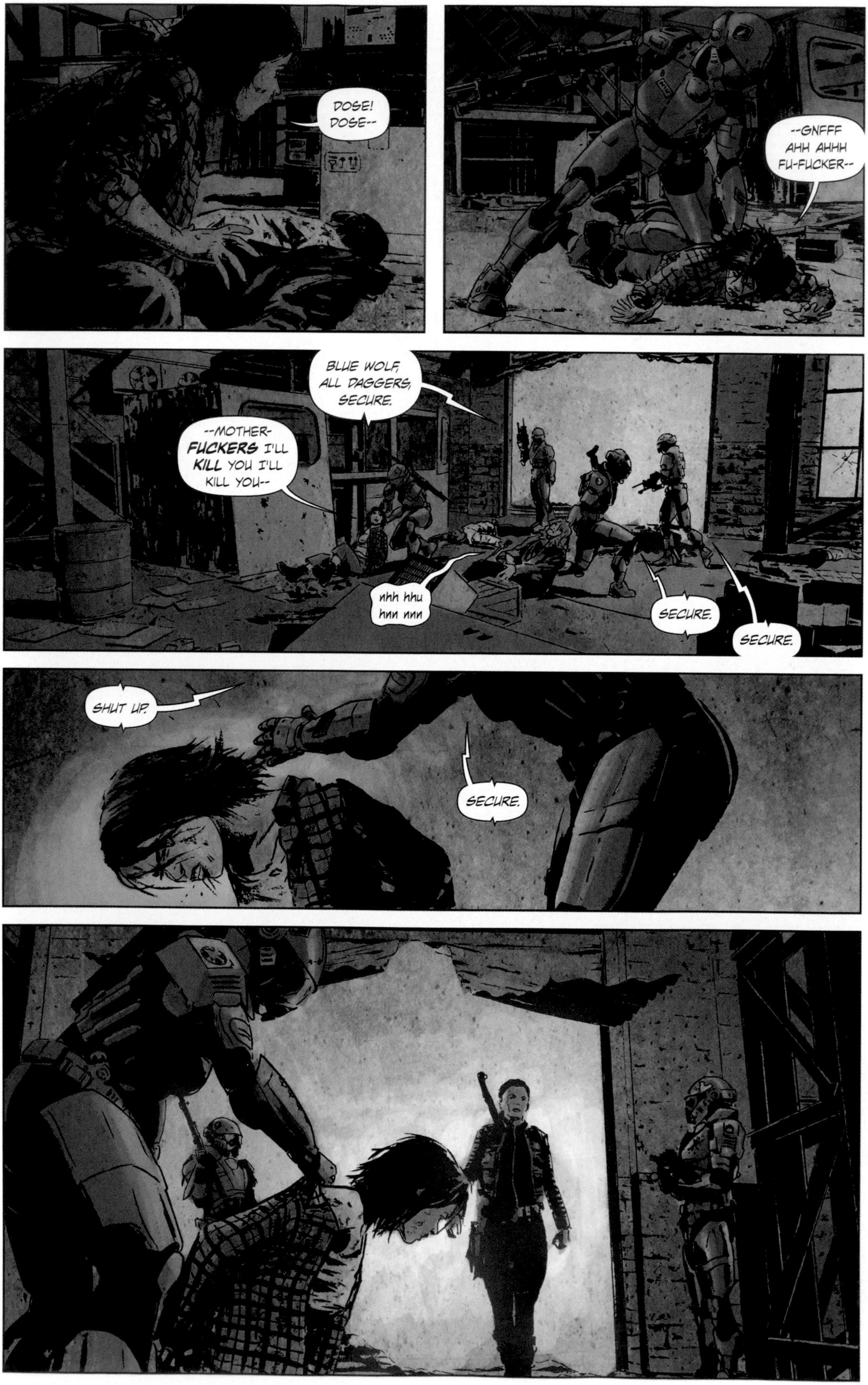
DOSE! DOSE--
--GNFFF AHH AHHH FU-FUCKER--
BLUE WOLF, ALL DAGGERS, SECURE.
--MOTHER-FUCKERS I'LL KILL YOU I'LL KILL YOU--
nhh hhu hnn nnn
SECURE.
SECURE.
SHUT UP.
SECURE.

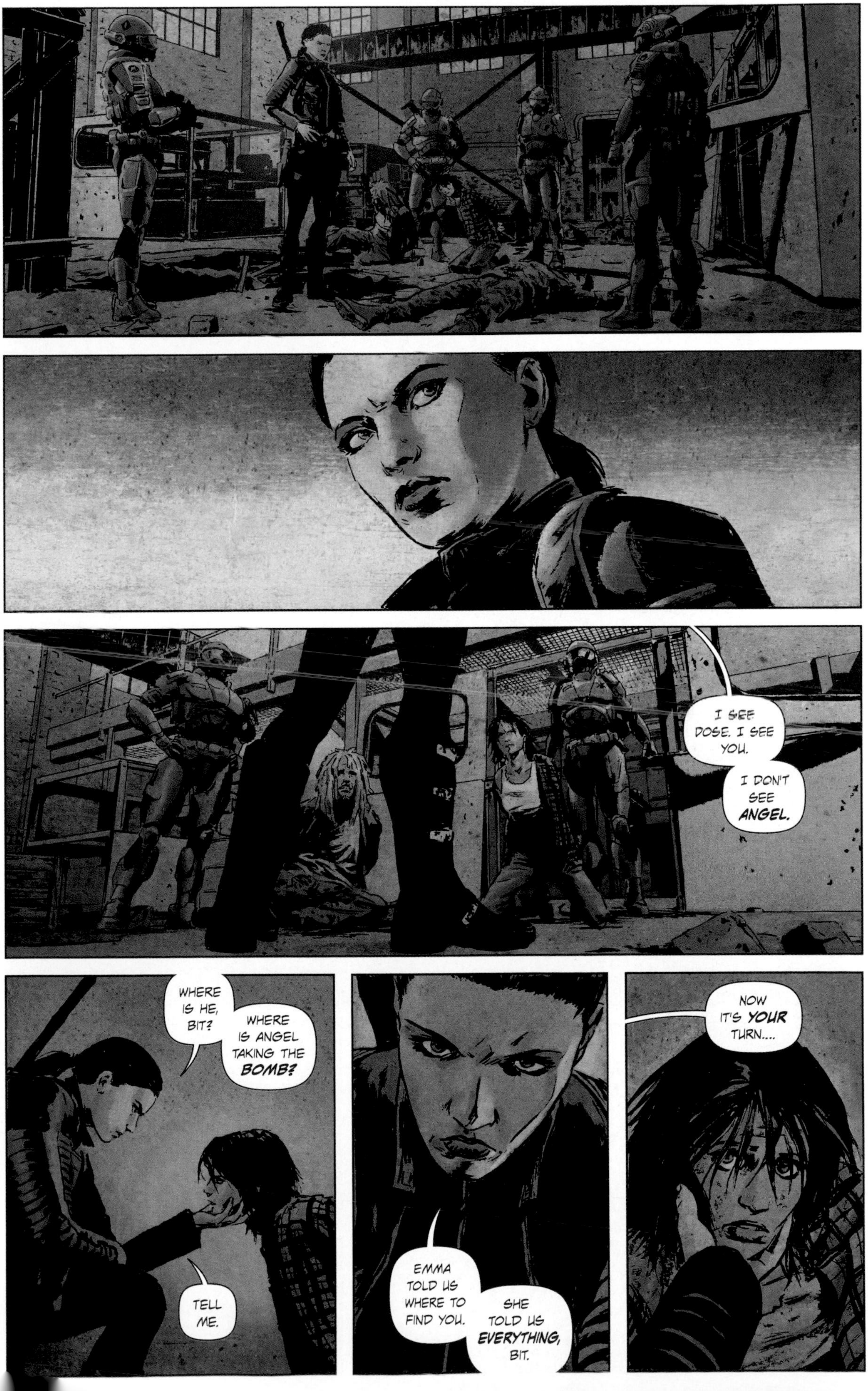
I SEE DOSE. I SEE YOU.
I DON'T SEE ANGEL.
WHERE IS HE, BIT?
WHERE IS ANGEL TAKING THE BOMB?
TELL ME.
EMMA TOLD US WHERE TO FIND YOU.
SHE TOLD US EVERYTHING, BIT.
NOW IT'S YOUR TURN....

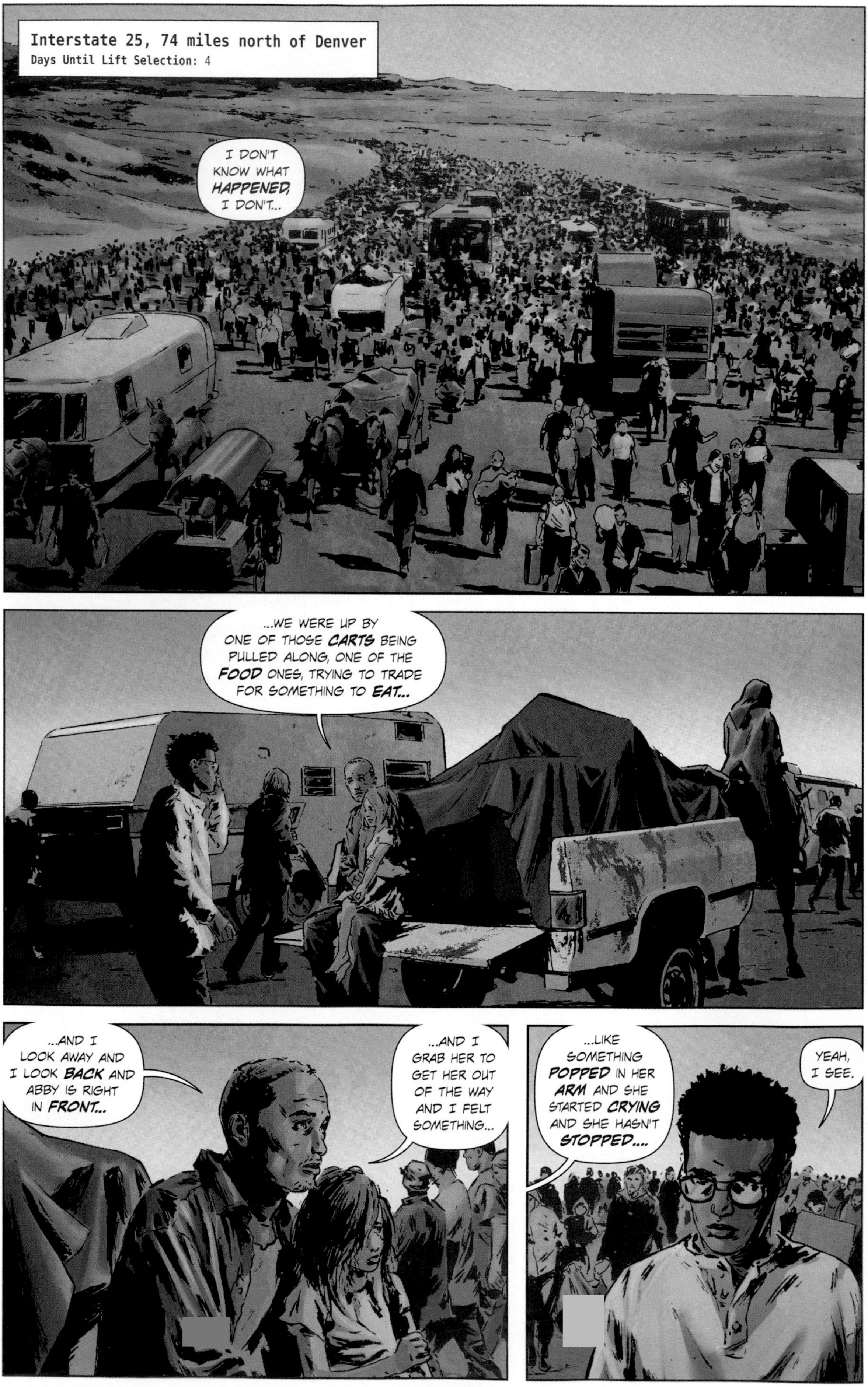
Interstate 25, 74 miles north of Denver
Days Until Lift Selection: 4
I DON'T KNOW WHAT HAPPENED, I DON'T...
...WE WERE UP BY ONE OF THOSE CARTS BEING PULLED ALONG, ONE OF THE FOOD ONES, TRYING TO TRADE FOR SOMETHING TO EAT...
...AND I LOOK AWAY AND I LOOK BACK AND ABBY IS RIGHT IN FRONT...
...AND I GRAB HER TO GET HER OUT OF THE WAY AND I FELT SOMETHING...
...LIKE SOMETHING POPPED IN HER ARM AND SHE STARTED CRYING AND SHE HASN'T STOPPED....
YEAH, I SEE.

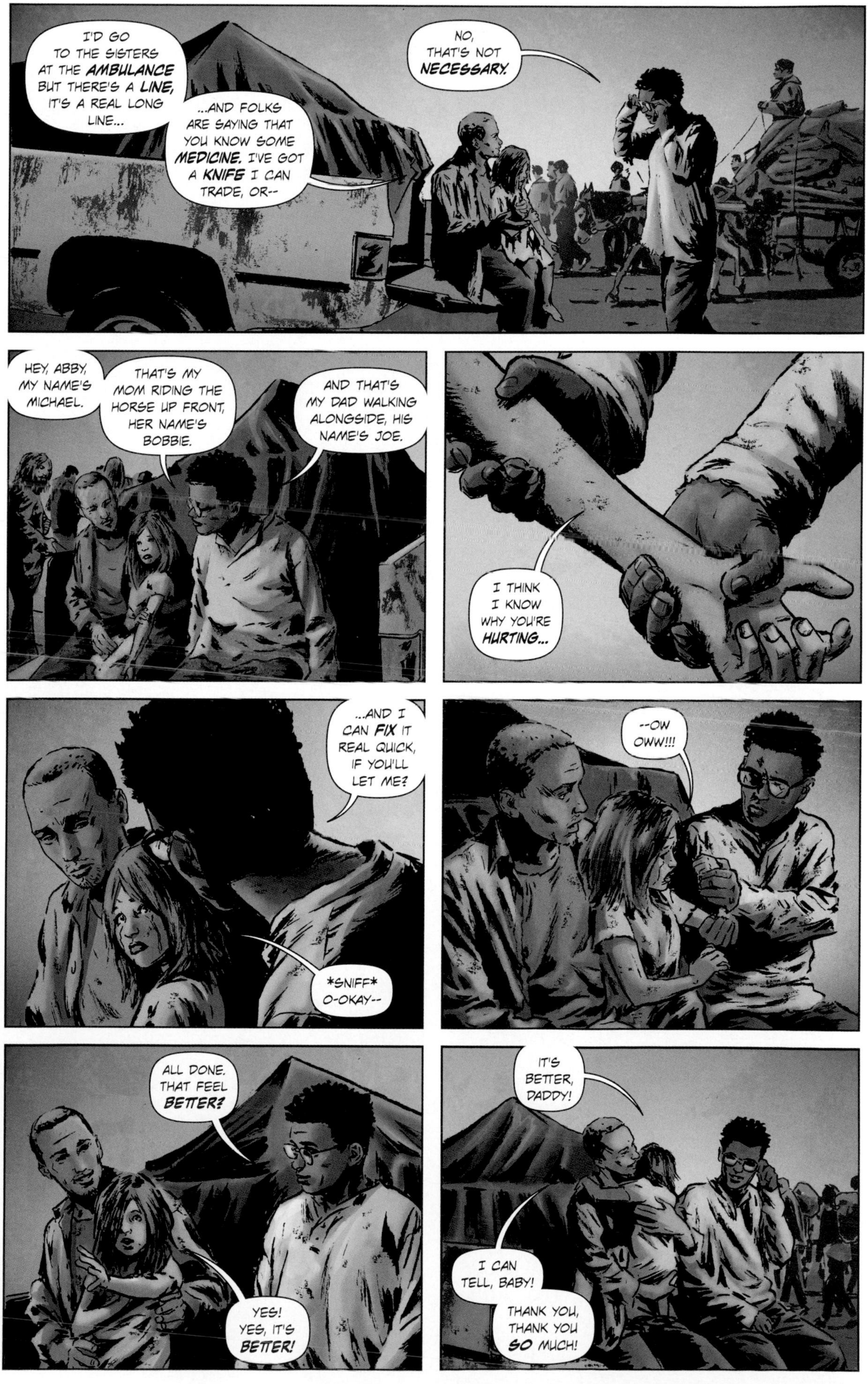
I'D GO TO THE SISTERS AT THE AMBULANCE BUT THERE'S A LINE, IT'S A REAL LONG LINE...
...AND FOLKS ARE SAYING THAT YOU KNOW SOME MEDICINE. I'VE GOT A KNIFE I CAN TRADE, OR--
NO, THAT'S NOT NECESSARY.
HEY, ABBY, MY NAME'S MICHAEL.
THAT'S MY MOM RIDING THE HORSE UP FRONT, HER NAME'S BOBBIE.
AND THAT'S MY DAD WALKING ALONGSIDE, HIS NAME'S JOE.
I THINK I KNOW WHY YOU'RE HURTING...
...AND I CAN FIX IT REAL QUICK, IF YOU'LL LET ME?
*SNIFF* O-OKAY--
--OW OWW!!!
ALL DONE. THAT FEEL BETTER?
YES! YES, IT'S BETTER!
IT'S BETTER, DADDY!
I CAN TELL, BABY!
THANK YOU, THANK YOU SO MUCH!

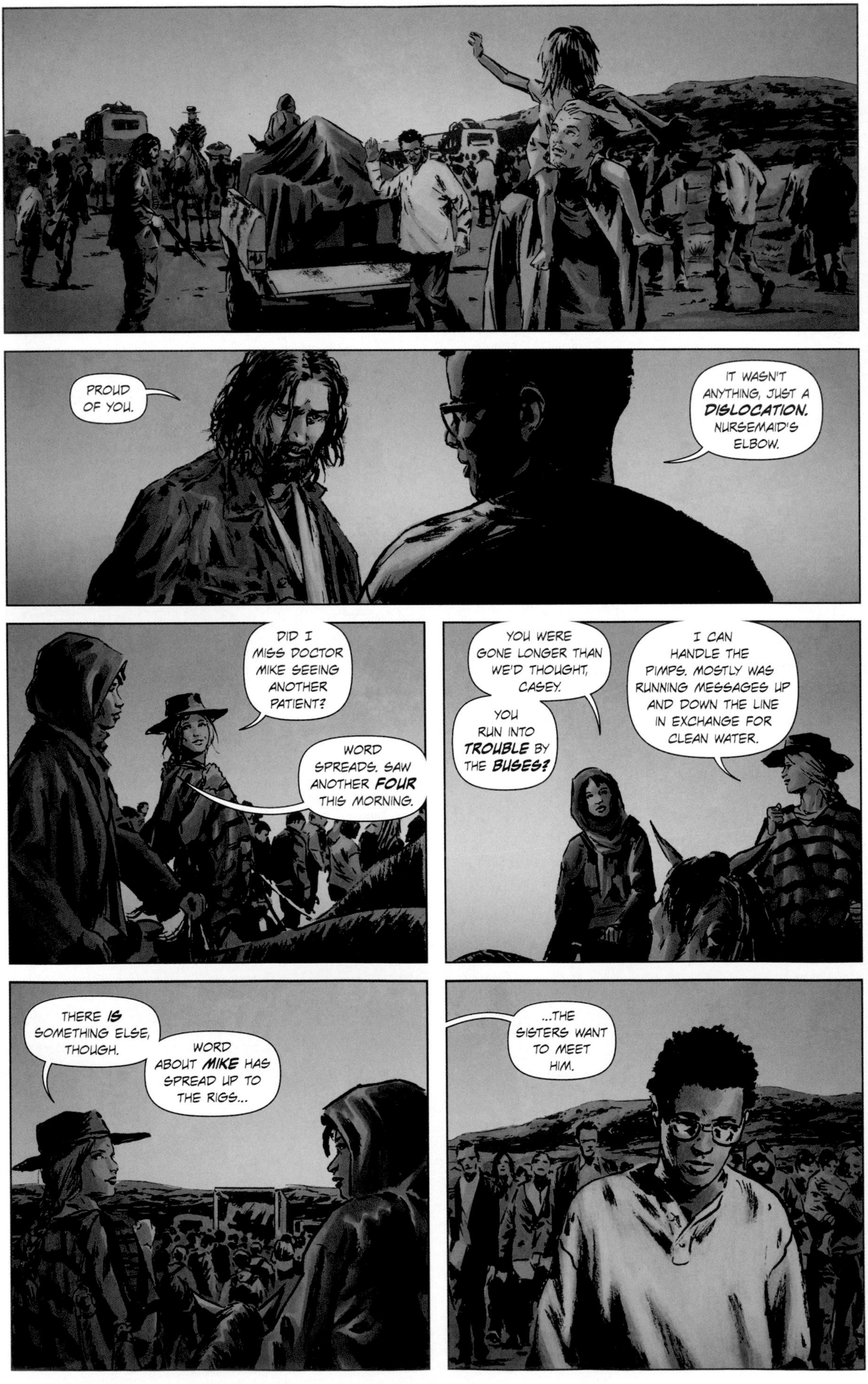
PROUD OF YOU.
IT WASN'T ANYTHING, JUST A **DISLOCATION.** NURSEMAID'S ELBOW.
DID I MISS DOCTOR MIKE SEEING ANOTHER PATIENT?
WORD SPREADS. SAW ANOTHER **FOUR** THIS MORNING.
YOU WERE GONE LONGER THAN WE'D THOUGHT, CASEY.
YOU RUN INTO **TROUBLE** BY THE **BUSES?**
I CAN HANDLE THE PIMPS. MOSTLY WAS RUNNING MESSAGES UP AND DOWN THE LINE IN EXCHANGE FOR CLEAN WATER.
THERE **IS** SOMETHING ELSE, THOUGH.
WORD ABOUT **MIKE** HAS SPREAD UP TO THE RIGS...
...THE SISTERS WANT TO MEET HIM.

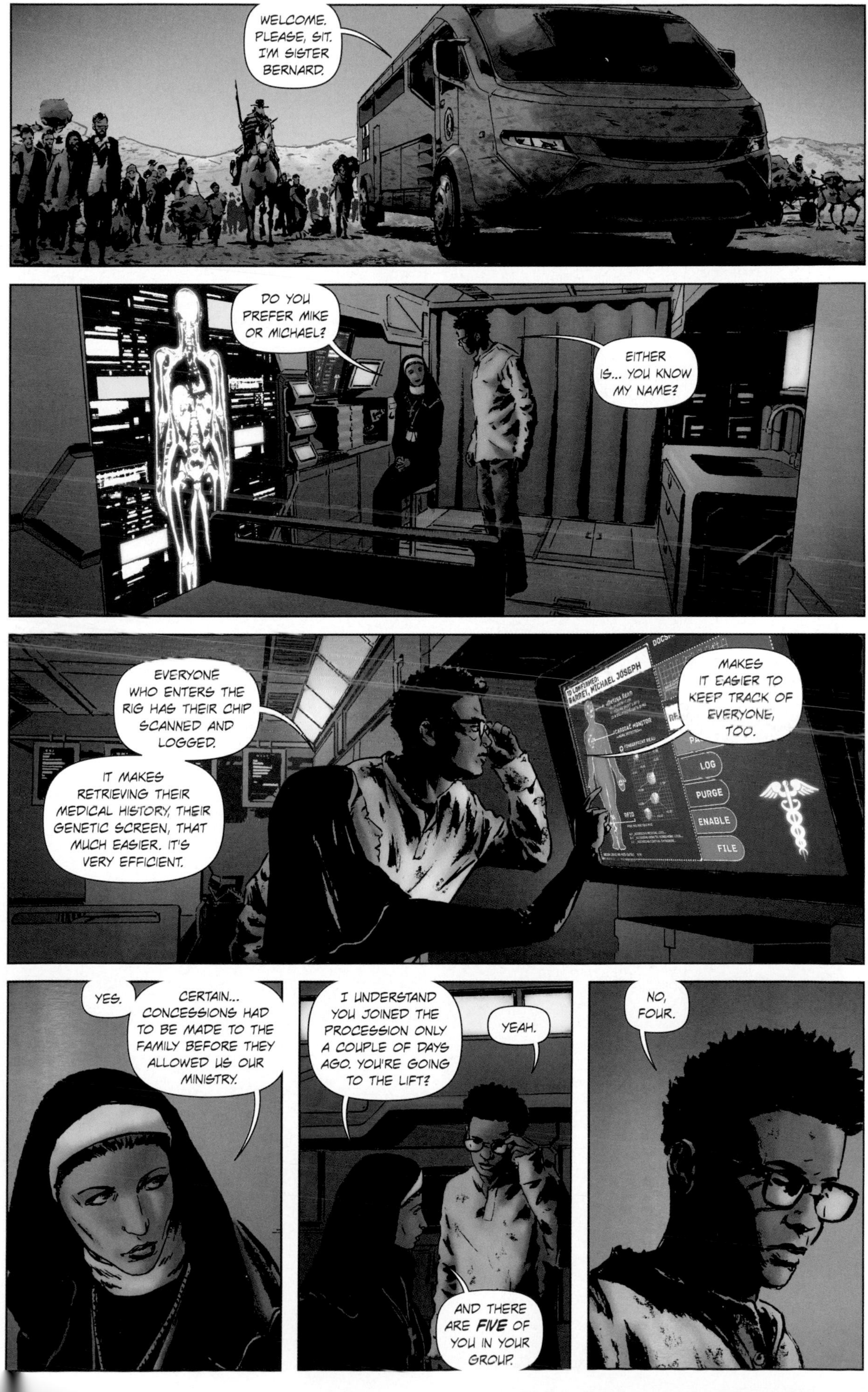
WELCOME. PLEASE, SIT. I'M SISTER BERNARD.
DO YOU PREFER MIKE OR MICHAEL?
EITHER IS... YOU KNOW MY NAME?
EVERYONE WHO ENTERS THE RIG HAS THEIR CHIP SCANNED AND LOGGED.
IT MAKES RETRIEVING THEIR MEDICAL HISTORY, THEIR GENETIC SCREEN, THAT MUCH EASIER. IT'S VERY EFFICIENT.
BARDEI, MICHAEL JOSEPH
CARDIAC MONITOR
FINGERPRINT READ
RFID
LOG
PURGE
ENABLE
FILE
MAKES IT EASIER TO KEEP TRACK OF EVERYONE, TOO.
YES.
CERTAIN... CONCESSIONS HAD TO BE MADE TO THE FAMILY BEFORE THEY ALLOWED US OUR MINISTRY.
I UNDERSTAND YOU JOINED THE PROCESSION ONLY A COUPLE OF DAYS AGO. YOU'RE GOING TO THE LIFT?
YEAH.
AND THERE ARE FIVE OF YOU IN YOUR GROUP.
NO, FOUR.

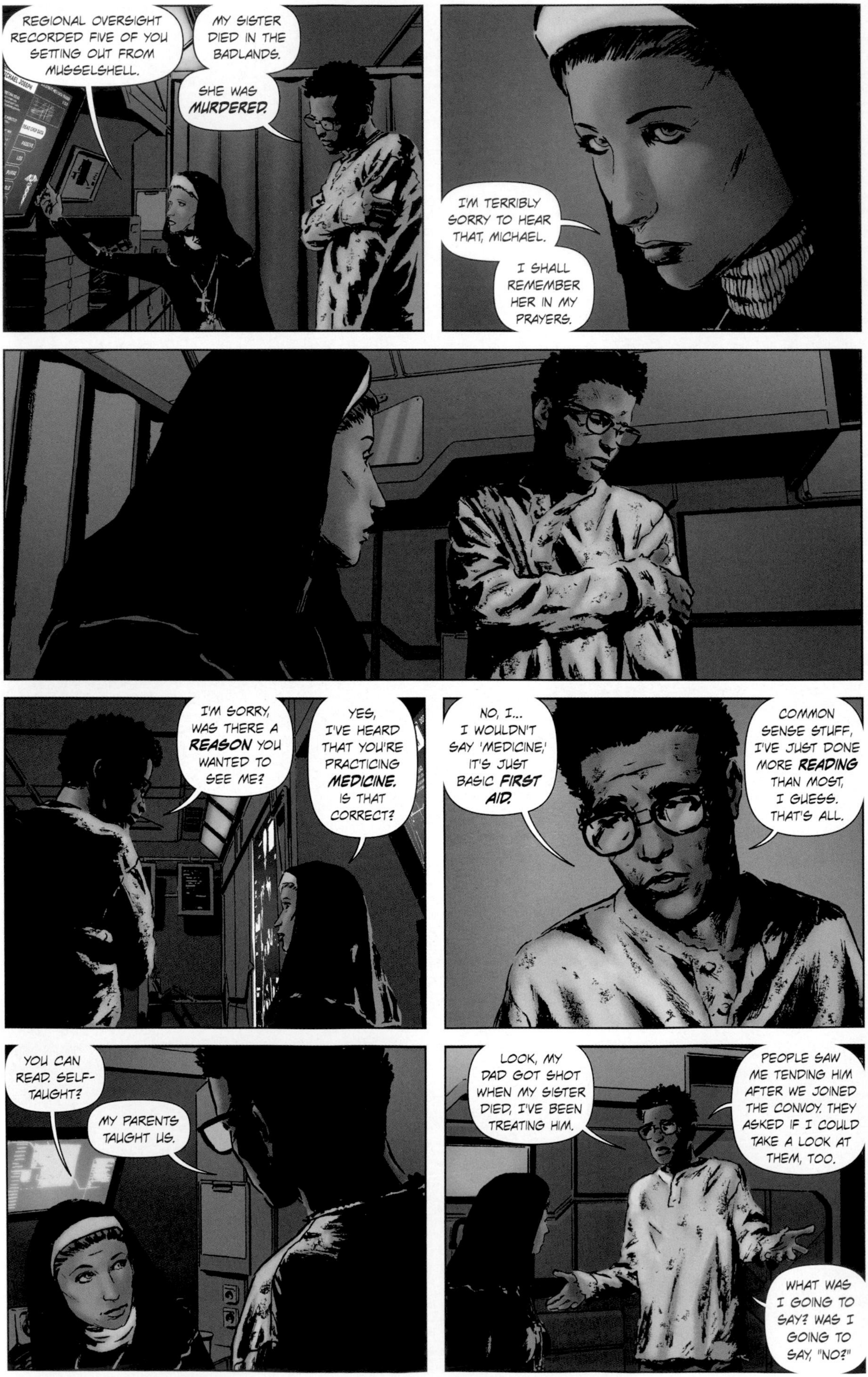
REGIONAL OVERSIGHT RECORDED FIVE OF YOU SETTING OUT FROM MUSSELSHELL.
MY SISTER DIED IN THE BADLANDS.
SHE WAS MURDERED.
I'M TERRIBLY SORRY TO HEAR THAT, MICHAEL.
I SHALL REMEMBER HER IN MY PRAYERS.
I'M SORRY, WAS THERE A REASON YOU WANTED TO SEE ME?
YES, I'VE HEARD THAT YOU'RE PRACTICING MEDICINE. IS THAT CORRECT?
NO, I... I WOULDN'T SAY 'MEDICINE,' IT'S JUST BASIC FIRST AID.
COMMON SENSE STUFF, I'VE JUST DONE MORE READING THAN MOST, I GUESS. THAT'S ALL.
YOU CAN READ. SELF-TAUGHT?
MY PARENTS TAUGHT US.
LOOK, MY DAD GOT SHOT WHEN MY SISTER DIED, I'VE BEEN TREATING HIM.
PEOPLE SAW ME TENDING HIM AFTER WE JOINED THE CONVOY. THEY ASKED IF I COULD TAKE A LOOK AT THEM, TOO.
WHAT WAS I GOING TO SAY? WAS I GOING TO SAY, "NO?"

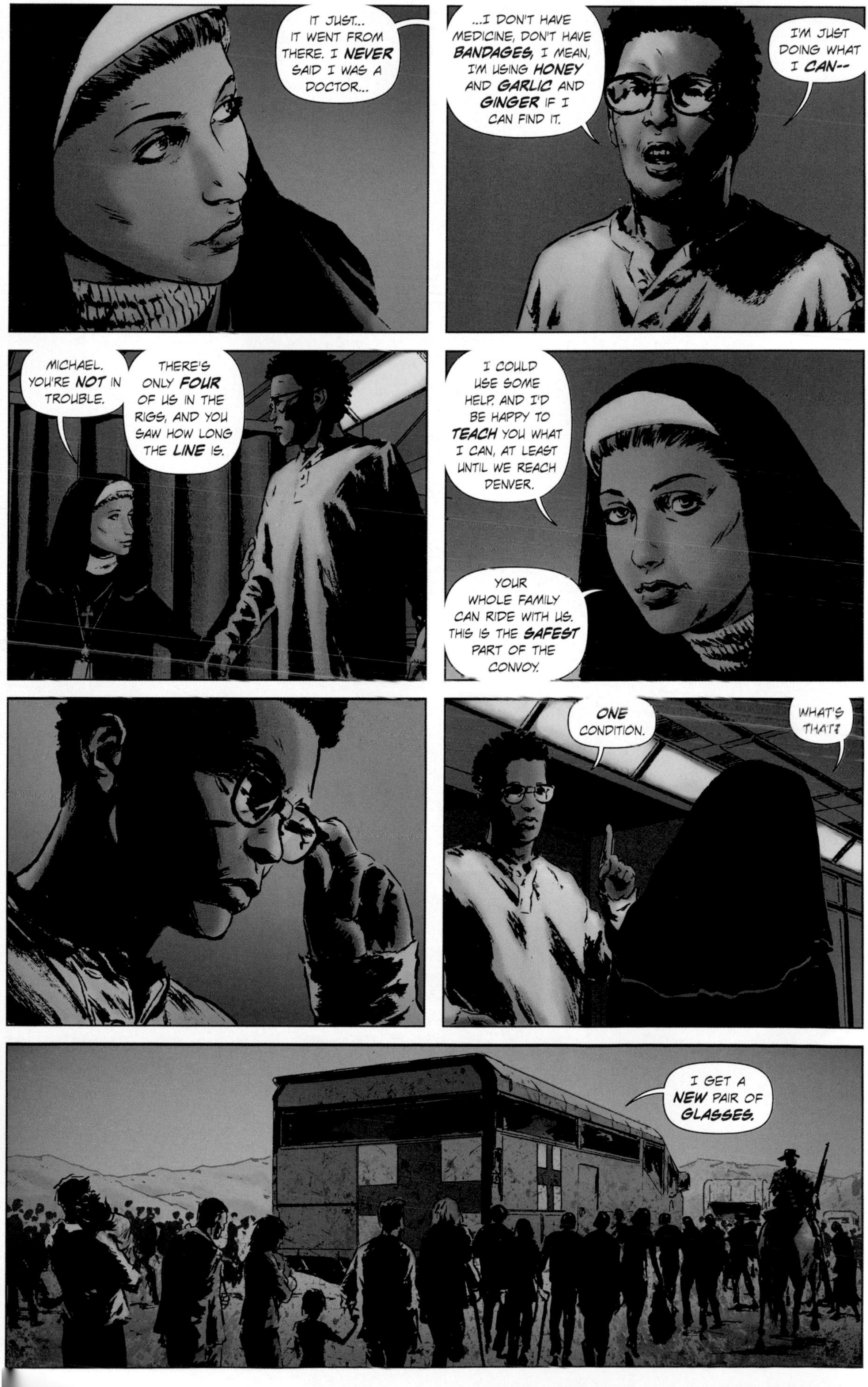

IT JUST... IT WENT FROM THERE. I NEVER SAID I WAS A DOCTOR...
...I DON'T HAVE MEDICINE, DON'T HAVE BANDAGES, I MEAN, I'M USING HONEY AND GARLIC AND GINGER IF I CAN FIND IT.
I'M JUST DOING WHAT I CAN--
MICHAEL. YOU'RE NOT IN TROUBLE.
THERE'S ONLY FOUR OF US IN THE RIGS, AND YOU SAW HOW LONG THE LINE IS.
I COULD USE SOME HELP. AND I'D BE HAPPY TO TEACH YOU WHAT I CAN, AT LEAST UNTIL WE REACH DENVER.
YOUR WHOLE FAMILY CAN RIDE WITH US. THIS IS THE SAFEST PART OF THE CONVOY.
ONE CONDITION.
WHAT'S THAT?
I GET A NEW PAIR OF GLASSES.

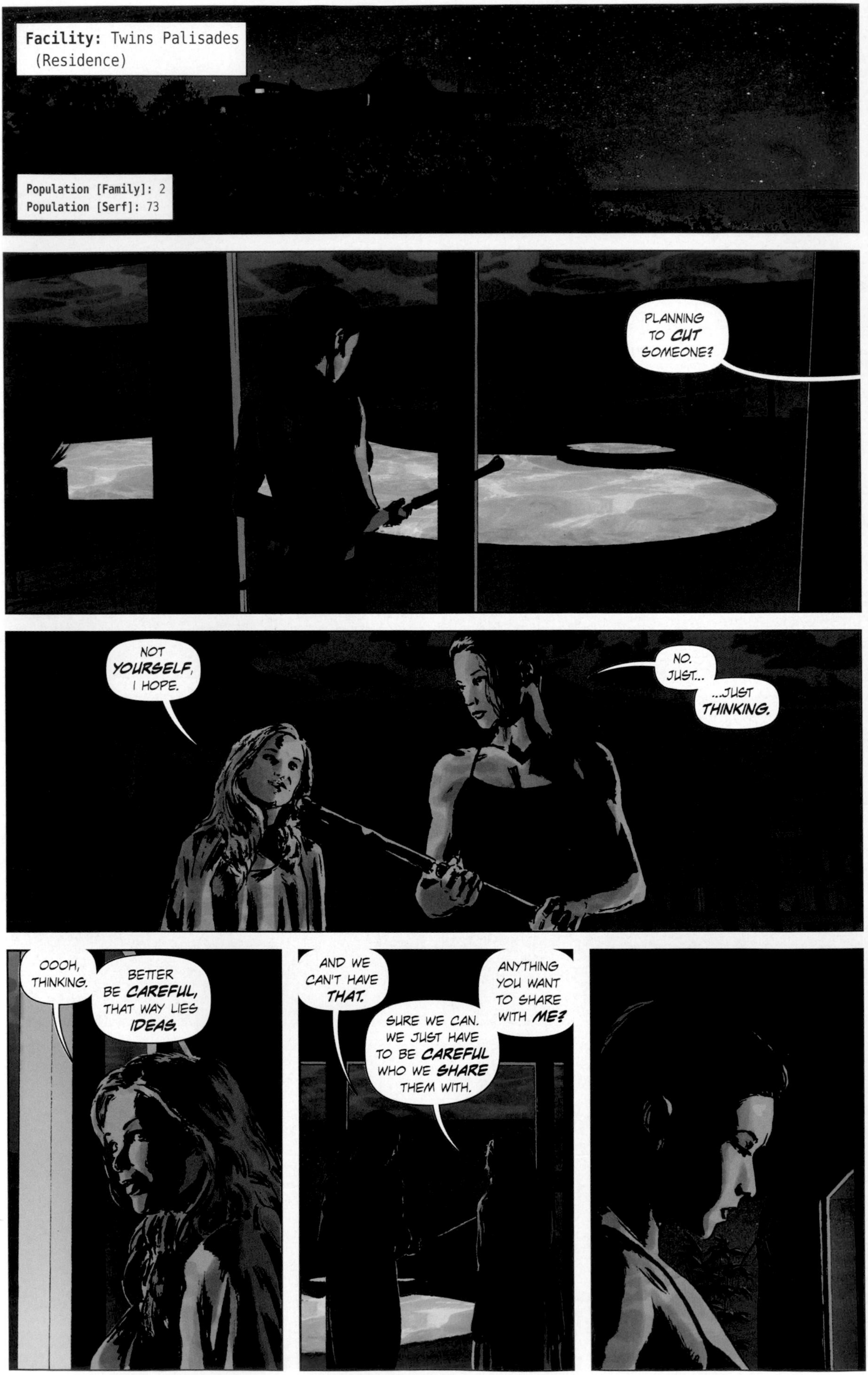
Facility: Twins Palisades (Residence)
Population [Family]: 2
Population [Serf]: 73
PLANNING TO CUT SOMEONE?
NOT YOURSELF, I HOPE.
NO. JUST...
...JUST THINKING.
OOOH, THINKING.
BETTER BE CAREFUL, THAT WAY LIES IDEAS.
AND WE CAN'T HAVE THAT.
SURE WE CAN. WE JUST HAVE TO BE CAREFUL WHO WE SHARE THEM WITH.
ANYTHING YOU WANT TO SHARE WITH ME?

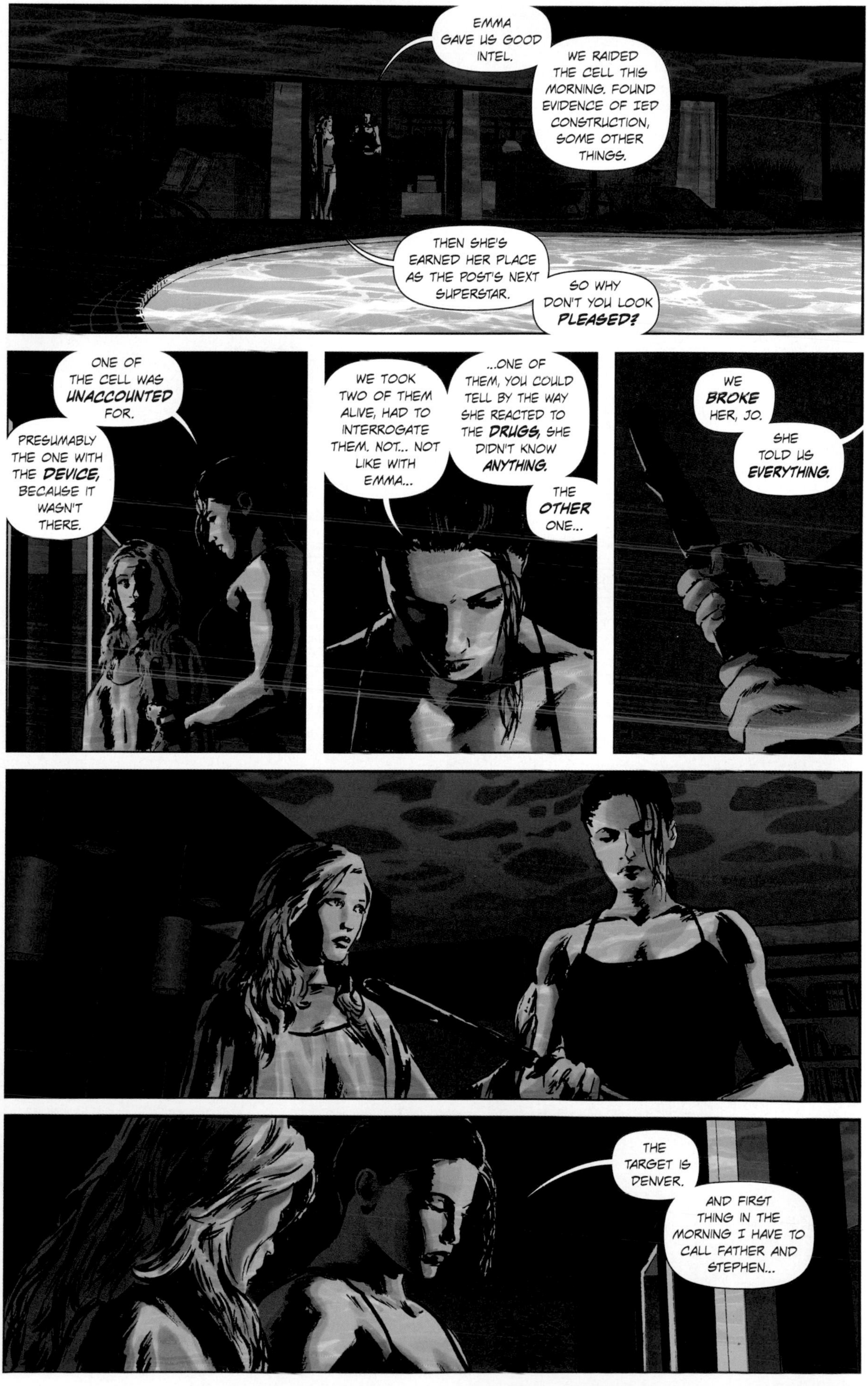
EMMA GAVE US GOOD INTEL.
WE RAIDED THE CELL THIS MORNING. FOUND EVIDENCE OF IED CONSTRUCTION, SOME OTHER THINGS.
THEN SHE'S EARNED HER PLACE AS THE POST'S NEXT SUPERSTAR.
SO WHY DON'T YOU LOOK PLEASED?
ONE OF THE CELL WAS UNACCOUNTED FOR.
PRESUMABLY THE ONE WITH THE DEVICE, BECAUSE IT WASN'T THERE.
WE TOOK TWO OF THEM ALIVE, HAD TO INTERROGATE THEM. NOT... NOT LIKE WITH EMMA...
...ONE OF THEM, YOU COULD TELL BY THE WAY SHE REACTED TO THE DRUGS, SHE DIDN'T KNOW ANYTHING.
THE OTHER ONE...
WE BROKE HER, JO.
SHE TOLD US EVERYTHING.
THE TARGET IS DENVER.
AND FIRST THING IN THE MORNING I HAVE TO CALL FATHER AND STEPHEN...

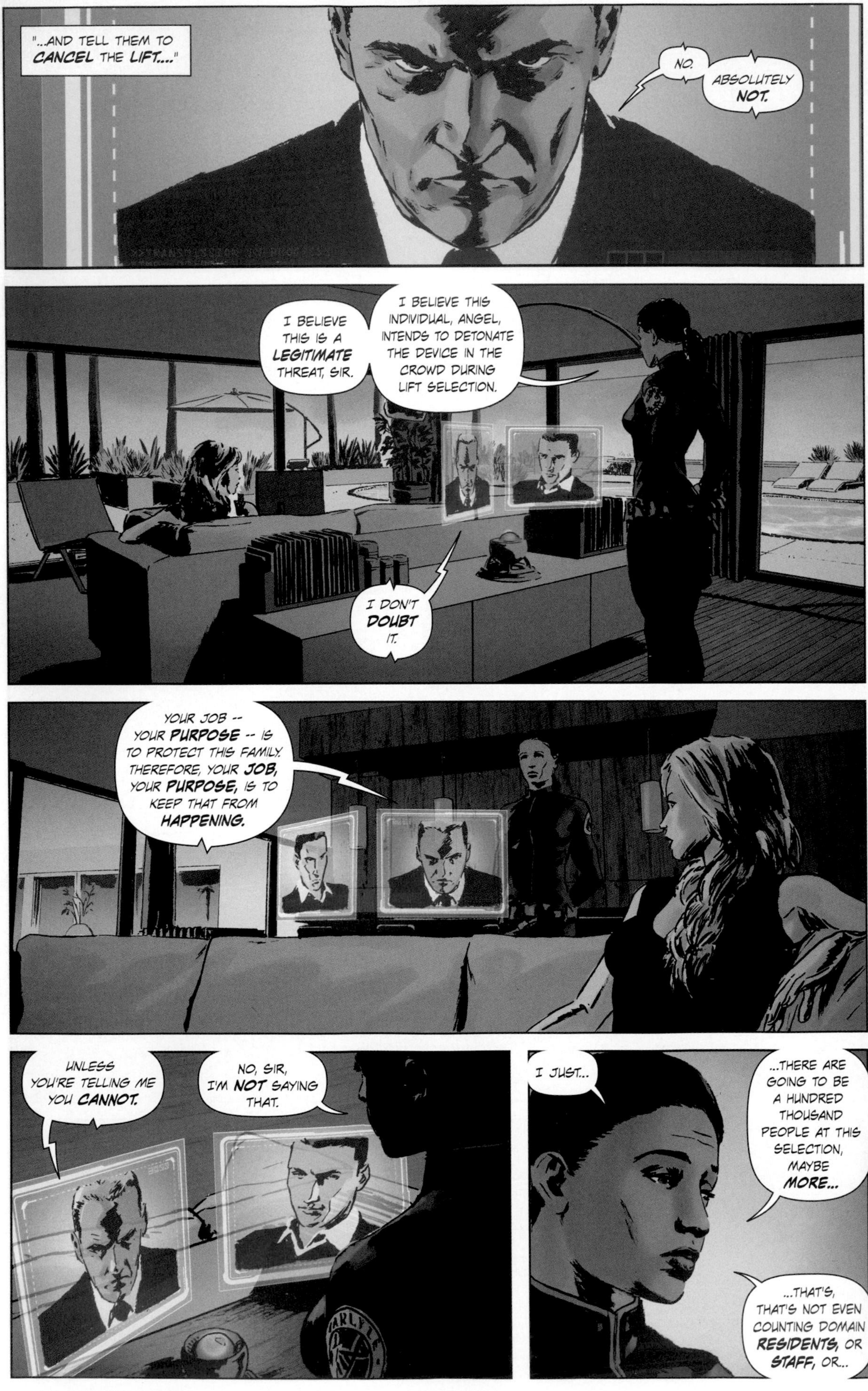
"...AND TELL THEM TO CANCEL THE LIFT...."
NO.
ABSOLUTELY NOT.
I BELIEVE THIS IS A LEGITIMATE THREAT, SIR.
I BELIEVE THIS INDIVIDUAL, ANGEL, INTENDS TO DETONATE THE DEVICE IN THE CROWD DURING LIFT SELECTION.
I DON'T DOUBT IT.
YOUR JOB -- YOUR PURPOSE -- IS TO PROTECT THIS FAMILY. THEREFORE, YOUR JOB, YOUR PURPOSE, IS TO KEEP THAT FROM HAPPENING.
UNLESS YOU'RE TELLING ME YOU CANNOT.
NO, SIR, I'M NOT SAYING THAT.
I JUST...
...THERE ARE GOING TO BE A HUNDRED THOUSAND PEOPLE AT THIS SELECTION, MAYBE MORE...
...THAT'S, THAT'S NOT EVEN COUNTING DOMAIN RESIDENTS, OR STAFF, OR...

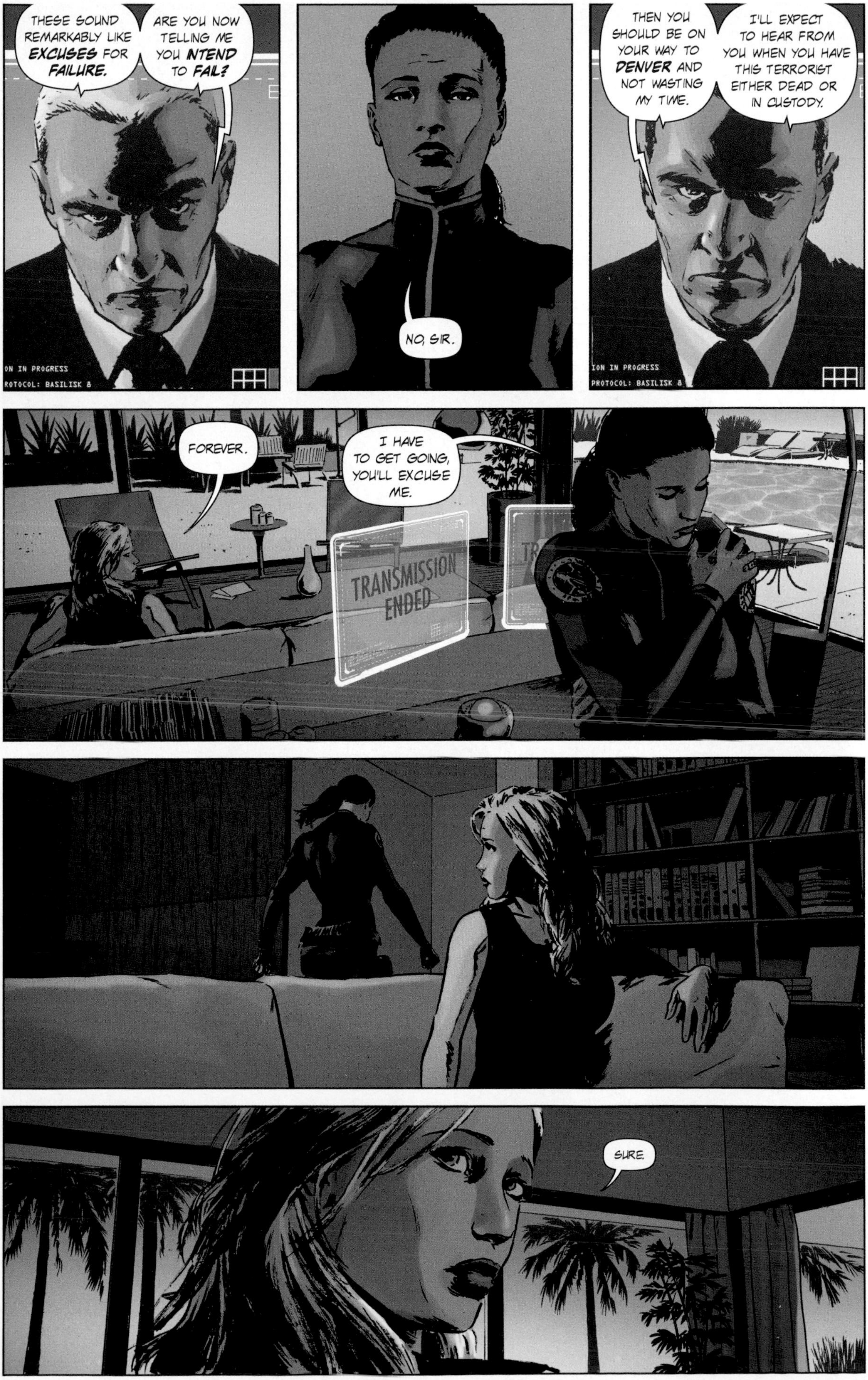
THESE SOUND REMARKABLY LIKE EXCUSES FOR FAILURE.
ARE YOU NOW TELLING ME YOU INTEND TO FAIL?
ON IN PROGRESS
ROTOCOL: BASILISK 8
NO, SIR.
THEN YOU SHOULD BE ON YOUR WAY TO DENVER AND NOT WASTING MY TIME.
I'LL EXPECT TO HEAR FROM YOU WHEN YOU HAVE THIS TERRORIST EITHER DEAD OR IN CUSTODY.
ION IN PROGRESS
PROTOCOL: BASILISK 8
FOREVER.
I HAVE TO GET GOING, YOU'LL EXCUSE ME.
TRANSMISSION ENDED
SURE.

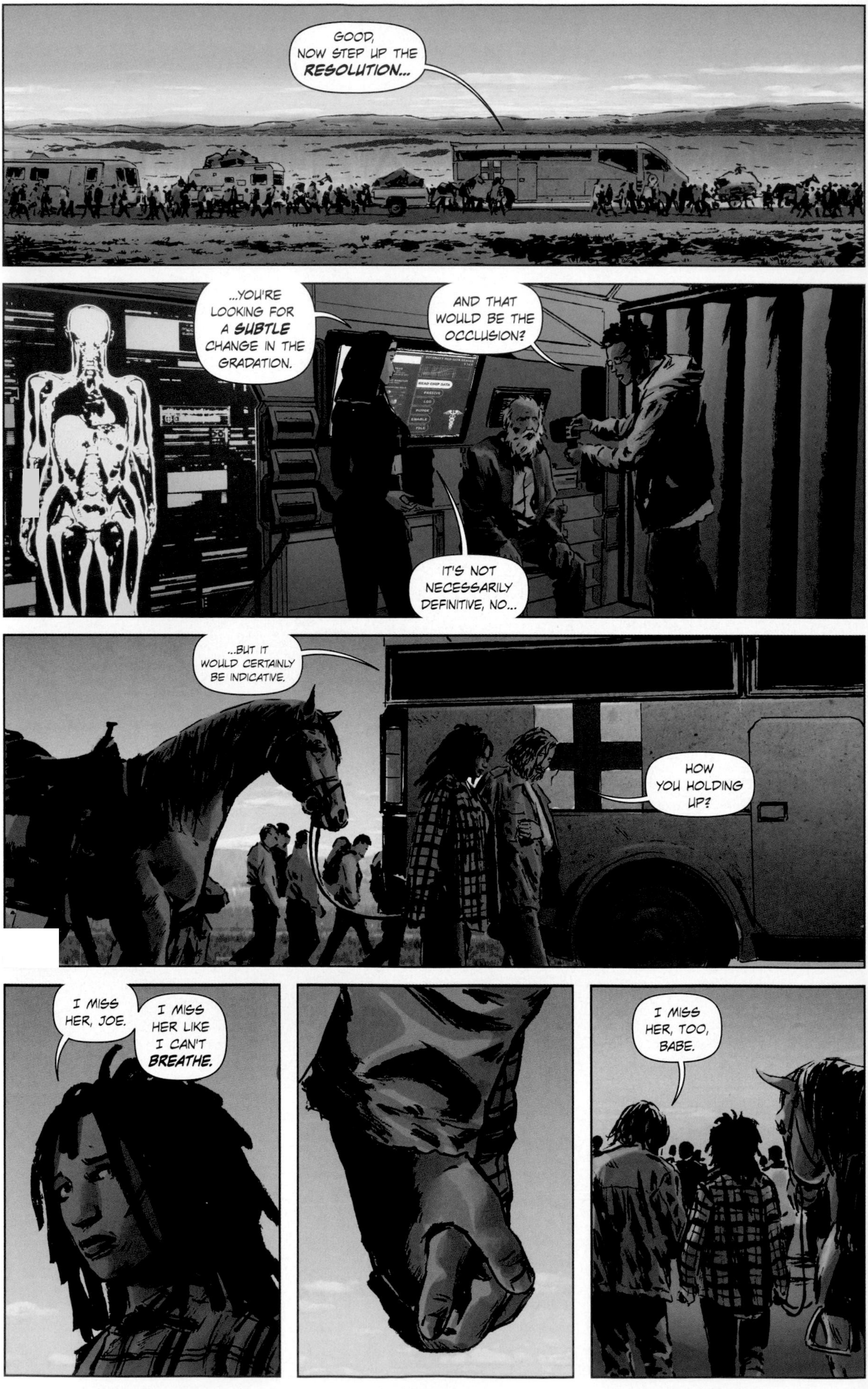
GOOD, NOW STEP UP THE RESOLUTION...
...YOU'RE LOOKING FOR A SUBTLE CHANGE IN THE GRADATION.
AND THAT WOULD BE THE OCCLUSION?
IT'S NOT NECESSARILY DEFINITIVE, NO...
...BUT IT WOULD CERTAINLY BE INDICATIVE.
HOW YOU HOLDING UP?
I MISS HER, JOE.
I MISS HER LIKE I CAN'T BREATHE.
I MISS HER, TOO, BABE.

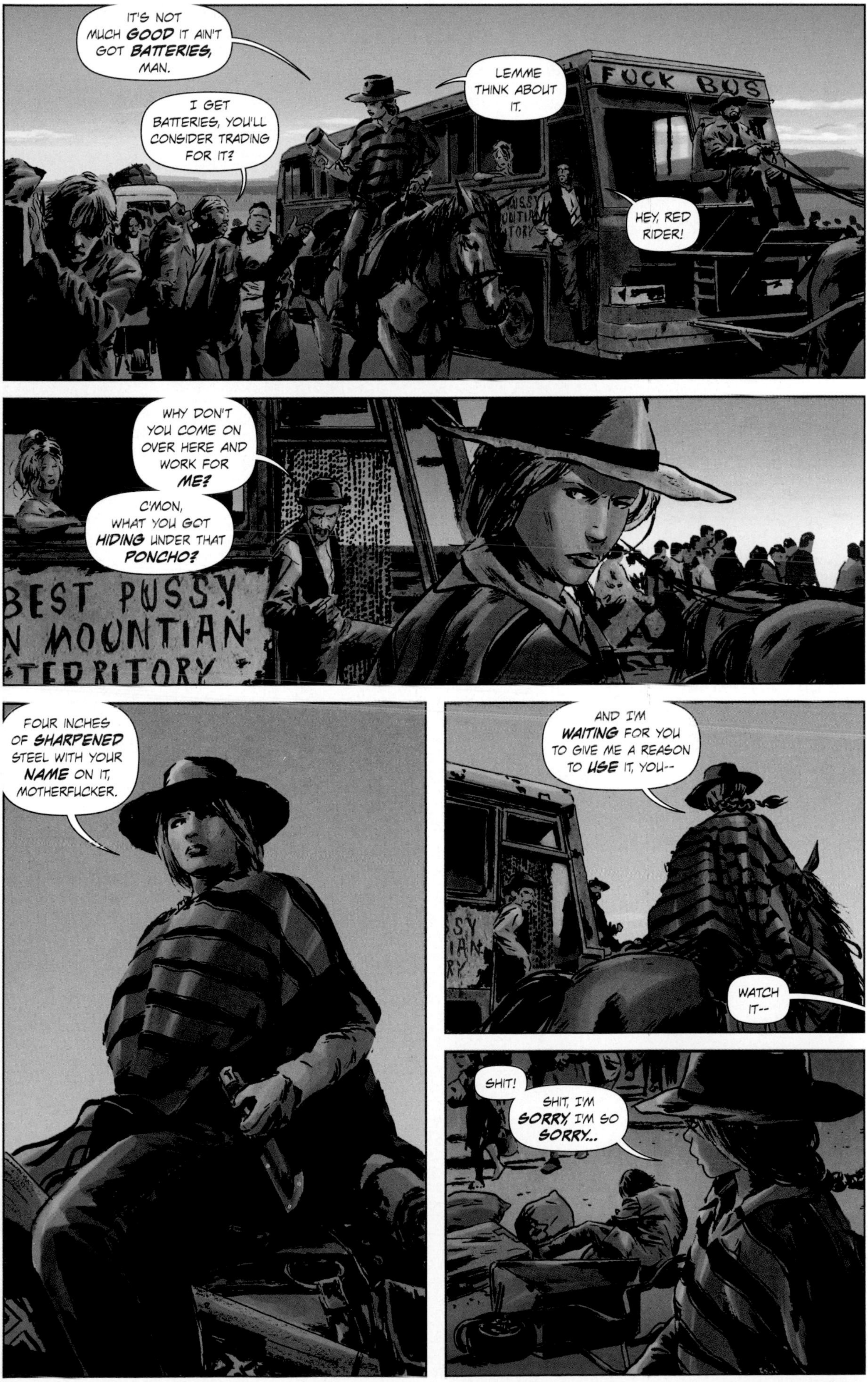
IT'S NOT MUCH **GOOD** IT AIN'T GOT **BATTERIES,** MAN.
I GET BATTERIES, YOU'LL CONSIDER TRADING FOR IT?
LEMME THINK ABOUT IT.
FUCK BUS
HEY, RED RIDER!
WHY DON'T YOU COME ON OVER HERE AND WORK FOR **ME?**
C'MON, WHAT YOU GOT **HIDING** UNDER THAT **PONCHO?**
BEST PUSSY
N MOUNTIAN
FOUR INCHES OF **SHARPENED** STEEL WITH YOUR **NAME** ON IT, MOTHERFUCKER.
AND I'M **WAITING** FOR YOU TO GIVE ME A REASON TO **USE** IT, YOU--
WATCH IT--
SHIT!
SHIT, I'M **SORRY,** I'M SO **SORRY...**

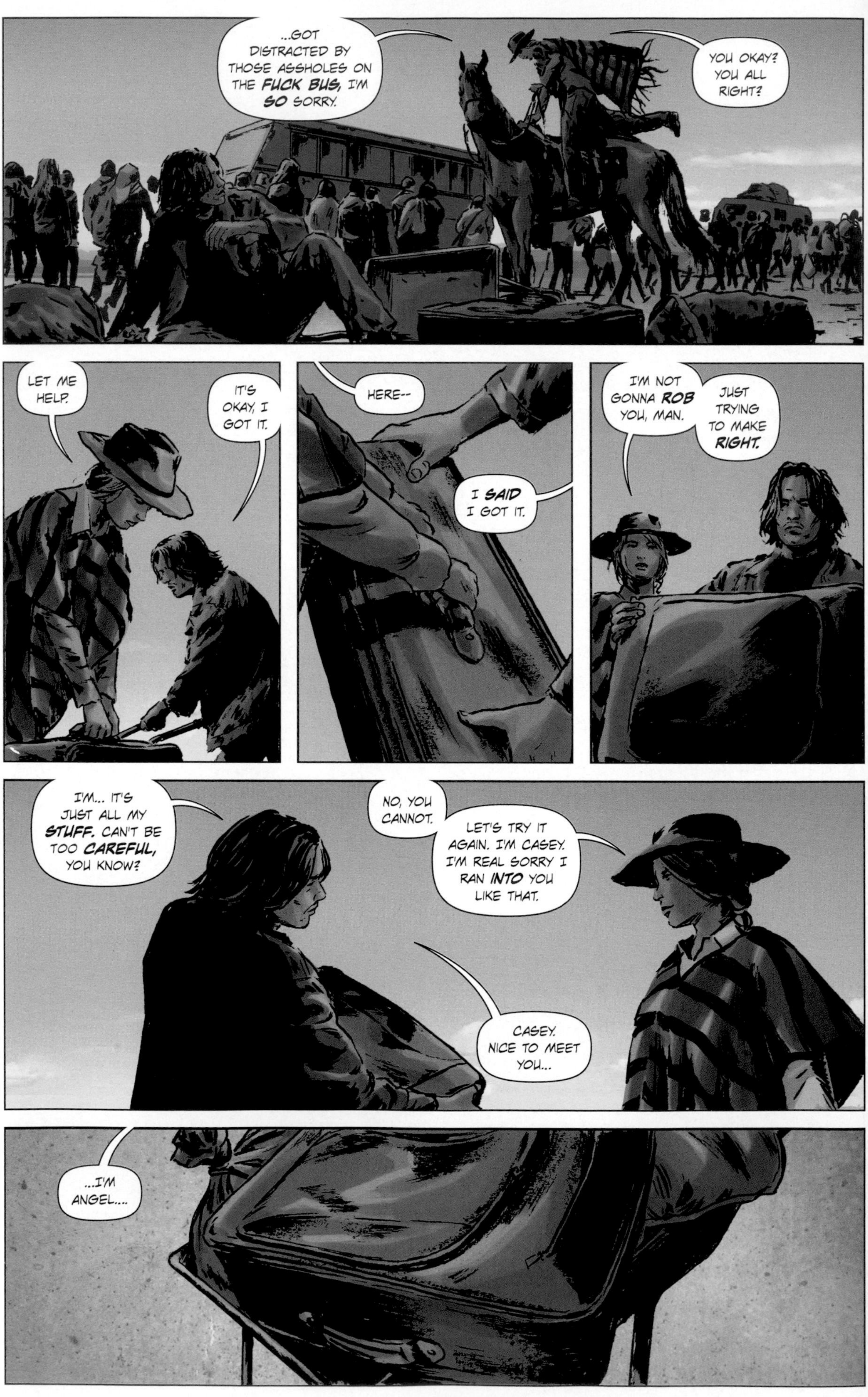
...GOT DISTRACTED BY THOSE ASSHOLES ON THE FUCK BUS, I'M SO SORRY.
YOU OKAY? YOU ALL RIGHT?
LET ME HELP.
IT'S OKAY, I GOT IT.
HERE--
I SAID I GOT IT.
I'M NOT GONNA ROB YOU, MAN.
JUST TRYING TO MAKE RIGHT.
I'M... IT'S JUST ALL MY STUFF. CAN'T BE TOO CAREFUL, YOU KNOW?
NO, YOU CANNOT.
LET'S TRY IT AGAIN. I'M CASEY. I'M REAL SORRY I RAN INTO YOU LIKE THAT.
CASEY. NICE TO MEET YOU...
...I'M ANGEL....

CARLYLE

ODERINT DUM METUANT

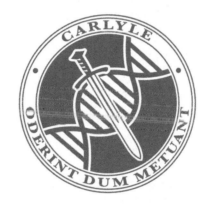

CARLYLE

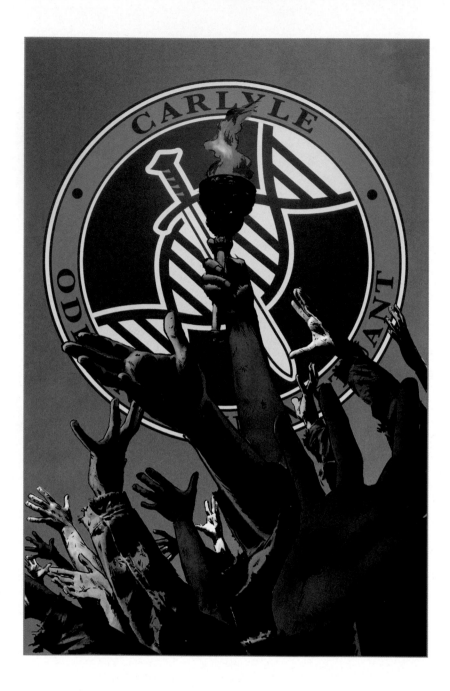

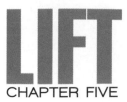

# LIFT
CHAPTER FIVE

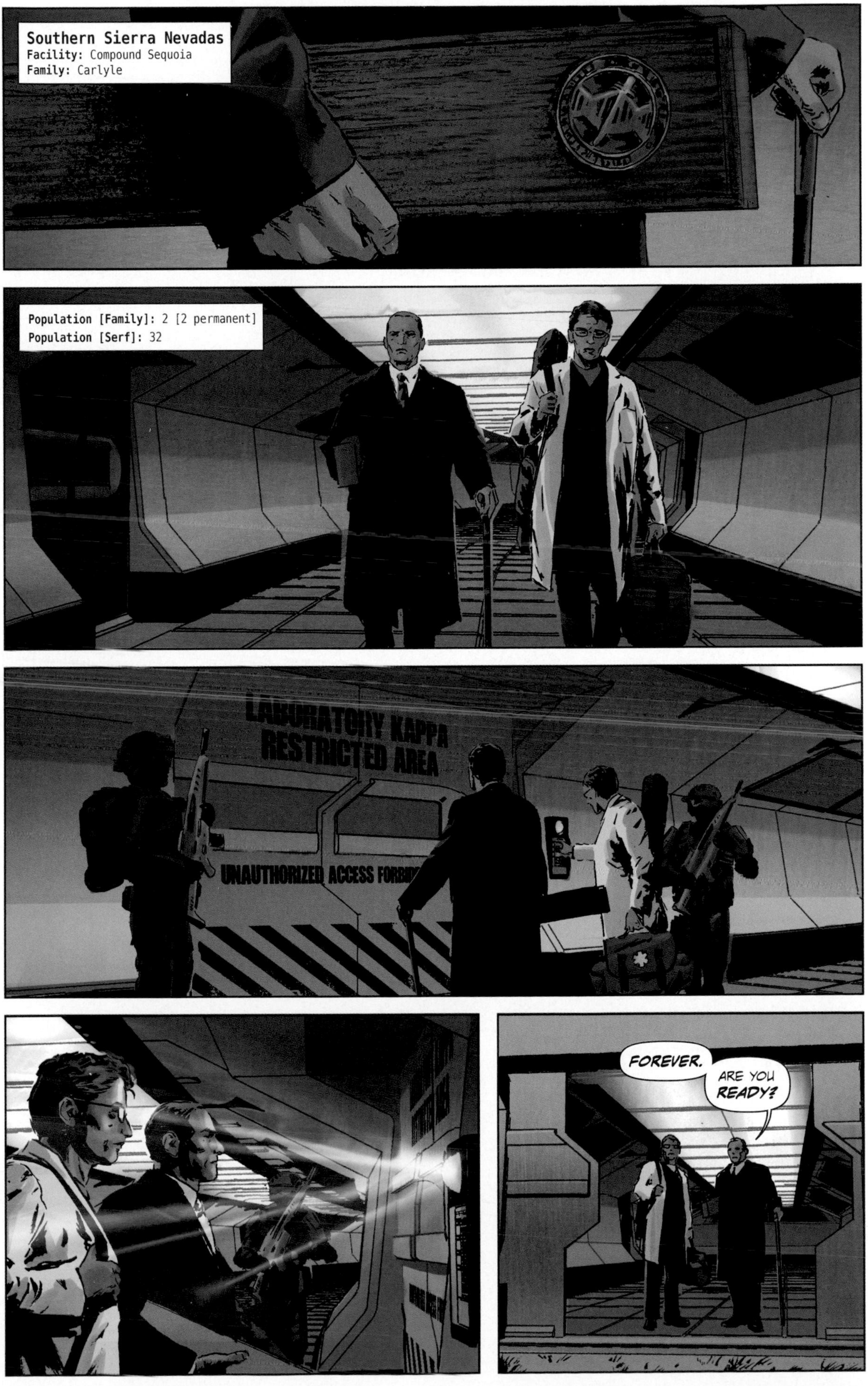
Southern Sierra Nevadas
Facility: Compound Sequoia
Family: Carlyle
Population [Family]: 2 [2 permanent]
Population [Serf]: 32
LABORATORY KAPPA
RESTRICTED AREA
UNAUTHORIZED ACCESS FORBID
FOREVER.
ARE YOU READY?

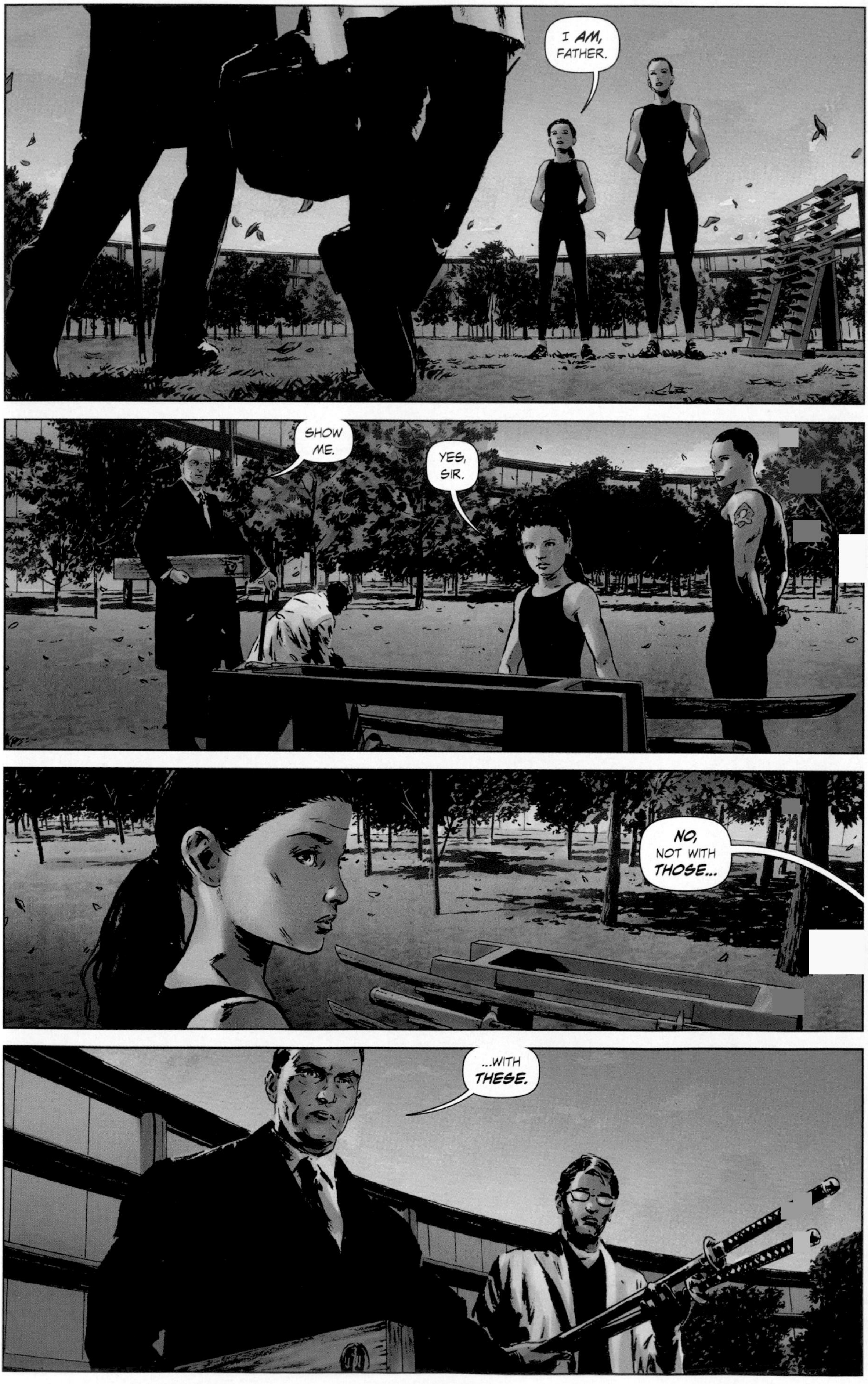
I AM, FATHER.
SHOW ME.
YES, SIR.
NO, NOT WITH THOSE...
...WITH THESE.

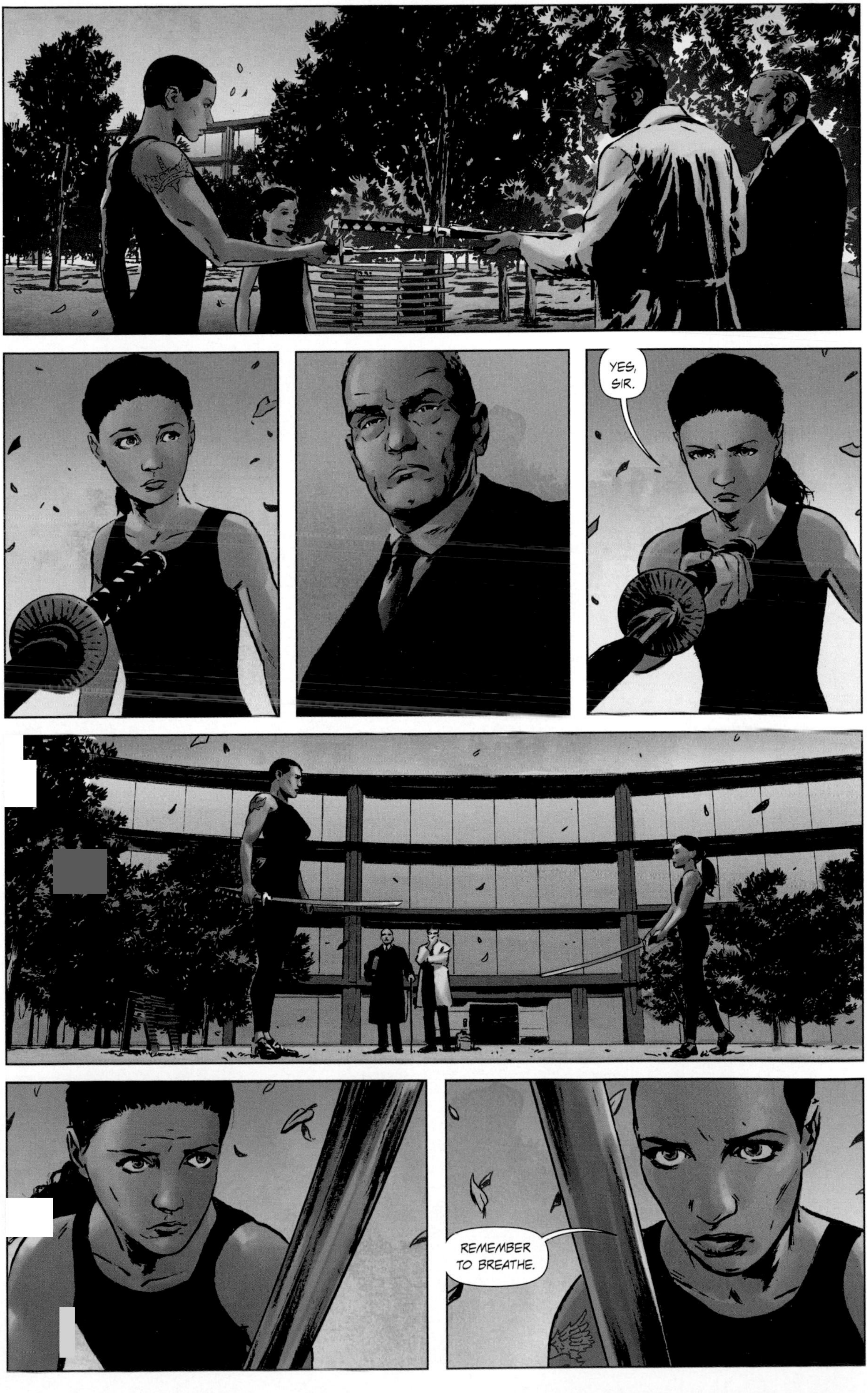
YES, SIR.
REMEMBER TO BREATHE.

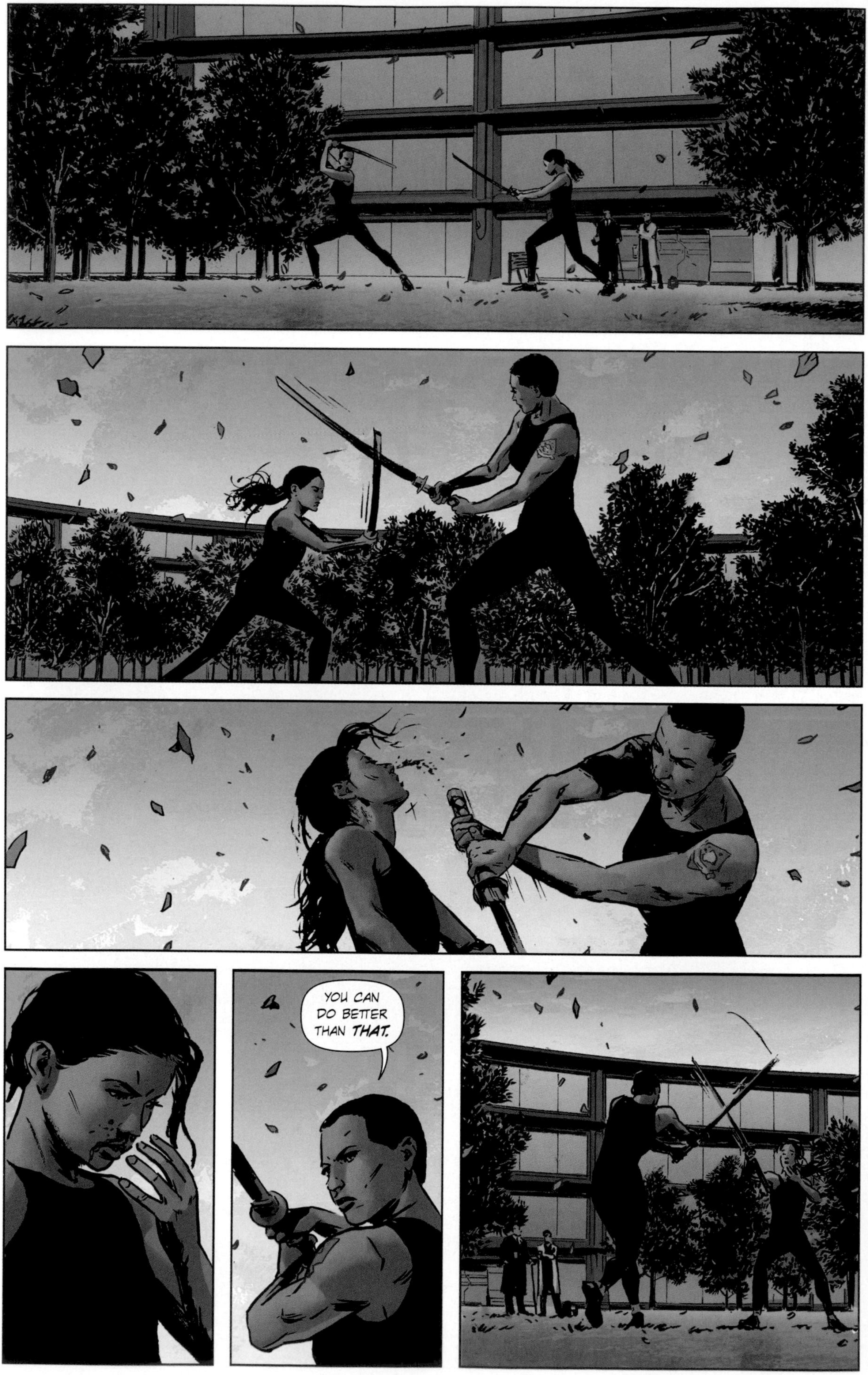
YOU CAN DO BETTER THAN THAT.

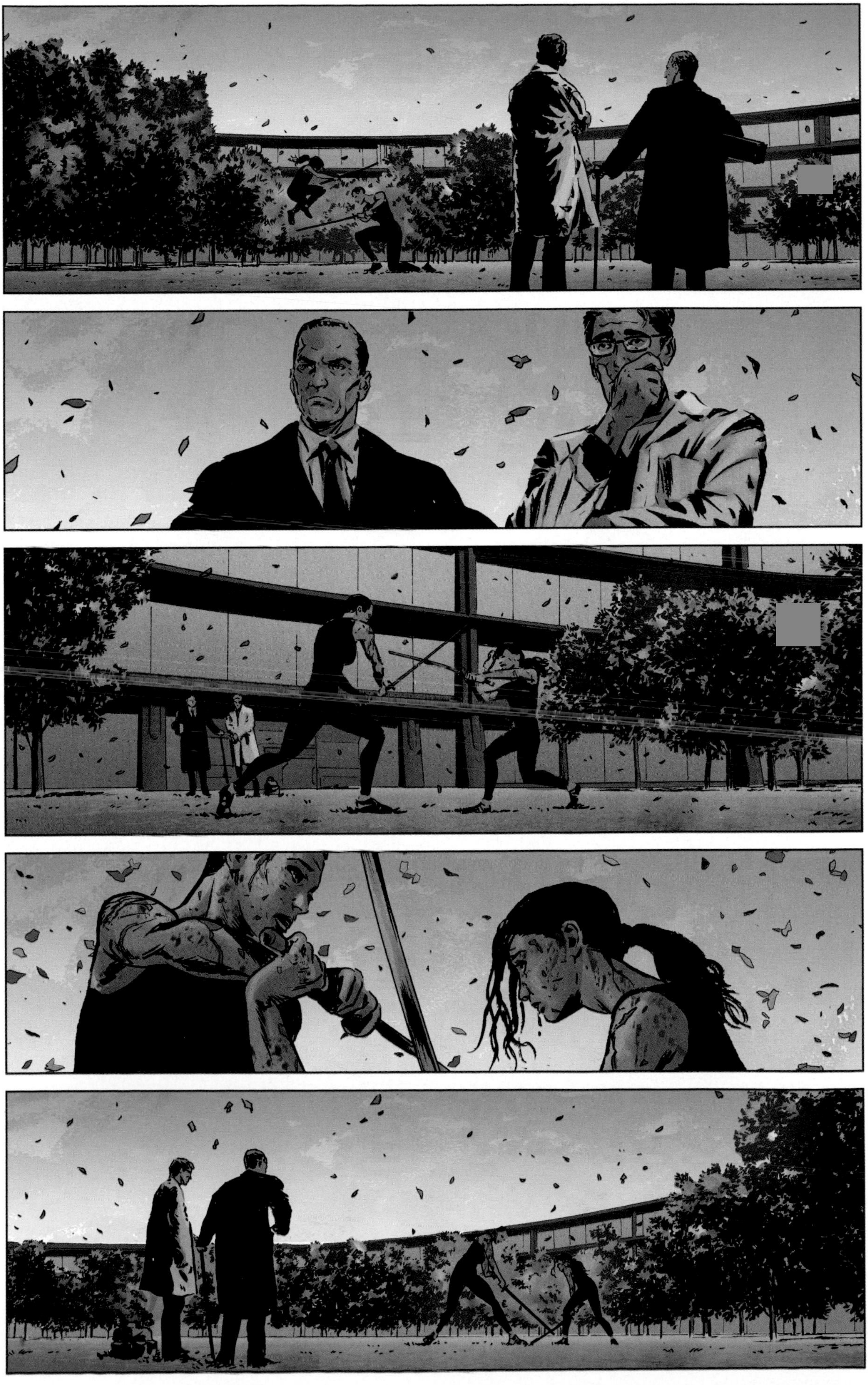

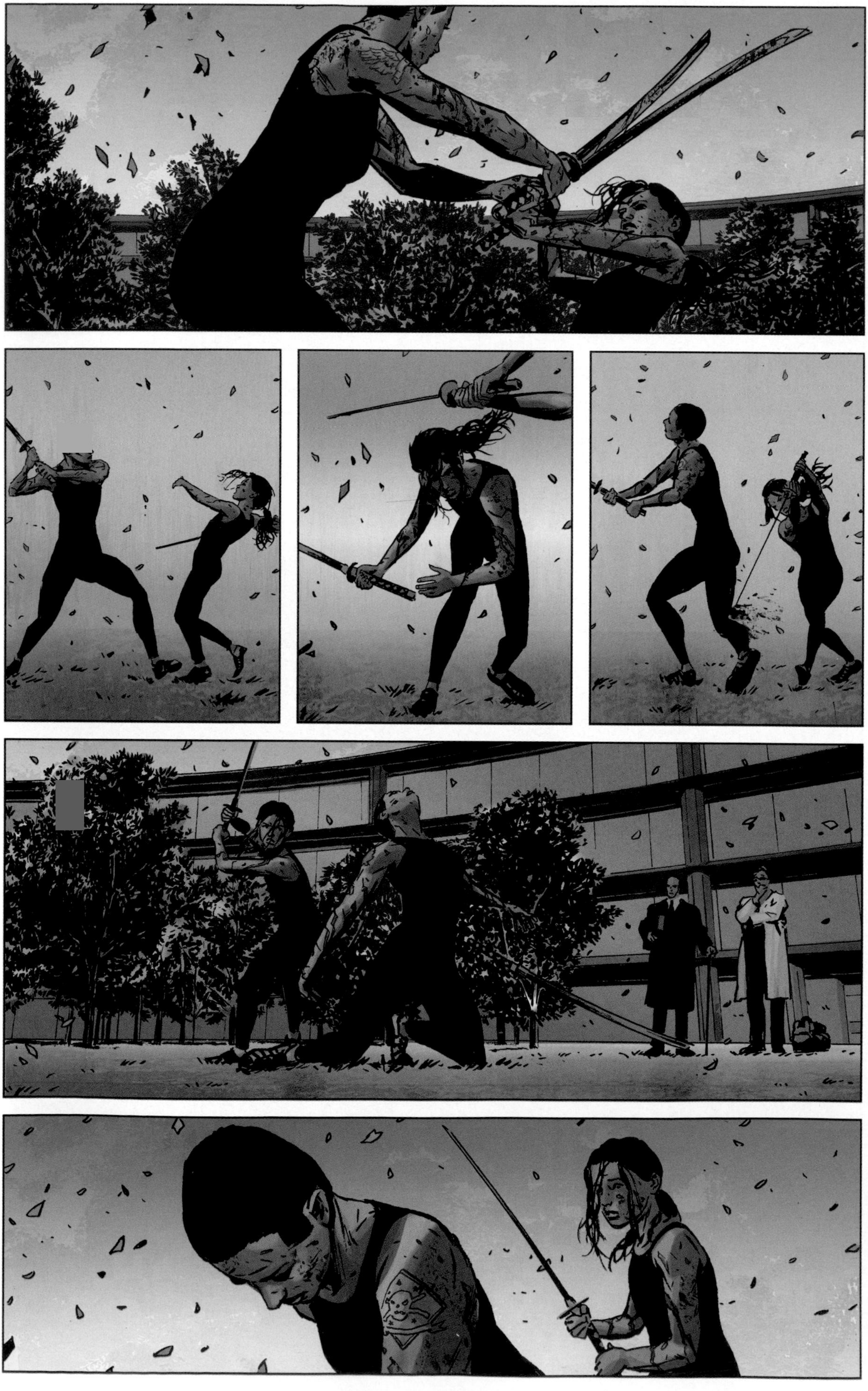

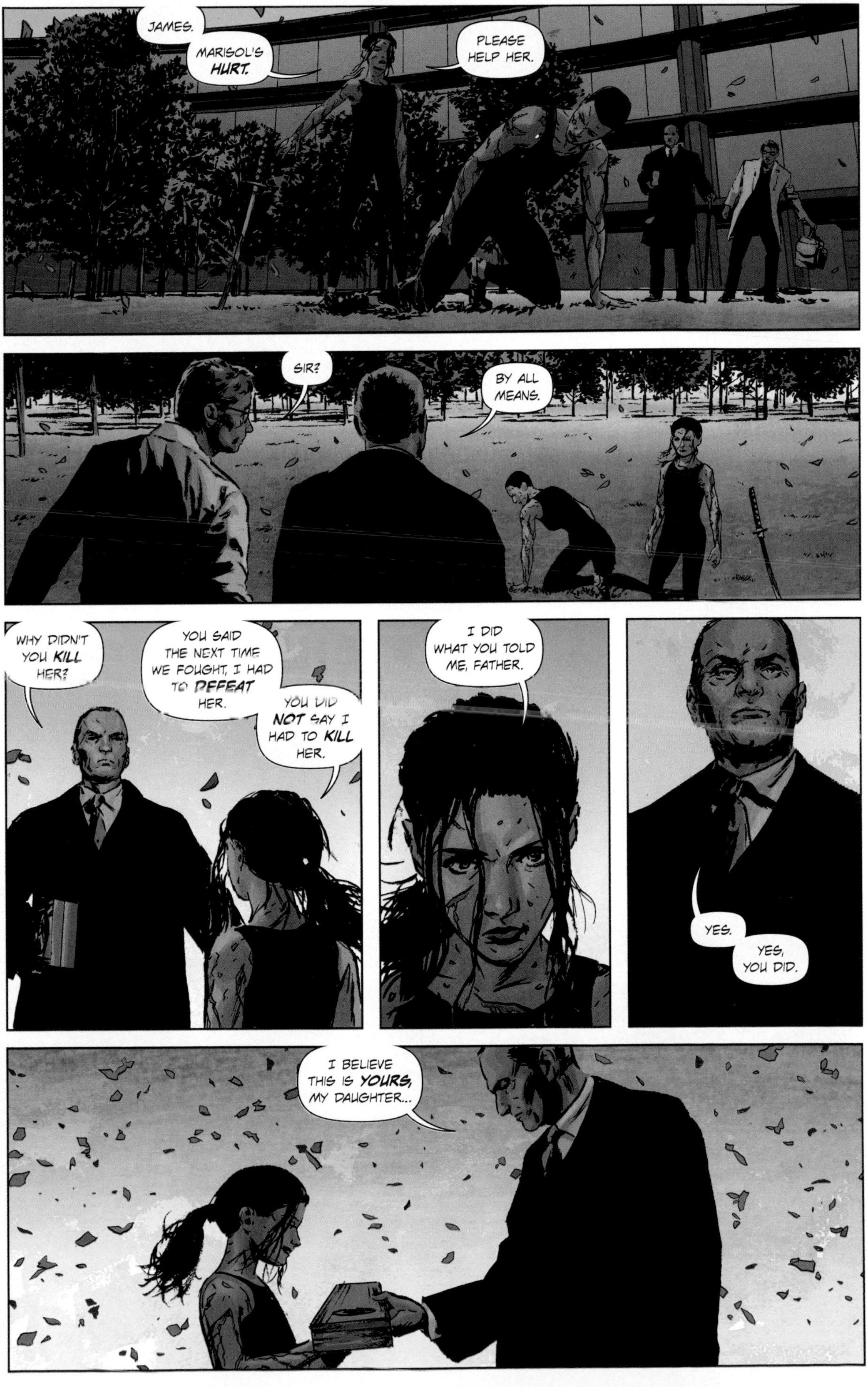
JAMES.
MARISOL'S HURT.
PLEASE HELP HER.
SIR?
BY ALL MEANS.
WHY DIDN'T YOU KILL HER?
YOU SAID THE NEXT TIME WE FOUGHT, I HAD TO DEFEAT HER.
YOU DID NOT SAY I HAD TO KILL HER.
I DID WHAT YOU TOLD ME, FATHER.
YES.
YES, YOU DID.
I BELIEVE THIS IS YOURS, MY DAUGHTER...

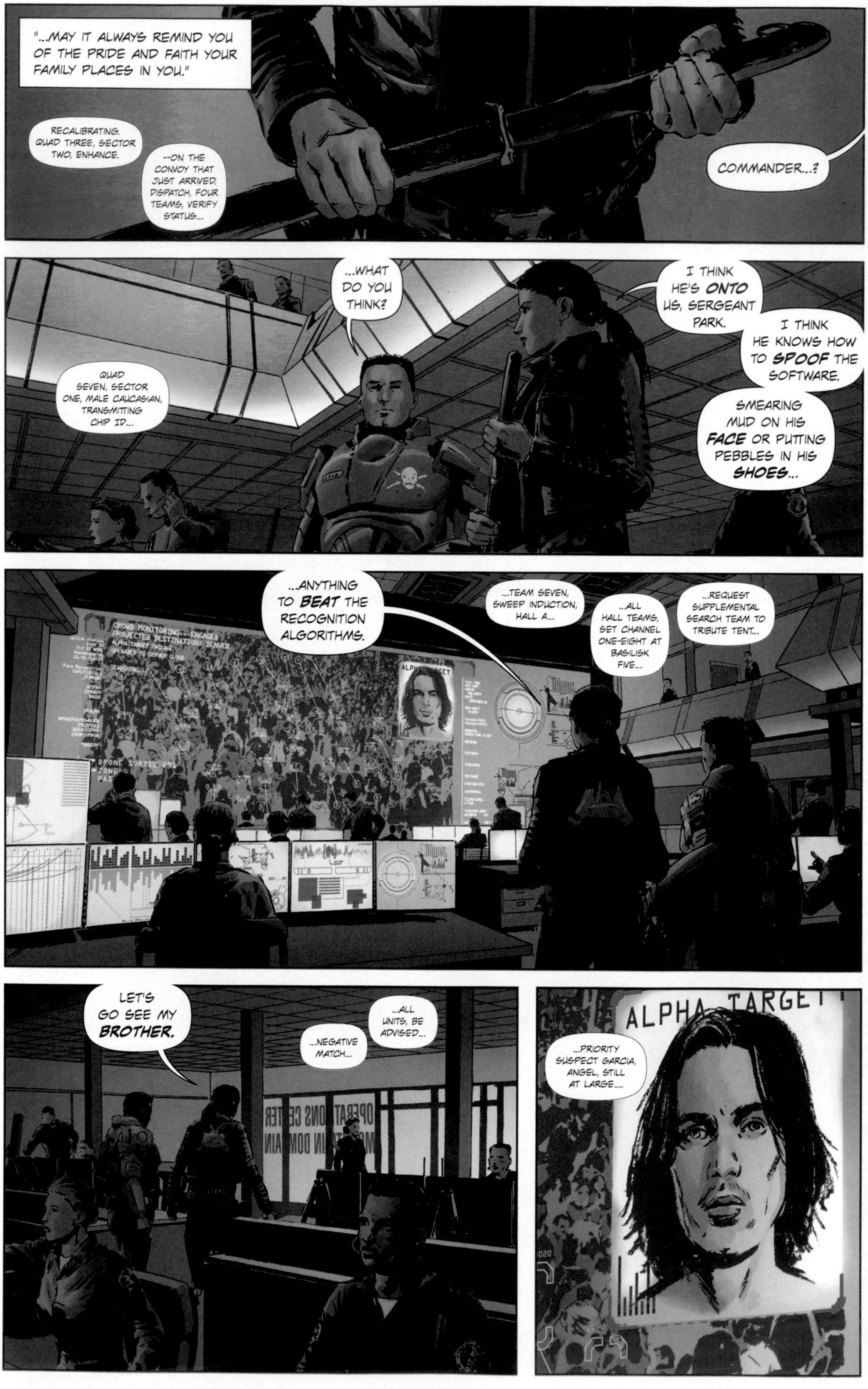
"...MAY IT ALWAYS REMIND YOU OF THE PRIDE AND FAITH YOUR FAMILY PLACES IN YOU."
RECALIBRATING. QUAD THREE, SECTOR TWO, ENHANCE.
--ON THE CONVOY THAT JUST ARRIVED. DISPATCH, FOUR TEAMS, VERIFY STATUS...
COMMANDER...?
...WHAT DO YOU THINK?
QUAD SEVEN, SECTOR ONE, MALE CAUCASIAN, TRANSMITTING CHIP ID...
I THINK HE'S ONTO US, SERGEANT PARK.
I THINK HE KNOWS HOW TO SPOOF THE SOFTWARE.
SMEARING MUD ON HIS FACE OR PUTTING PEBBLES IN HIS SHOES...
...ANYTHING TO BEAT THE RECOGNITION ALGORITHMS.
CROWD MONITORING--ENGAGED
PROJECTED DESTINATION: DENVER
ALPHA TARGET
DRONE SORTIE
ZONE
...TEAM SEVEN, SWEEP INDUCTION, HALL A...
...ALL HALL TEAMS, SET CHANNEL ONE-EIGHT AT BASILISK FIVE...
...REQUEST SUPPLEMENTAL SEARCH TEAM TO TRIBUTE TENT...
LET'S GO SEE MY BROTHER.
...NEGATIVE MATCH...
...ALL UNITS, BE ADVISED...
OPERATIONS CENTER
ALPHA TARGET
...PRIORITY SUSPECT GARCIA, ANGEL, STILL AT LARGE....

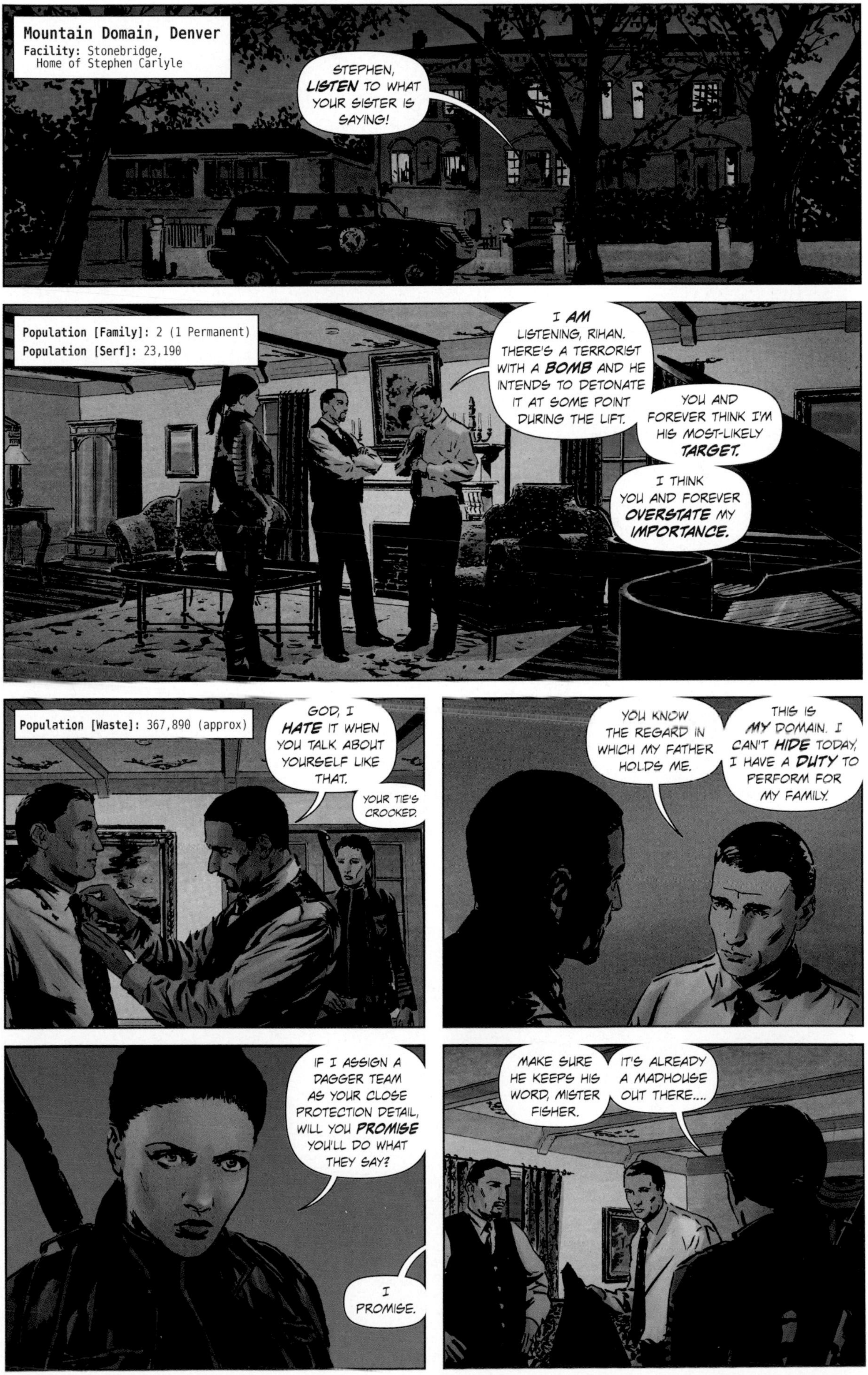
Mountain Domain, Denver
Facility: Stonebridge, Home of Stephen Carlyle
STEPHEN, LISTEN TO WHAT YOUR SISTER IS SAYING!
Population [Family]: 2 (1 Permanent)
Population [Serf]: 23,190
I AM LISTENING, RIHAN. THERE'S A TERRORIST WITH A BOMB AND HE INTENDS TO DETONATE IT AT SOME POINT DURING THE LIFT.
YOU AND FOREVER THINK I'M HIS MOST-LIKELY TARGET.
I THINK YOU AND FOREVER OVERSTATE MY IMPORTANCE.
Population [Waste]: 367,890 (approx)
GOD, I HATE IT WHEN YOU TALK ABOUT YOURSELF LIKE THAT.
YOUR TIE'S CROOKED.
YOU KNOW THE REGARD IN WHICH MY FATHER HOLDS ME.
THIS IS MY DOMAIN. I CAN'T HIDE TODAY, I HAVE A DUTY TO PERFORM FOR MY FAMILY.
IF I ASSIGN A DAGGER TEAM AS YOUR CLOSE PROTECTION DETAIL, WILL YOU PROMISE YOU'LL DO WHAT THEY SAY?
I PROMISE.
MAKE SURE HE KEEPS HIS WORD, MISTER FISHER.
IT'S ALREADY A MADHOUSE OUT THERE....

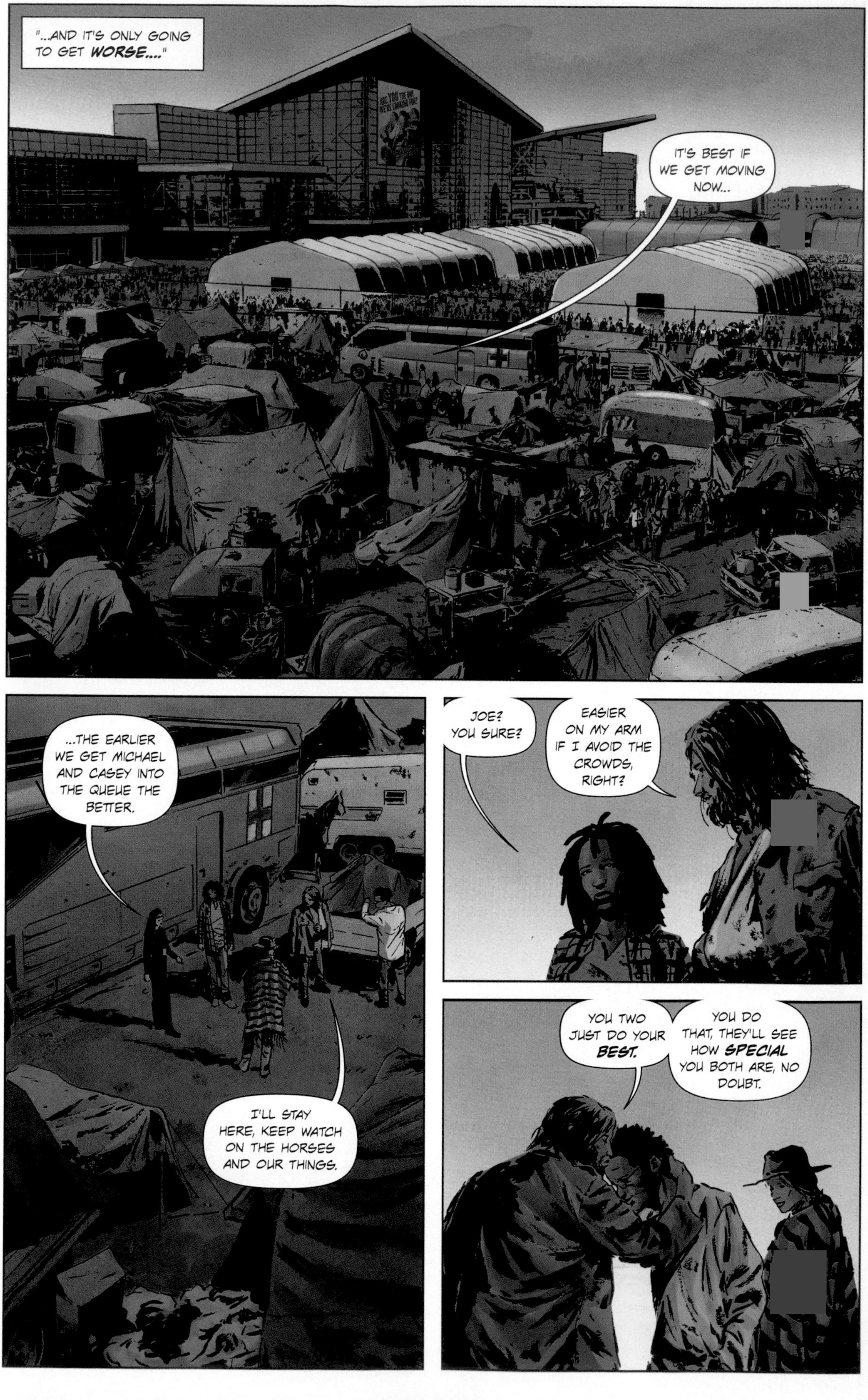
"...AND IT'S ONLY GOING TO GET **WORSE....**"
IT'S BEST IF WE GET MOVING NOW...
...THE EARLIER WE GET MICHAEL AND CASEY INTO THE QUEUE THE BETTER.
I'LL STAY HERE, KEEP WATCH ON THE HORSES AND OUR THINGS.
JOE? YOU SURE?
EASIER ON MY ARM IF I AVOID THE CROWDS, RIGHT?
YOU TWO JUST DO YOUR **BEST.**
YOU DO THAT, THEY'LL SEE HOW **SPECIAL** YOU BOTH ARE, NO DOUBT.

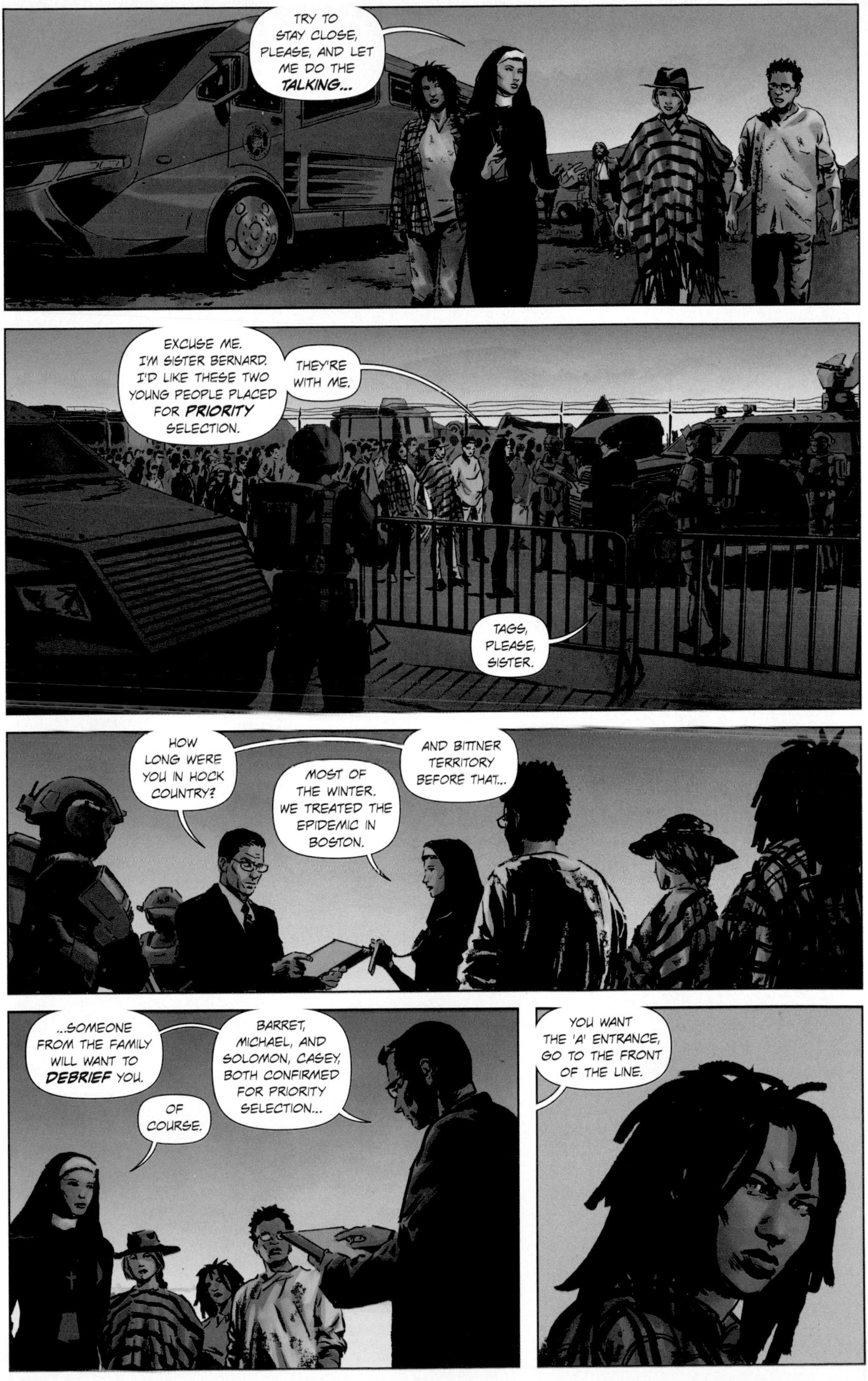
TRY TO STAY CLOSE, PLEASE, AND LET ME DO THE TALKING...
EXCUSE ME. I'M SISTER BERNARD. I'D LIKE THESE TWO YOUNG PEOPLE PLACED FOR PRIORITY SELECTION.
THEY'RE WITH ME.
TAGS, PLEASE, SISTER.
HOW LONG WERE YOU IN HOCK COUNTRY?
MOST OF THE WINTER. WE TREATED THE EPIDEMIC IN BOSTON.
AND BITTNER TERRITORY BEFORE THAT...
...SOMEONE FROM THE FAMILY WILL WANT TO DEBRIEF YOU.
BARRET, MICHAEL, AND SOLOMON, CASEY, BOTH CONFIRMED FOR PRIORITY SELECTION...
OF COURSE.
YOU WANT THE 'A' ENTRANCE, GO TO THE FRONT OF THE LINE.

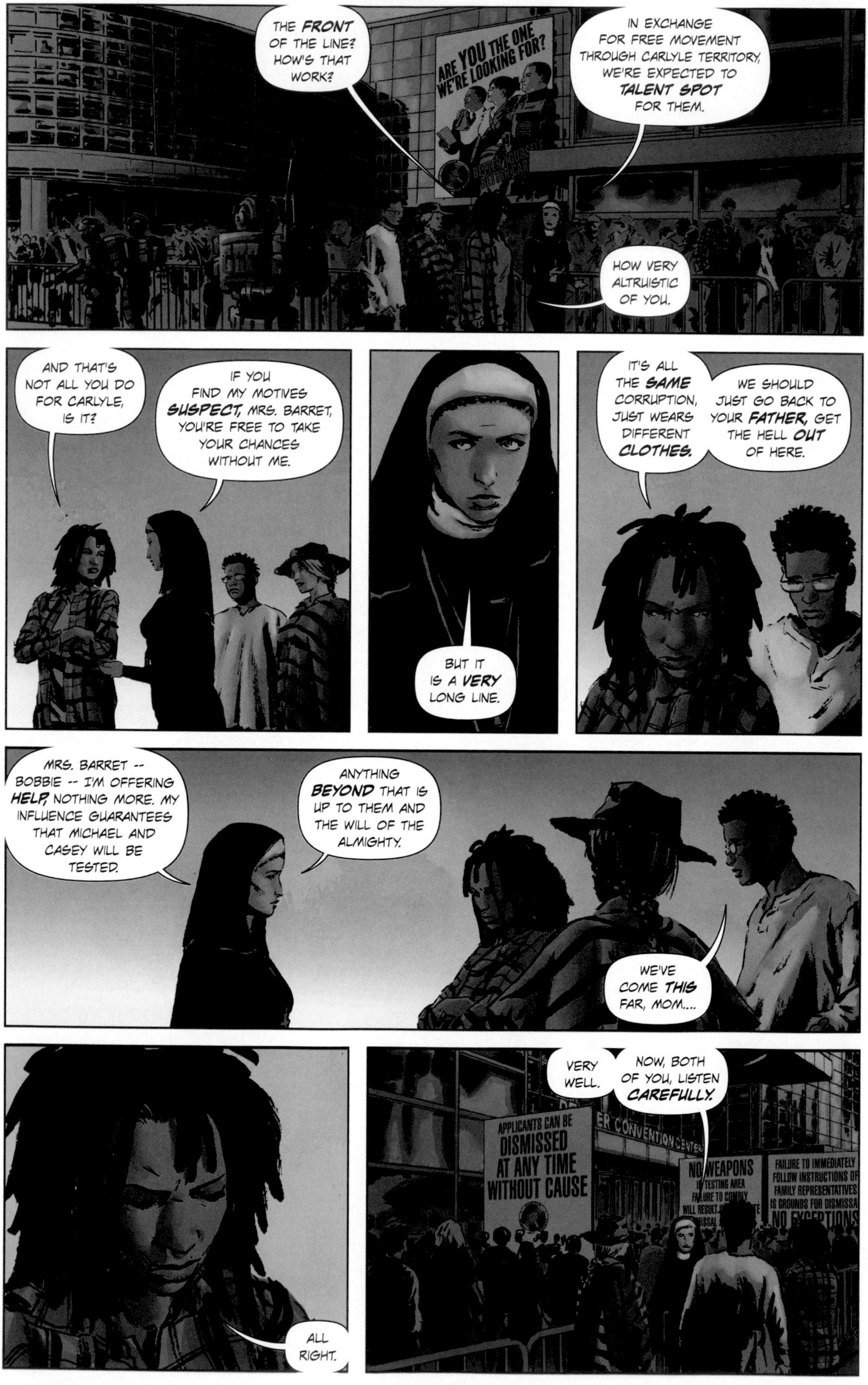
THE FRONT OF THE LINE? HOW'S THAT WORK?
ARE YOU THE ONE WE'RE LOOKING FOR?
IN EXCHANGE FOR FREE MOVEMENT THROUGH CARLYLE TERRITORY, WE'RE EXPECTED TO TALENT SPOT FOR THEM.
HOW VERY ALTRUISTIC OF YOU.
AND THAT'S NOT ALL YOU DO FOR CARLYLE, IS IT?
IF YOU FIND MY MOTIVES SUSPECT, MRS. BARRET, YOU'RE FREE TO TAKE YOUR CHANCES WITHOUT ME.
BUT IT IS A VERY LONG LINE.
IT'S ALL THE SAME CORRUPTION, JUST WEARS DIFFERENT CLOTHES.
WE SHOULD JUST GO BACK TO YOUR FATHER, GET THE HELL OUT OF HERE.
MRS. BARRET -- BOBBIE -- I'M OFFERING HELP, NOTHING MORE. MY INFLUENCE GUARANTEES THAT MICHAEL AND CASEY WILL BE TESTED.
ANYTHING BEYOND THAT IS UP TO THEM AND THE WILL OF THE ALMIGHTY.
WE'VE COME THIS FAR, MOM....
ALL RIGHT.
VERY WELL.
NOW, BOTH OF YOU, LISTEN CAREFULLY.
APPLICANTS CAN BE DISMISSED AT ANY TIME WITHOUT CAUSE
CONVENTION CENTER
FAILURE TO IMMEDIATELY FOLLOW INSTRUCTIONS OF FAMILY REPRESENTATIVES IS GROUNDS FOR DISMISSA

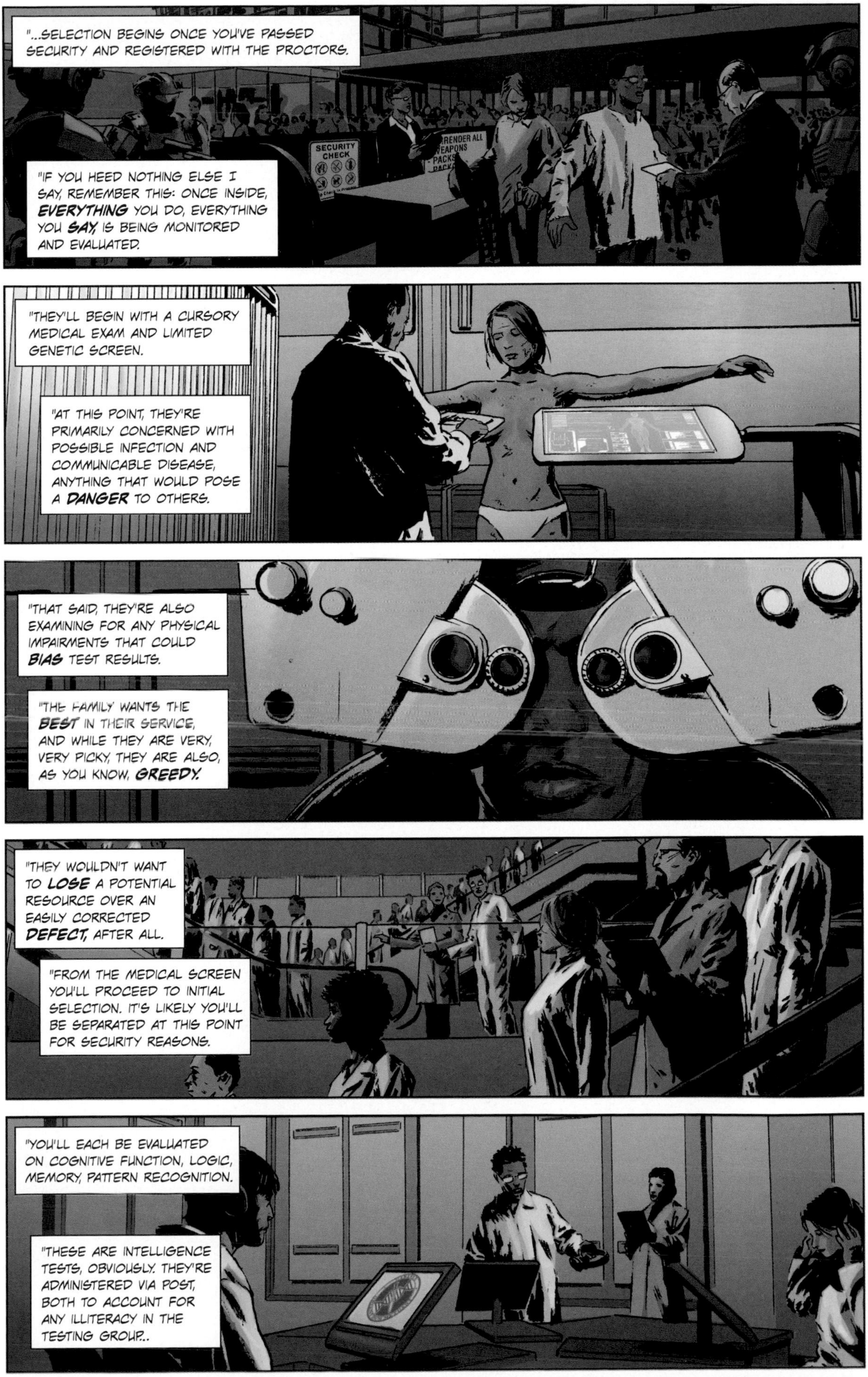
"...SELECTION BEGINS ONCE YOU'VE PASSED SECURITY AND REGISTERED WITH THE PROCTORS.
SECURITY CHECK
"IF YOU HEED NOTHING ELSE I SAY, REMEMBER THIS: ONCE INSIDE, **EVERYTHING** YOU DO, EVERYTHING YOU **SAY,** IS BEING MONITORED AND EVALUATED.
"THEY'LL BEGIN WITH A CURSORY MEDICAL EXAM AND LIMITED GENETIC SCREEN.
"AT THIS POINT, THEY'RE PRIMARILY CONCERNED WITH POSSIBLE INFECTION AND COMMUNICABLE DISEASE, ANYTHING THAT WOULD POSE A **DANGER** TO OTHERS.
"THAT SAID, THEY'RE ALSO EXAMINING FOR ANY PHYSICAL IMPAIRMENTS THAT COULD **BIAS** TEST RESULTS.
"THE FAMILY WANTS THE **BEST** IN THEIR SERVICE, AND WHILE THEY ARE VERY, VERY PICKY, THEY ARE ALSO, AS YOU KNOW, **GREEDY.**
"THEY WOULDN'T WANT TO **LOSE** A POTENTIAL RESOURCE OVER AN EASILY CORRECTED **DEFECT,** AFTER ALL.
"FROM THE MEDICAL SCREEN YOU'LL PROCEED TO INITIAL SELECTION. IT'S LIKELY YOU'LL BE SEPARATED AT THIS POINT FOR SECURITY REASONS.
"YOU'LL EACH BE EVALUATED ON COGNITIVE FUNCTION, LOGIC, MEMORY, PATTERN RECOGNITION.
"THESE ARE INTELLIGENCE TESTS, OBVIOUSLY. THEY'RE ADMINISTERED VIA POST, BOTH TO ACCOUNT FOR ANY ILLITERACY IN THE TESTING GROUP...

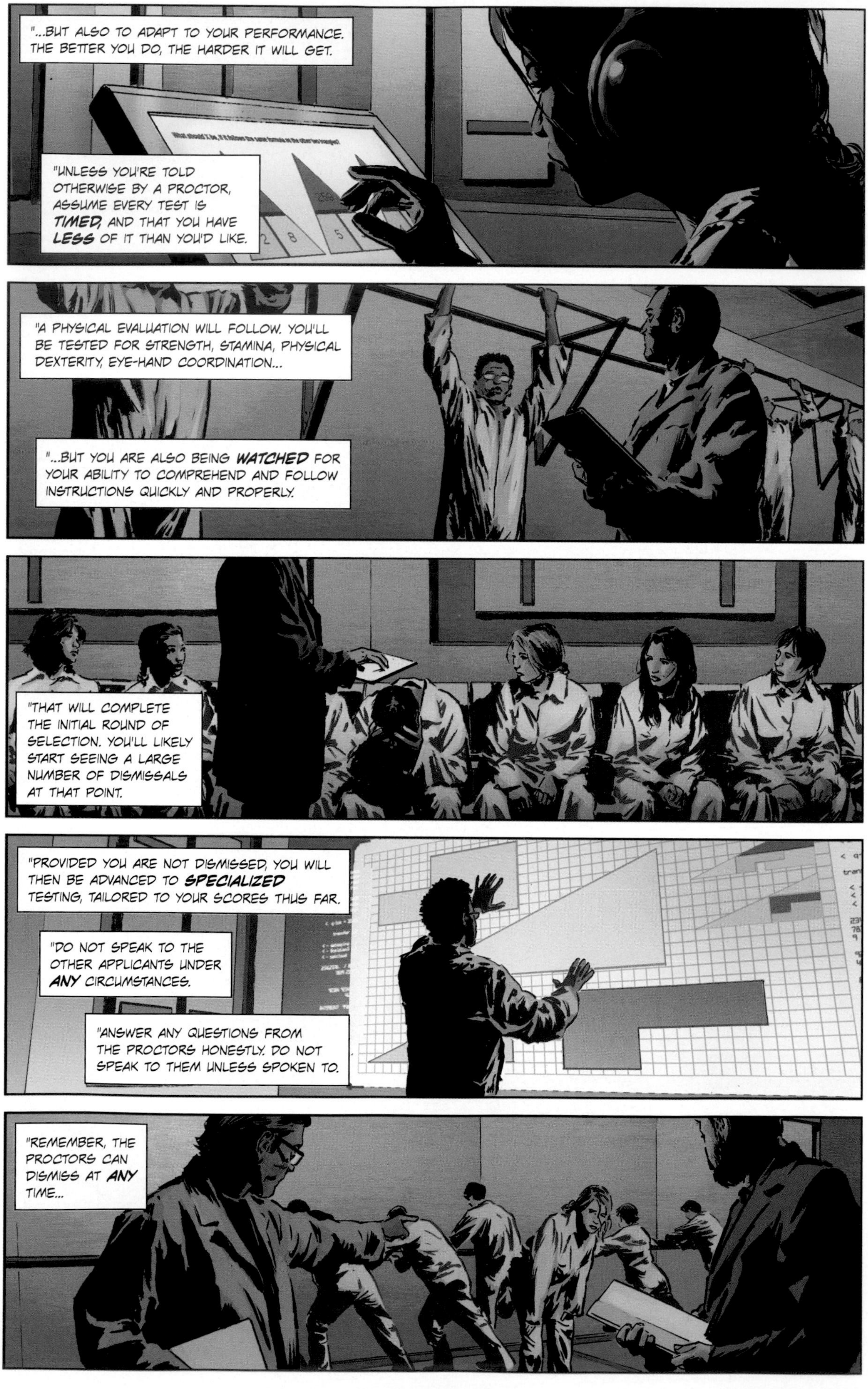
"...BUT ALSO TO ADAPT TO YOUR PERFORMANCE. THE BETTER YOU DO, THE HARDER IT WILL GET.
"UNLESS YOU'RE TOLD OTHERWISE BY A PROCTOR, ASSUME EVERY TEST IS TIMED, AND THAT YOU HAVE LESS OF IT THAN YOU'D LIKE.
"A PHYSICAL EVALUATION WILL FOLLOW. YOU'LL BE TESTED FOR STRENGTH, STAMINA, PHYSICAL DEXTERITY, EYE-HAND COORDINATION...
"...BUT YOU ARE ALSO BEING WATCHED FOR YOUR ABILITY TO COMPREHEND AND FOLLOW INSTRUCTIONS QUICKLY AND PROPERLY.
"THAT WILL COMPLETE THE INITIAL ROUND OF SELECTION. YOU'LL LIKELY START SEEING A LARGE NUMBER OF DISMISSALS AT THAT POINT.
"PROVIDED YOU ARE NOT DISMISSED, YOU WILL THEN BE ADVANCED TO SPECIALIZED TESTING, TAILORED TO YOUR SCORES THUS FAR.
"DO NOT SPEAK TO THE OTHER APPLICANTS UNDER ANY CIRCUMSTANCES.
"ANSWER ANY QUESTIONS FROM THE PROCTORS HONESTLY. DO NOT SPEAK TO THEM UNLESS SPOKEN TO.
"REMEMBER, THE PROCTORS CAN DISMISS AT ANY TIME...

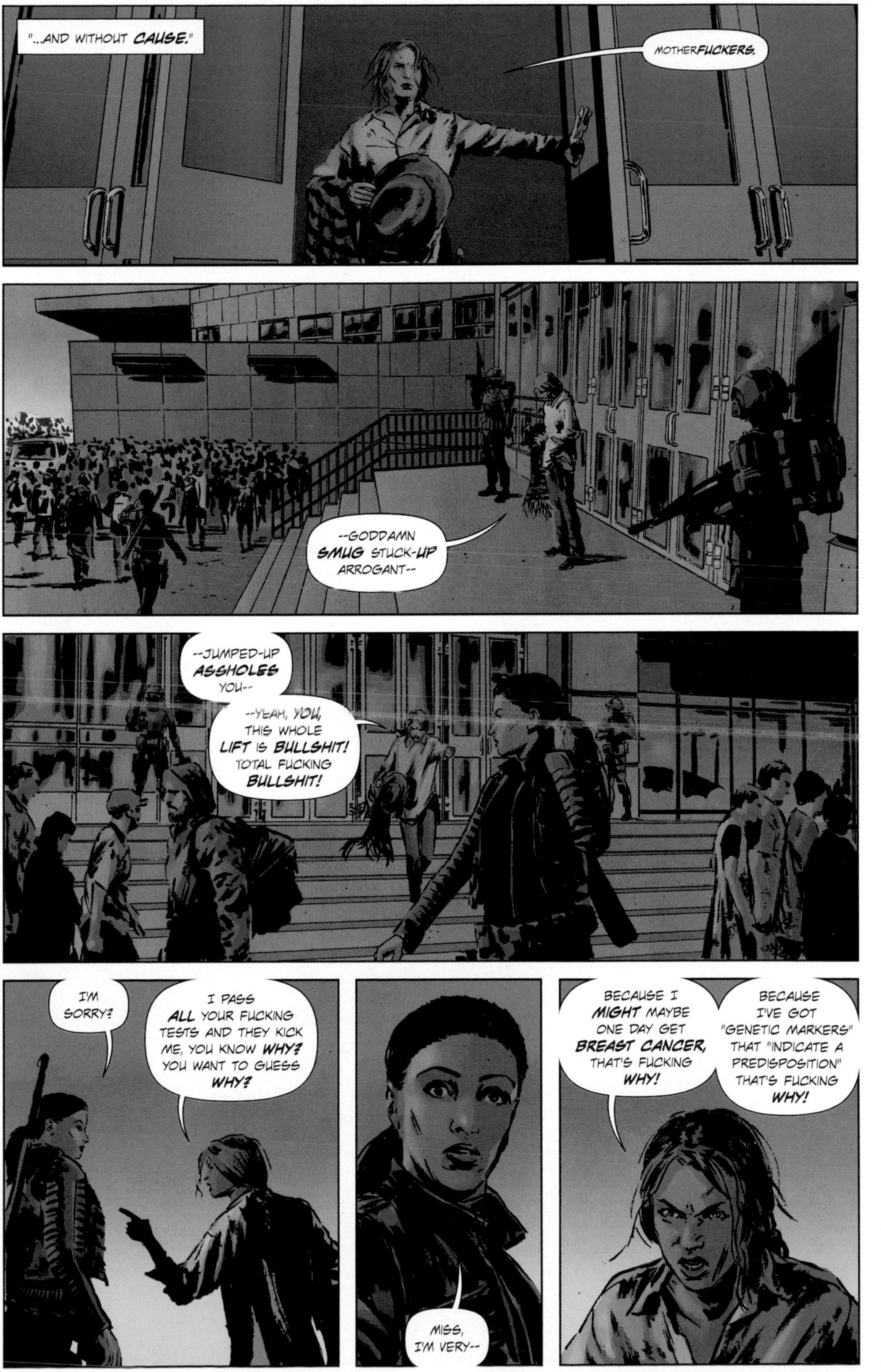
"...AND WITHOUT CAUSE."
MOTHERFUCKERS.
--GODDAMN SMUG STUCK-UP ARROGANT--
--JUMPED-UP ASSHOLES YOU--
--YEAH, YOU, THIS WHOLE LIFT IS BULLSHIT! TOTAL FUCKING BULLSHIT!
I'M SORRY?
I PASS ALL YOUR FUCKING TESTS AND THEY KICK ME, YOU KNOW WHY? YOU WANT TO GUESS WHY?
MISS, I'M VERY--
BECAUSE I MIGHT MAYBE ONE DAY GET BREAST CANCER, THAT'S FUCKING WHY!
BECAUSE I'VE GOT "GENETIC MARKERS" THAT "INDICATE A PREDISPOSITION" THAT'S FUCKING WHY!

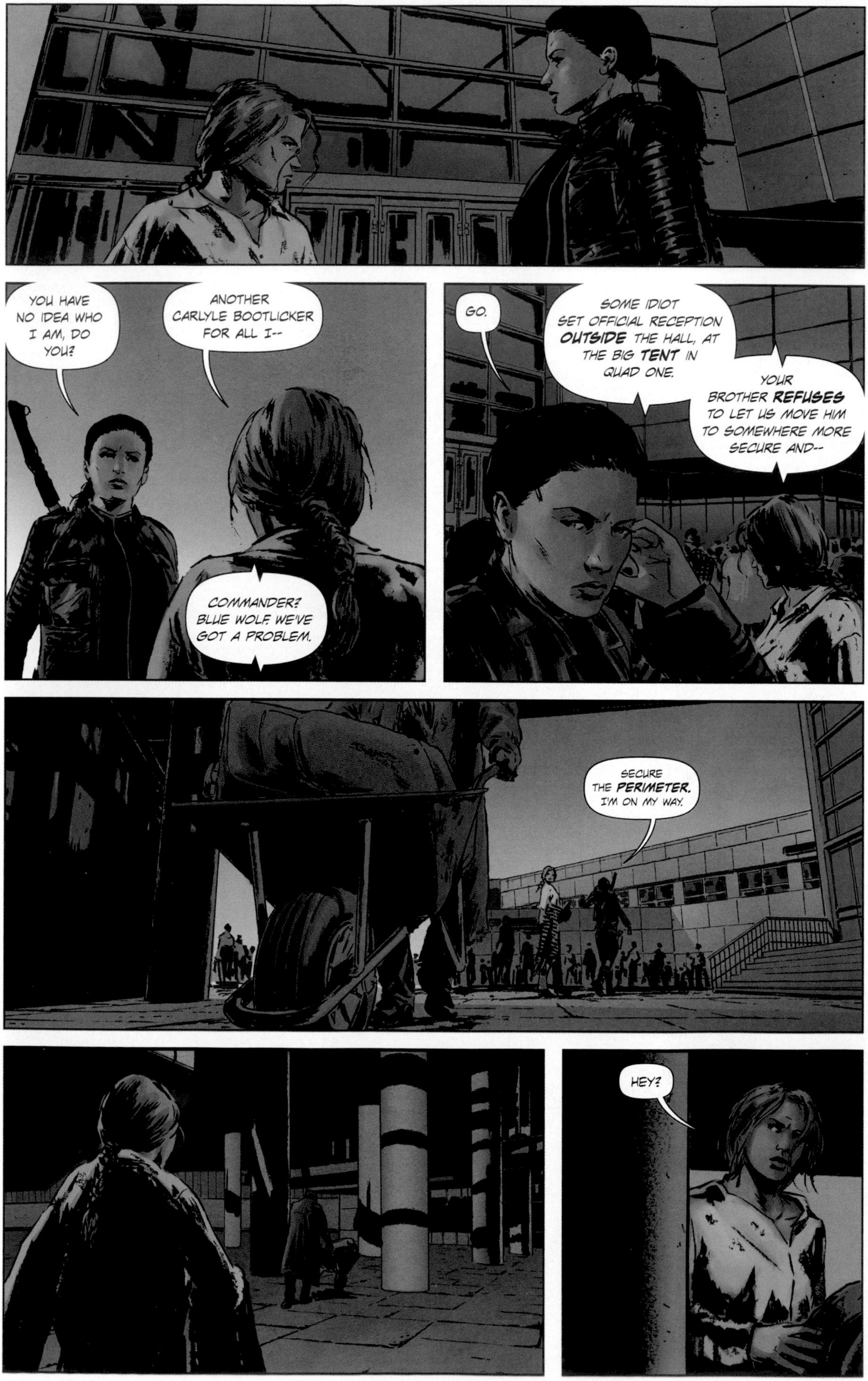
YOU HAVE NO IDEA WHO I AM, DO YOU?
ANOTHER CARLYLE BOOTLICKER FOR ALL I--
COMMANDER? BLUE WOLF. WE'VE GOT A PROBLEM.
GO.
SOME IDIOT SET OFFICIAL RECEPTION OUTSIDE THE HALL, AT THE BIG TENT IN QUAD ONE.
YOUR BROTHER REFUSES TO LET US MOVE HIM TO SOMEWHERE MORE SECURE AND--
SECURE THE PERIMETER. I'M ON MY WAY.
HEY?

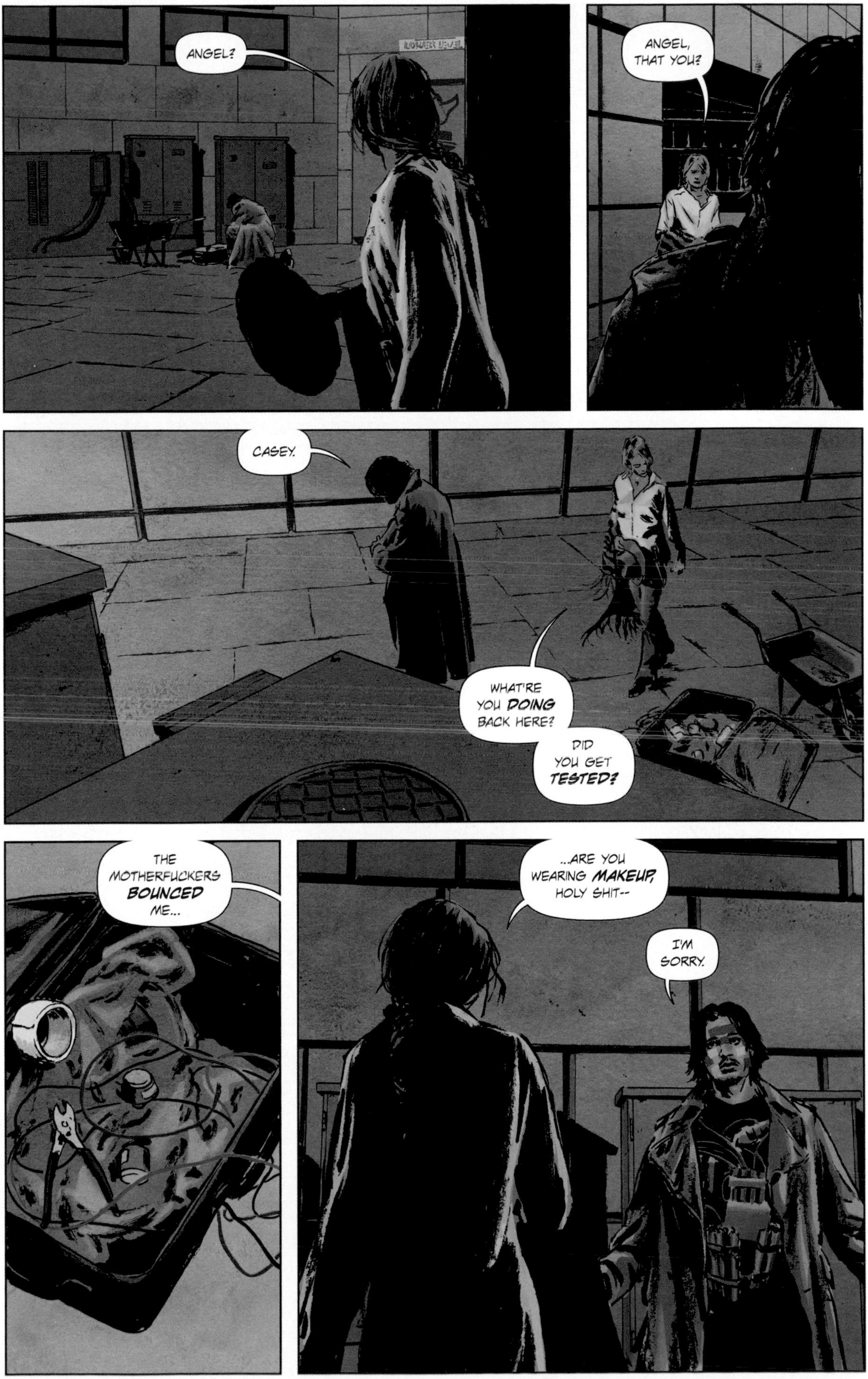
ANGEL?
ANGEL, THAT YOU?
CASEY.
WHAT'RE YOU DOING BACK HERE?
DID YOU GET TESTED?
THE MOTHERFUCKERS BOUNCED ME...
...ARE YOU WEARING MAKEUP, HOLY SHIT--
I'M SORRY.

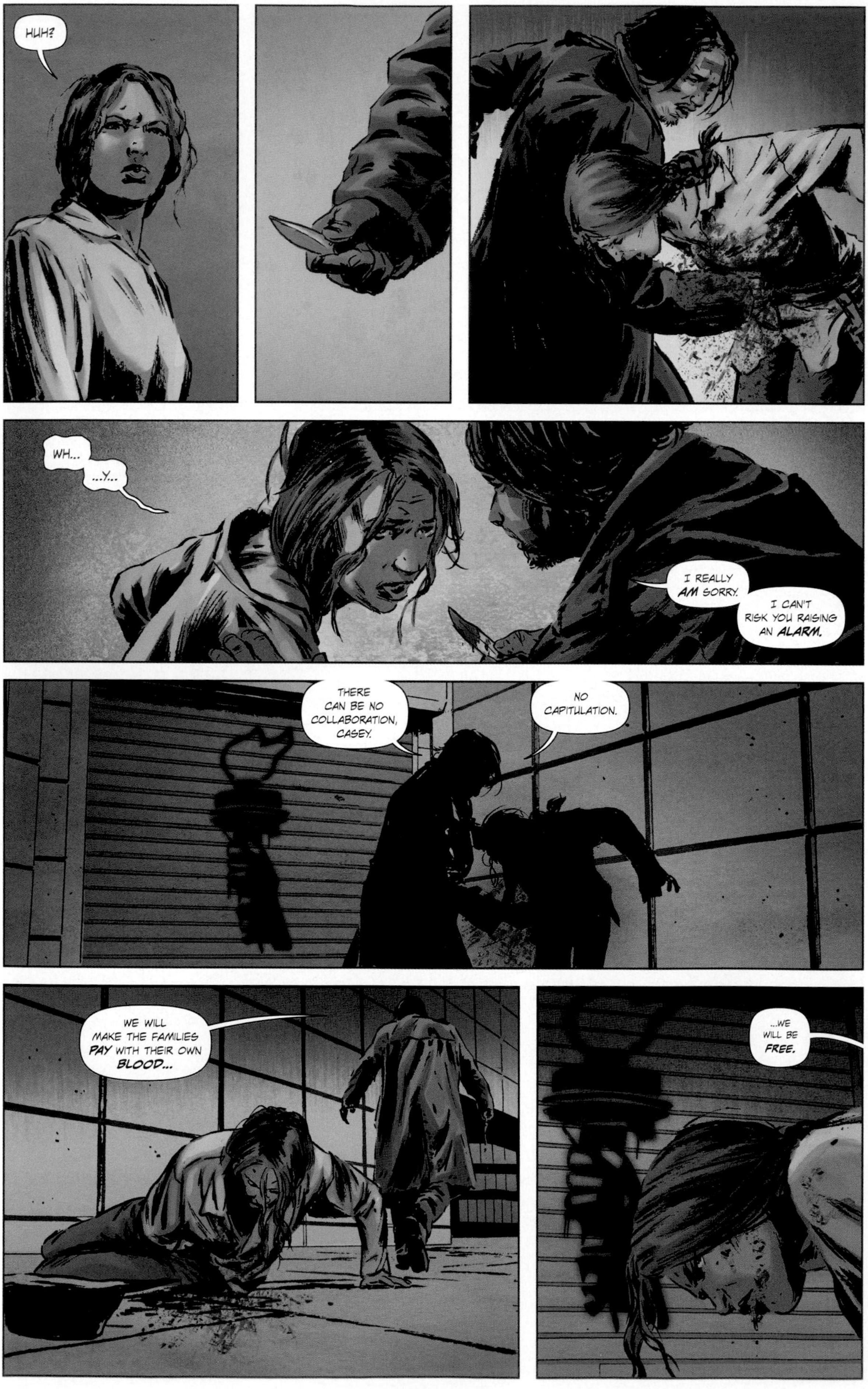
HUH?
WH...
...Y...
I REALLY AM SORRY.
I CAN'T RISK YOU RAISING AN ALARM.
THERE CAN BE NO COLLABORATION, CASEY.
NO CAPITULATION.
WE WILL MAKE THE FAMILIES PAY WITH THEIR OWN BLOOD...
...WE WILL BE FREE.

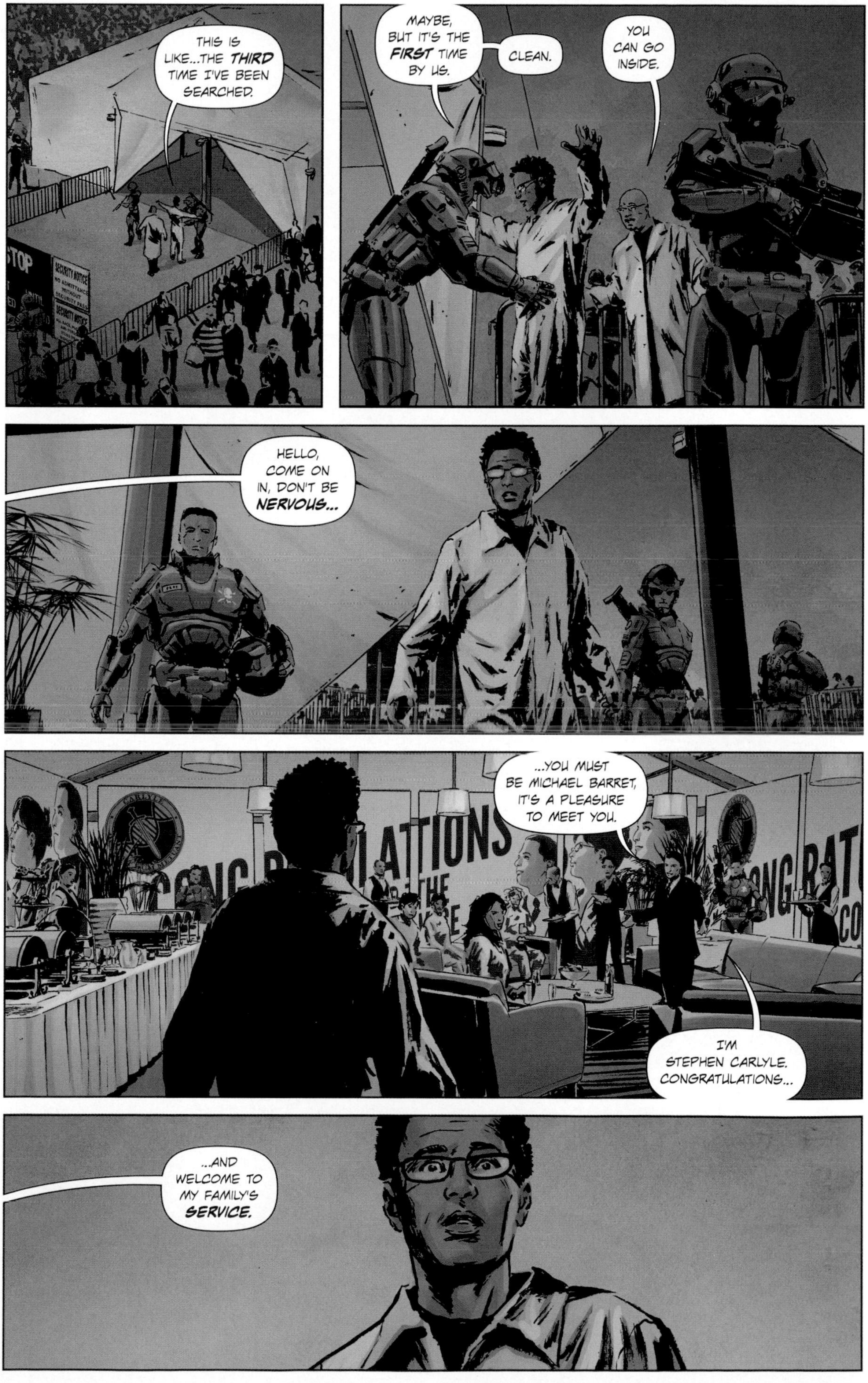
THIS IS LIKE...THE THIRD TIME I'VE BEEN SEARCHED.
STOP
MAYBE, BUT IT'S THE FIRST TIME BY US.
CLEAN.
YOU CAN GO INSIDE.
HELLO, COME ON IN, DON'T BE NERVOUS...
...YOU MUST BE MICHAEL BARRET, IT'S A PLEASURE TO MEET YOU.
I'M STEPHEN CARLYLE. CONGRATULATIONS...
...AND WELCOME TO MY FAMILY'S SERVICE.

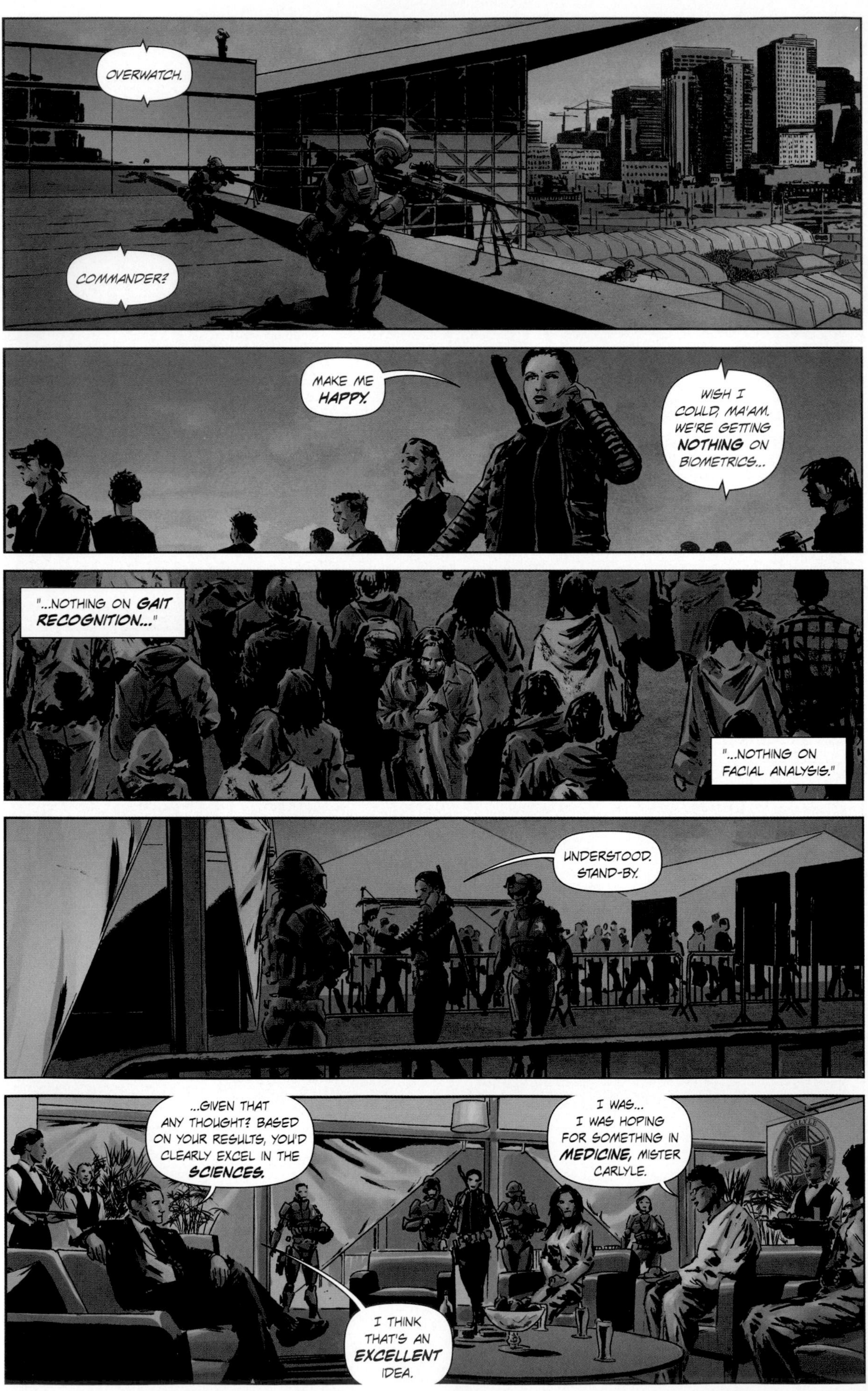
OVERWATCH.
COMMANDER?
MAKE ME HAPPY.
WISH I COULD, MA'AM. WE'RE GETTING NOTHING ON BIOMETRICS...
"...NOTHING ON GAIT RECOGNITION..."
"...NOTHING ON FACIAL ANALYSIS."
UNDERSTOOD. STAND-BY.
...GIVEN THAT ANY THOUGHT? BASED ON YOUR RESULTS, YOU'D CLEARLY EXCEL IN THE SCIENCES.
I WAS... I WAS HOPING FOR SOMETHING IN MEDICINE, MISTER CARLYLE.
I THINK THAT'S AN EXCELLENT IDEA.

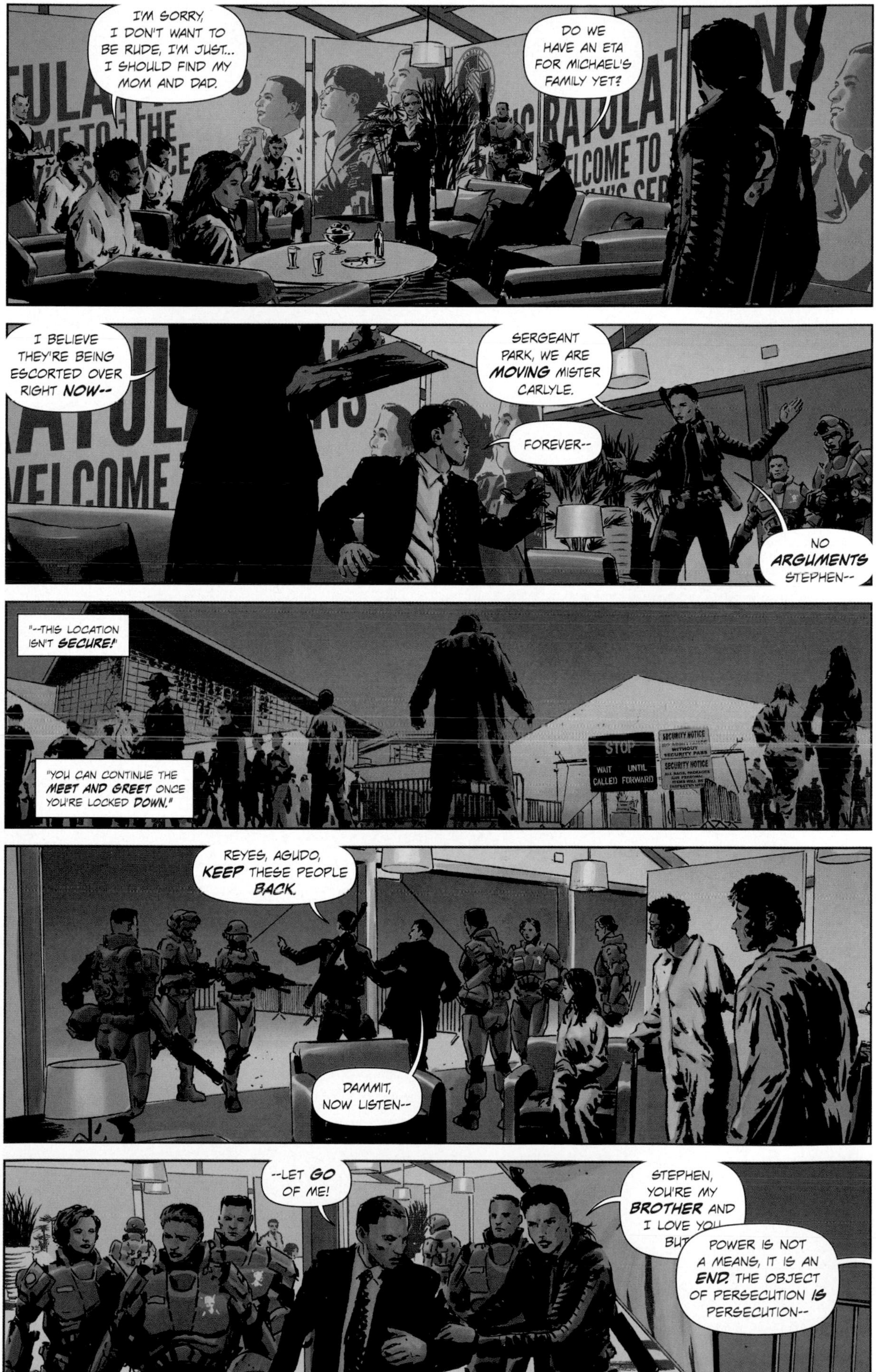
I'M SORRY, I DON'T WANT TO BE RUDE, I'M JUST... I SHOULD FIND MY MOM AND DAD.
DO WE HAVE AN ETA FOR MICHAEL'S FAMILY YET?
I BELIEVE THEY'RE BEING ESCORTED OVER RIGHT **NOW--**
SERGEANT PARK, WE ARE **MOVING** MISTER CARLYLE.
FOREVER--
NO **ARGUMENTS** STEPHEN--
"--THIS LOCATION ISN'T **SECURE!**"
"YOU CAN CONTINUE THE **MEET AND GREET** ONCE YOU'RE LOCKED **DOWN.**"
STOP
WAIT UNTIL CALLED FORWARD
SECURITY NOTICE
REYES, AGUDO, **KEEP** THESE PEOPLE **BACK.**
DAMMIT, NOW LISTEN--
--LET **GO** OF ME!
STEPHEN, YOU'RE MY **BROTHER** AND I LOVE YOU BUT
POWER IS NOT A MEANS, IT IS AN **END.** THE OBJECT OF PERSECUTION **IS** PERSECUTION--

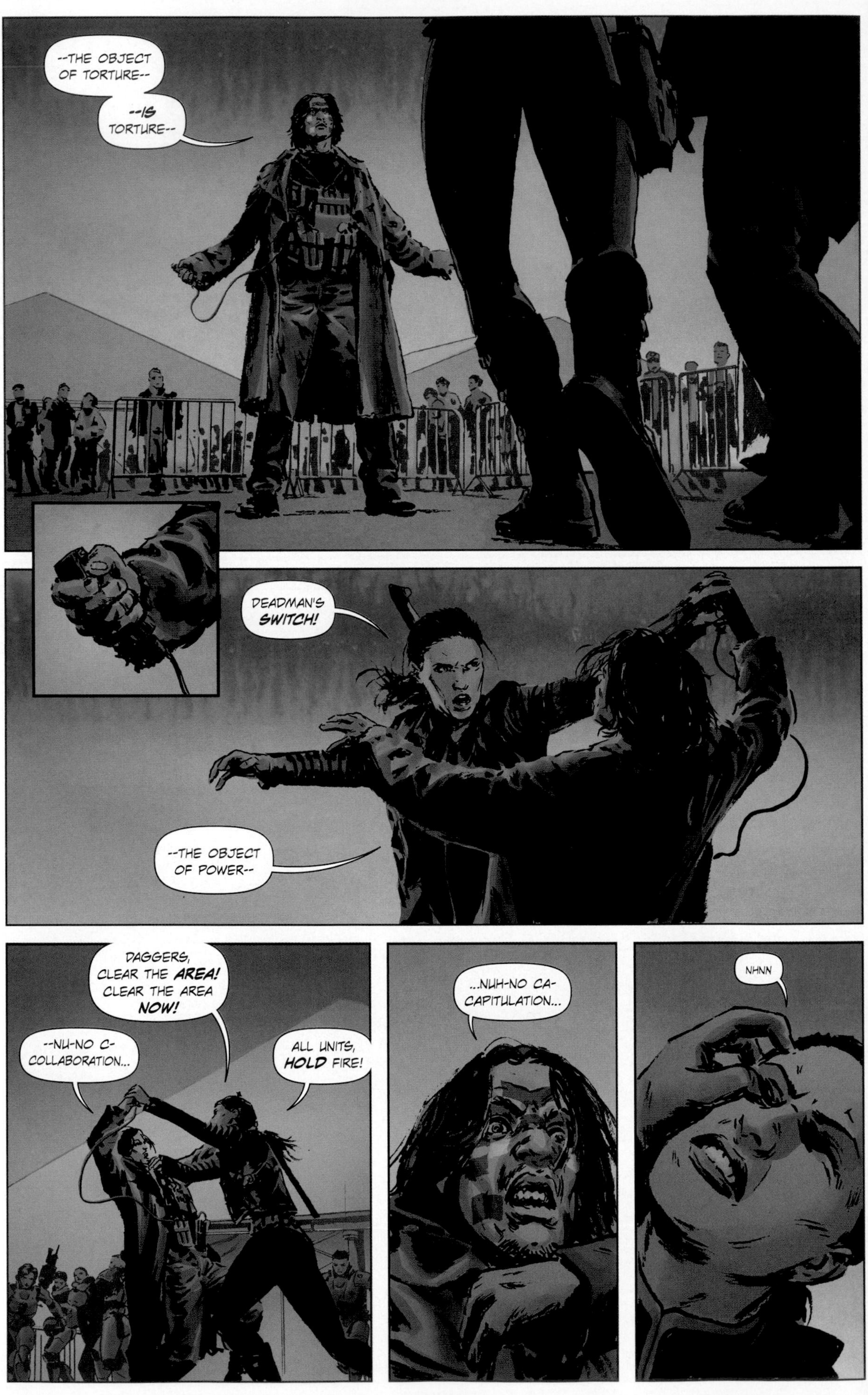
--THE OBJECT OF TORTURE--
--IS TORTURE--
DEADMAN'S SWITCH!
--THE OBJECT OF POWER--
DAGGERS, CLEAR THE AREA! CLEAR THE AREA NOW!
--NU-NO C-COLLABORATION...
ALL UNITS, HOLD FIRE!
...NUH-NO CA-CAPITULATION...
NHNN

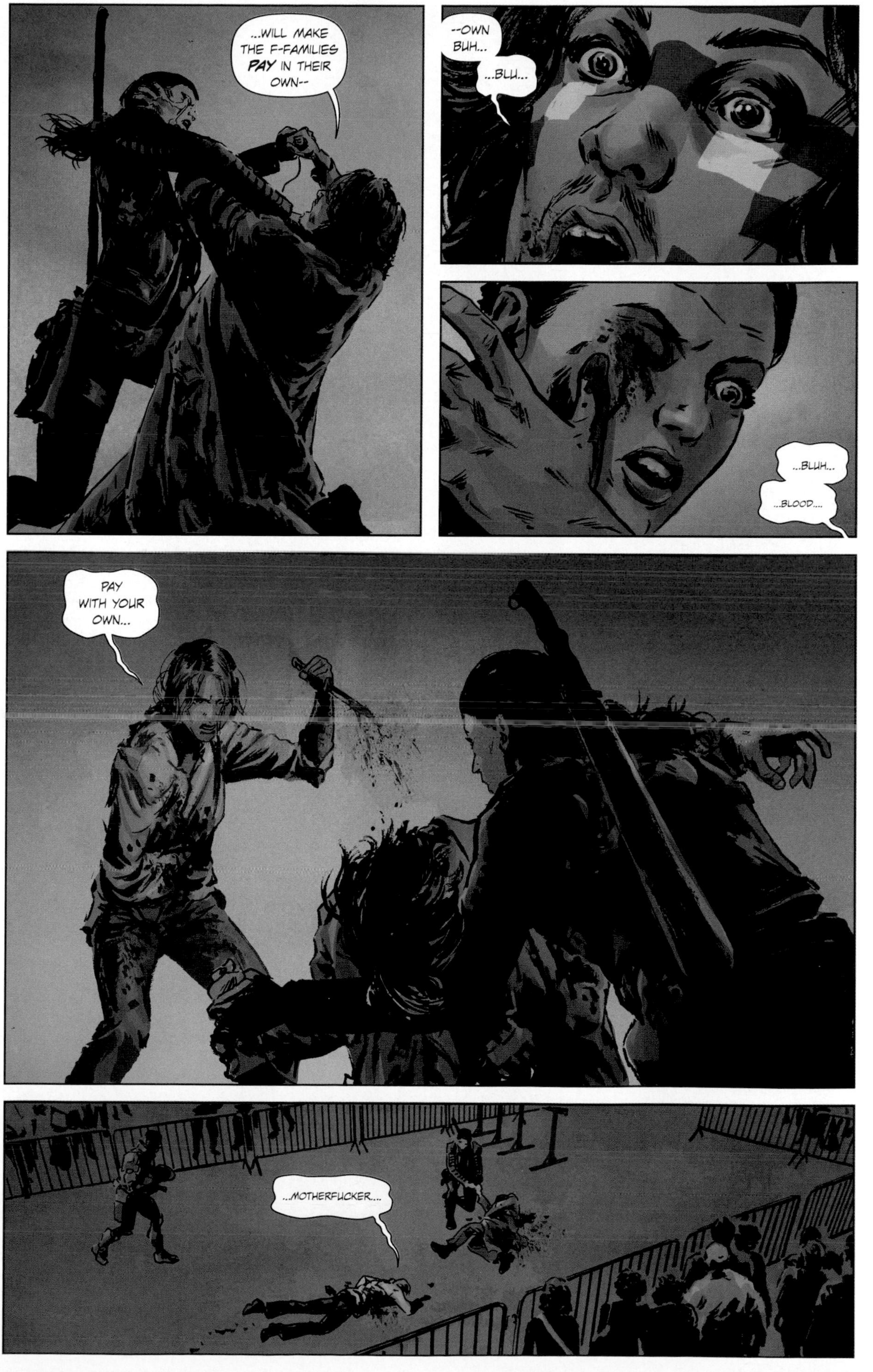
...WILL MAKE THE F-FAMILIES PAY IN THEIR OWN--
--OWN BUH...
...BLU...
...BLUH...
...BLOOD...
PAY WITH YOUR OWN...
...MOTHERFUCKER...

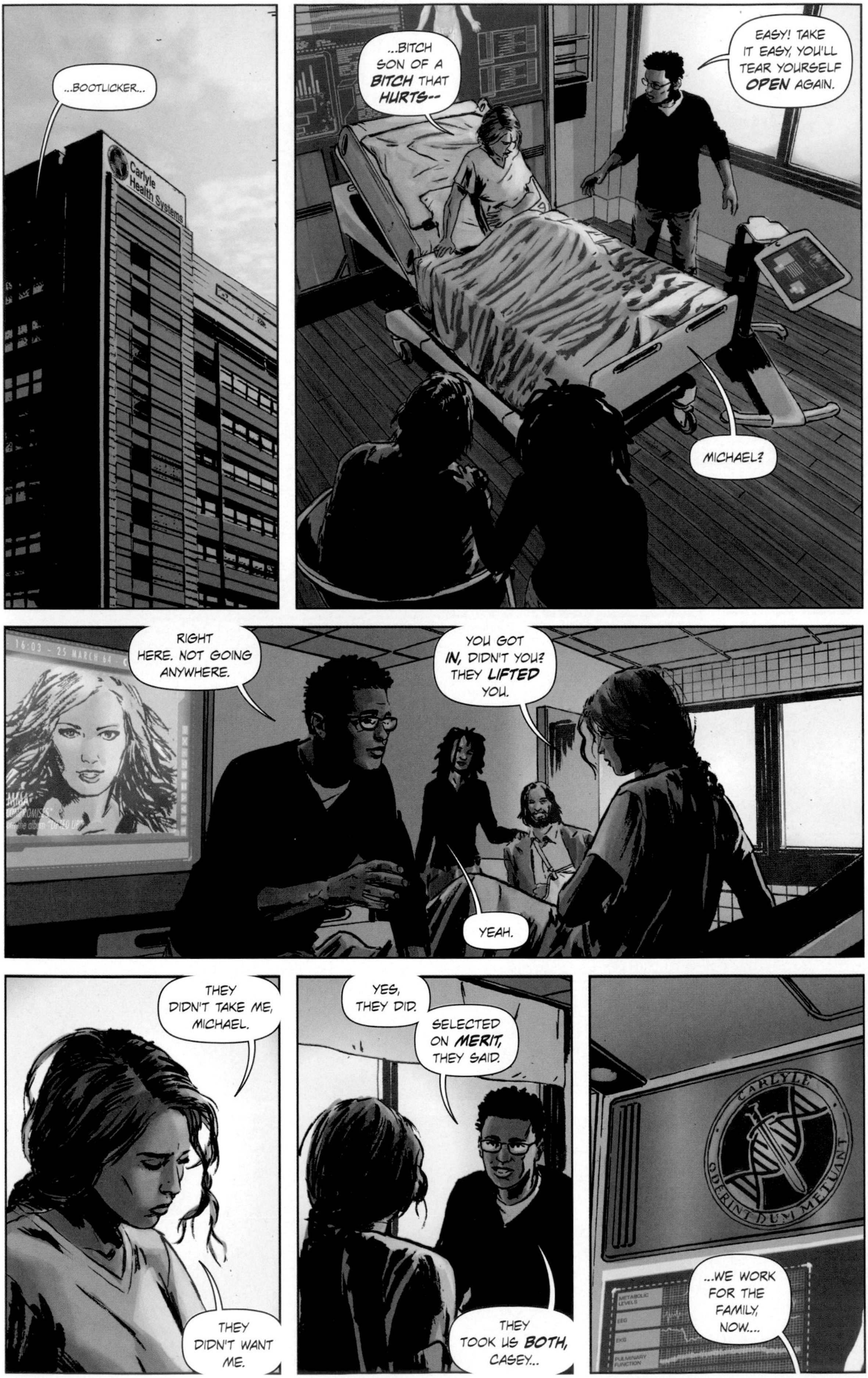

...BOOTLICKER...
Carlyle Health Systems
...BITCH SON OF A BITCH THAT HURTS--
EASY! TAKE IT EASY, YOU'LL TEAR YOURSELF OPEN AGAIN.
MICHAEL?
16:03 - 25 MARCH 64
RIGHT HERE. NOT GOING ANYWHERE.
YOU GOT IN, DIDN'T YOU? THEY LIFTED YOU.
YEAH.
THEY DIDN'T TAKE ME, MICHAEL.
THEY DIDN'T WANT ME.
YES, THEY DID.
SELECTED ON MERIT, THEY SAID.
THEY TOOK US BOTH, CASEY...
CARLYLE
ODERINT DUM METUANT
METABOLIC LEVELS
EEG
EKG
PULMINARY FUNCTION
...WE WORK FOR THE FAMILY, NOW....